STATE-SOCIETY RELATIONS IN MEXICO

The Political Economy of Latin America Series
Series Editor: George Philip

State-Society Relations in Mexico

Clientelism, neoliberal state reform,
and the case of Conasupo

KENNETH EDWARD MITCHELL
Department of Political Science, Saint Peter's College, New Jersey, USA

Ashgate

Aldershot • Burlington USA • Singapore • Sydney

Published by
Ashgate Publishing Limited
Gower House
Croft Road
Aldershot
Hants GU11 3HR
England

Ashgate Publishing Company
131 Main Street
Burlington, VT 05401-5600 USA

Ashgate website: http://www.ashgate.com

British Library Cataloguing in Publication Data
Mitchell, Kenneth Edward
    State-society relations in Mexico : clientelism, neoliberal
    state reform, and the case of Conasupo. - (The political
    economy of Latin America)
    1.Conasupo 2.Subsidies - Mexico 3.Mexico - Social policy
    4.Mexico - Politics and government - 20th century
    I.Title
    320.9'72'09045

Library of Congress Control Number: 2001089037

ISBN 0 7546 1718 1

Printed in Great Britain by
Antony Rowe Ltd, Chippenham, Wiltshire

Contents

List of Figures

List of Graphs

List of Tables

Acknowledgements

I am indebted to my doctoral thesis supervisor Laurence Whitehead, for his time and input over the course of this investigation. Also I want to express gratitude to the scholars who found the time to discuss their thoughts on Mexican politics: Alan Knight, Leslie Skliar, George Philip, Jonathan Fox, Wayne Cornelius, Elaine Carey, Eduardo Zepeda, and Jorge Hernández Díaz. I also want to thank the institutions that have made available their resources and staff – Centre for U.S.-Mexican Studies, La Jolla, Ca., El Colegio de México, Mexico and Universidad de Buenos Aires, Argentina. Research that has been carried out in Mexico, Argentina and the United States would not have been possible without the financial support provided by St Hugh's College, Oxford, the Norman Chester Fund, Oxford, and the University of Oxford's Inter-Faculty Award for Latin American Research. In terms of institutional support, I also owe a debt of gratitude to David Robertson, St Hugh's College, Oxford, for taking the time to discuss broader issues related to research organisation and the discipline of political science.

This book is dedicated to Patricia Beatriz Salzman-Mitchell and Carol Ann Mitchell, whose support guided me through my time in Oxford, Mexico City and Buenos Aires. I also want to acknowledge several friends and scholars who endured too many discussions about the politics of tortillas – Drucilla Scribner, Neil Graves, Richard Enthoven, and Philip Howard. Finally, I want to thank two Saint Peter's College students who aided in the production of this book, Luis Mendez and Yanette Brito.

Principal Acronyms

ANDSA	National Warehouse System
BANRURAL	National Campesino Bank
BORUCONSA	Grain Marketing Branch of Conasupo
CAP	General Assembly of the National Agricultural Council
CFE	National Electricity Company
CMP	Conasupo *Modernización* Plan (1990-1994)
CNC	National Peasant Confederation
CNOP	National Confederation of Popular Organisations
CONASUPO	National Basic Foods Company
CT	Labour Congress
CTM	Confederation of Mexican Workers
DICONSA	Distribution Branch of Conasupo
DIF	Defence of the Family Agency
FIDELIST	Tortilla Programme Commission
ICONSA	Processing Branch of Conasupo
IMPECSA	Retail Branch of Conasupo
IMSS	Mexican Social Security Institute
INFONAVIT	National Housing Fund
INI	National Indigenous Institute
LICONSA	The Milk Processing/Distributing Branch of Conasupo
MASECA	Private Tortilla Firm (*Molinos Aztecas*)
MICONSA	The Corn Flour/Tortilla Processing Branch of Conasupo
PACE	Conasupo's Programme of Direct Producer Subsidies
PAN	National Action Party
PASE	Conasupo's Campeche Pilot Scheme
PEMEX	National Oil Company
PRD	Democratic Revolutionary Party
PRI	Institutional Revolutionary Party
PROFECO	Federal Consumer Office
PROGRESA	Programme of Health, Education and Nutrition (1997-present)
PRONAL	National Food Programme (1983-1987)
SAM	Mexican Agricultural System (1978-1982)
SARH	Ministry of Agriculture
SECOFI	Ministry of Commerce
SOLIDARITY	National Solidarity Programme (1989-1994)
SRA	The Ministry of Agrarian Reform

1 State-Society Relations in Mexico: Clientelism, Neoliberal State Reform, and the Case of Conasupo

Introduction

Social policy is the quintessential lever available to Mexican presidents to manage state-society relations in general and assuage social tension in moments of economic and political crisis (Collier and Collier, 1979; Rubio and Newell, 1984; Story, 1986). Today, in Mexico and elsewhere in Latin America, the provision of social resources is being rethought in an era of democratisation and market-oriented reform. Moreover the provision of social resources has been an essential part of the Mexican system of governance under the Institutional Revolutionary Party (PRI). Thus it is an opportune moment to re-evaluate the variables that influence its design and articulation 'in the field' so that it can be linked to the larger issue of continuity and discontinuity in Mexican state-society relations.

Discussing broader dynamics of Mexican social policy, Ward (1993: 613) writes:

> As well as providing a temporary palliative to offset some of the negative outcomes of rapid urbanization and economic growth based upon low wage rates and trickle-down, social policy provides an arena through which *scarce societal resources may be negotiated.* (...emphasis added)

Negotiation, in this context, appeals to a particular forum, namely a dialogue joining local populations and executive representatives, which nurtures as well as reflects laden social norms around welfare provision that

1

are predicated on subtle and more overt exchange or clientele relationships. Discussing the PRI – in power continuously between 1929 and December 2000 – Kaufman Purcell and Purcell (1980: 223) observe,

> Though it formally incorporates working class, peasant, and middle-class groups, it is not the primary locus of interclass or intergroup bargaining; the most important aspects of this bargaining take place in *ad hoc*, informal settings.

The social programmes evaluated in this research often provide these '*ad hoc*, informal settings'. In this context, political capital for the government springs from two sources: output, the final distribution of goods, and process, the establishment of local-executive forums that ultimately furnish a stage for the executive, or his immediate interlocutors, to engage community leaders.[1] A national opinion poll (*Reforma*, 5 April 1997) asked, 'in general who represents your interests' and the top two answers (in order) were the municipal president and the president of the Republic. The bottom three answers (of a long list) were political parties, federal deputies and federal senators. That preference is given to the most local and the most national figures, emphasises the importance of the executive-local bridge in Mexican state-society relations.

This idea of negotiation also appeals to processes inside the government involving the equilibration of 'modern' (neoliberal or technocratic) and 'antiquated' (clientelistic, corporatist or populist) policy currents. Scholars reflecting on the Carlos Salinas years (1988-1994) propose different analytic devices to frame the dynamics of negotiation in social policy, in either its state-society or intra-state variants. For example, Dresser's (1994) study of The National Solidarity Programme (Solidarity) embraces the term 'neo-populism' and Bartra's (1991) investigation of rural sector policy changes speaks of 'efficient neocorporatism' to describe a conflation of common and not so common modes of negotiation. Nevertheless beneath disparate labels, scholars almost universally agree that in moments of crisis Mexican presidents seize the social policy lever to foster legitimacy and to maintain continuity among the government and strategic populations.

The National Basic Foods Company (Conasupo) offers fertile

ground to probe the accepted boundaries of continuity and discontinuity in Mexico. First developed in 1961, Conasupo, by 1988, subsidised food consumption of 30 million Mexicans and delivered producer subsidies to hundreds of thousands of grain producers. In 1983, in a policy shift witnessed elsewhere in Latin America, President Miguel de la Madrid (1982-1988) proposed replacing the Mexican government's long-standing policy of general consumption subsidies for food with various targeting schemes, to be handled by Conasupo. After several policy debacles, de la Madrid reasserted this policy goal in 1986. His successors reasserted it in 1988, 1991, 1994 and 1997. In November 1996, a PRI deputy made these comments about the food subsidy policy of the Zedillo administration (1994-2000):

> ... a basic problem is that the general subsidies for bread and tortilla give the same benefit to people of high and low income. It is for this reason that we have been insisting that in place of a policy of general subsidies for basics, it would be better to have a selective subsidy for those that most need it... We are insisting that the subsidies are not generalised but focused, and with luck, benefits can be increased to those that really need it (*Reforma*, 7 November 1996).

President de la Madrid outlined the same general objective in 1983.

This book analyses the Conasupo *Modernización* Plan (1990-1994), which promised to privatise various assets, to end general subsidies, to reduce a large Conasupo labour force, and to impose a neoliberal or 'needs-based' alternative at the parastatal. Yet, amid this reform agenda there was also a pledge to inflate the number of Conasupo consumers to 50 million. Blending neoliberalism (discontinuity) and populism (continuity) is a recurrent feature in Conasupo policy after 1982 and it helps to explain why Mexico has been able to manage the transition away from general subsidies without incurring a 'breakdown' in traditional state-society arrangements.

In this same time frame, Mexico is seen to be anomalous. In other Latin American countries, management of basic food consumption by democratically elected governments has proven more volatile. For example, Venezuelan President Carlos Andrés Pérez entered office in 1988 and introduced a series of market-oriented measures in February 1989, including cuts in general food subsidies. This sparked violent food riots in Caracas; an episode that Pérez never recovered from (Philip, 1998, 1992b). Likewise, in 1988 Argentine President Raúl Alfonsín watched spiralling food prices prompt middle-class Argentines to loot supermarkets in Buenos Aires and Rosario. Social pressure eventually forced Alfonsín to leave office before the end of his constitutional mandate (Smith *et al.*, 1994).

Failing to achieve certain social policy goals is something Mexico shares with other nations, and problems in targeting scarce resources occurs north of the Mexican border and elsewhere (Weir, Orloff and Skocpol, 1988; Anagnoson, 1980). The policy experience in this area is however testimony to the primacy of safe delivery of basic foodstuffs (notably corn) as part of a wider scheme of the Mexican government (1) to preserve political stability in a society characterised by high income inequality and (2) to protect the living standards of strategic populations (by supplementing household consumption and not necessarily wage increases) to whom the ruling elite appeals for legitimation. In this sense, Conasupo belongs with The National Oil Company (PEMEX), The Mexican Social Security Institute (IMSS), The Institute for Social Security and Services for Public Employees (ISSSTE), and The National Housing Fund (Infonavit), parastatals that engender symbolic, nationalistic, and political significance beyond the commodities under their discretion.

Why, since 1983, has the Mexican government that managed radical reform elsewhere in the public sector, found it so difficult to deliver consumption and production subsidies to poor households? More theoretically, how, as Mexican society experienced significant economic and political transformations, did the abstract 'patron' survive, along with the legitimacy of their informal, arbitrary, clientele politics, when both modernisation theory and the 'virtuous circle' of neoliberalism predicted the contrary? This book investigates these two questions. In particular, it evaluates long-running resource commitments between state and society that three Mexican presidents (de la Madrid, Salinas, and Zedillo) have struggled to place on a neoliberal ('discontinuous') foundation. Clientele norms in the provision of Conasupo's subsidies, involving official unions, consumers in Mexico City and grain producers in certain rural zones, contributed to long-observed patterns in state-society relations. This case study documents how these arrangements evolved after 1982 and especially under the policy management of President Salinas.

By misjudging the constraints on Conasupo, Mexican policymakers have, since 1983, suffered one policy fiasco after another in this area. Despite the relentless pressure on the old state-society model predicted by neoliberal and modernisation theory, clientele norms around Conasupo services have often been resilient to political and economic transformations that underlie general theorising about Mexican state-society relations. Therefore changes in social policy – and this case study of Conasupo is a revealing example – lend an instructive means for investigating the purchase of the conventional theoretical wisdom governing our understandings of state-society relations in Mexico, that is, the broader issue of continuity and discontinuity.

The rest of this opening chapter develops a broad analytic framework in which to examine the dynamics of continuity and discontinuity in Mexican state-society relations. The next section reviews a selection of literature from the late 1970s, 1980s and 1990s; it also presents different perspectives that put social policy at the centre of the continuity-discontinuity debate. It is found that the debate on continuity and discontinuity as well as discussions of a post-1982 'breakdown' of the old model produce an imprecise map of state-society relations. Although this section does not provide a definitive alternative, it offers some areas for discussion that improve the conventional framework.

After that the discussion turns to the methodological tools employed in this book. In particular, it is necessary to discuss how it proposes to conceive and evaluate 'clientele norms' and 'political culture' in the context of continuity and discontinuity at Conasupo. Lastly, a brief appendix furnishes an overview of Conasupo operations before Salinas entered office in 1988.

Interpreting the Boundaries of Continuity and Discontinuity

Hirschman (1970: 1) argues:

> No matter how well a society's basic institutions are devised, failures of

some actors to live up to the behaviour which is expected of them are bound to occur, if only for all kinds of accidental reasons.

Unavoidable lapses or the declining performance of private firms, political institutions or entire governments force citizens, as economic or political agents, to exercise one of three options: *exit*, withdraw from arrived-at arrangements, *voice*, pursue improvement within established institutions, or *loyalty*, acquiescence to institutional arrangements without actively trying to reverse the immediate slide. Hirschman's decision-oriented framework is useful for examining broader patterns in Mexican state-society relations.

Economic events in 1982, and the prolonged economic crisis they unleashed, pushed Mexico to the brink of bankruptcy, provoking a major lapse or clash with the prevailing expectations that most Mexicans held of their economic and political systems. A tradition that predicates political legitimacy on 'delivering the goods' through established channels or what Rodríguez (1997) denotes as the 'distributive state' amplified social tension vis-à-vis intermediary institutions. Indeed, the watershed of 1982-1983, punctuated by the nationalisation of the banking system, ushered in the decline in performance that activates Hirschman's tripartite formula. Different groups selected different choices. Many exercised *exit* and *loyalty* – in general, the space and institutional capacity to exert *voice* was constrained by the norms of the PRI's corporatist structures, an impotent judiciary, non-functioning public security forces, rigged elections and severe income inequality.

After 1982 some loyal partners elected to *exit*, choosing to disengage or distance themselves from the regime. Private sector groups, usually firms independent of government largesse according to Salas-Porras (1996), distanced themselves in order to pursue innovation using alternative means. Urban community associations in Mexico City, including parts of the Popular Urban Movement, left after corrupt relief operations in the aftermath of the 1985 earthquake convinced them that reconstruction necessitated new intermediary institutions linking state and society. The PRI's 1987 split prompted left-wing departures, and much of Mexico City opted to exit in the 1988 presidential election by voting against the PRI. Numerous middle class business-owners and farmers enlisted in the debtor's movement *El Barzón*, after the 1994-1995 economic crisis (Williams,

1996). Finally, there is no better illustration of the exit option, in the individual and economic context, than the millions that cross the northern border.

However, Mexican state-society relations have not obeyed a linear trajectory. Today's *exit*-er might tomorrow opt for *loyalty*, a development that is well illustrated by the post-1982 zigzag nature of electoral behaviour. In 1983 de la Madrid entered office facing only minor left and right wing challenges, though he upheld an unusual total of local National Action Party (PAN) victories in northern Mexico. In the 1985 mid-term election, however, he encountered meaningful PAN competition in Sonora, Nuevo León and other northern states. Voters (especially from Mexico City) abandoned the government in record numbers in the 1988 presidential election and in the 1997 mid-term election, while a clear recovery transpired in the 1991 mid-term and 1994 presidential elections. In 1998, the PRI recaptured the governorship of Chihuahua from the PAN and retained the governorships of most strategic states, marking another shift after its mid-term setback in 1997. However, in the 2000 presidential election the tide changed once again and Mexicans voted in the first non-PRI president in the post-revolutionary era.

Post-1982 shifts and realignments, though real and conspicuous, evolve alongside instances of continuity and *loyalty*. Though the PRI is no longer hegemonic nationally, it endures as a force in the political arena. In the poorer southern states of Mexico, the PRI continues to be the chief political actor. PRI corporatist institutions that many have written off, while diminished, remain fixtures in the interest aggregation-articulation process.[2] New intermediary institutions for state-society relations have also emerged since 1982, often, though not always, according to a well-known blueprint of centralised, clientelistic executive control. A decentralisation campaign based on *concertación* (formal corporatist dialogue) linked de la Madrid to communities and intermediary associations directly, and elements of the National Solidarity Programme (Solidarity) under Salinas and the Programme of Health, Education and Nutrition (Progresa) under Zedillo lend similar examples.

Post-1982 continuity also touches upon society's contact with other elements of the public sector: the law enforcement community, the military, the tax collector, the judicial system, the financial system, indigenous institutions, and, in some regions, the electoral system. A nation-wide opinion poll asked 'what is your opinion of the federal police' and a mere 13 percent of respondents answered favourably (*Reforma*, 3 May 1997). A pre-election national opinion poll (*Reforma*, 2 March 1997) found that 58 percent of Mexicans had 'no confidence' that the '1997 mid-term election would be clean'. Yet it is important to look at cases where institutional performance re-inforces continuity in conjunction with developments at a macro- or structural level. Mexico's income distribution and the socioeconomic gap between rural and urban areas have tended to deteriorate since 1982. Non-functioning or costly institutional channels and high income inequality combine to hinder society's capacity to curb government power and to secure a new model of state-society relations.

In the literature the tension between continuity and discontinuity, *loyalty* and *exit*, manifests itself differently over time. The discussion that follows tries to synthesise the general sentiment among scholars at different junctures since the 1970s to highlight a pattern of imprecision. In the 1970s, a partial consensus held that Mexican state-society relations engendered considerable stability. In pre-austerity, pre-1982 Mexico, research by Collier and Collier (1979, 1977) and Kaufman Purcell (1981, 1975) refer to multiple, often conflicting, material, geographical and ideological interests inside the public bureaucracy and society. Yet this observed complexity was depicted as manageable, sometimes even ritualised or institutionalised via informal tradeoffs or accommodations, furnishing a sense of order and stability. Kaufman Purcell and Purcell (1980: 194) assert:

> The Mexican State is a 'balancing act' because it is based on a constantly renewed political bargain among several ruling groups and interests representing a broad range of ideological tendencies and social bases.

The introductory comments of Fagen and Tuohy's (1972: 9) study of Jalapa, Veracruz, are representative:

> ...the physical aspects of the city – centralized, orderly; a core of modernity surrounded by substantial impoverishment – can stand as an introductory metaphor for its political life. Politics too is centralized, quite orderly, and organized around an active core of *políticos*,

bureaucrats, and a minority of citizens.

Stevens (1977: 227) writes:

> Decisions concerning distribution of social and economic goods are made according to pragmatic judgements about the need to balance economic growth and political stability. Changes in domestic or international political and economic conditions are reflected in decisions to expand or contract the benefits granted to participating groups.

In the 1970s, parastatals such as Conasupo and Infonavit, the corporatist branches of the PRI, and bureaucracies such as the Ministry of Agrarian Reform (SRA) and the National Indigenous Institute (INI) represented the apparatus used to perform this balancing act. Writing about Conasupo, Hall and Price (1982: 310 and 307) surmise:

> Conasupo was viewed as being particularly useful to the PRI because of its urban and rural constituencies... and [its] pricing policies have varied from administration to administration in response to the prevailing political atmosphere in the country.

The picture of the Mexican government managing society's immense diversity suddenly yielded to a sense of imminent and profound change after the 1982 crisis. Authors such as Rubio and Newell (1984), Bailey (1988, 1986), and Philip (1992, 1988, 1986) indicate that 1970s stability was in fact a facade masking longer-running tensions amid state-society relations that was largely sustained by excessive government spending.[3] Foreign debt forced the government to curtail previous levels of patronage and discontinue numerous parastatals, and for some, it threatened to unravel the PRI's nexus of intermediary arrangements that filled and managed the space between state and society. Research in the mid-1980s reported on public sector rationalisation, a promise to decentralise national life, and the emergence of new social movements. For some, these were symptomatic of ongoing systemic breakdown (Lustig, 1992; Hellman, 1983; Ruiz Dueñas, 1990; Foweraker and Craig, 1990). A new consensus started to emerge. Rapid political change, a trend throughout Latin America in the lost decade of the 1980s, loomed on the horizon in Mexico as the PAN accumulated more protest votes, as the PRI failed to reform itself, as an ascendant technocratic class squeezed traditional middle-class pathways to political power, and finally as Mexicans increasingly abstained from the ballot box, eroding a key pillar of PRI legitimacy. According to Gentleman (1987: 58):

> Mexico's model of political economy ... appears to be in disarray and offers little suggestion of potential success in overcoming the current economic impasse.

Levy (1986: 33) observed a transition in the areas of information and political socialisation, cornerstones of PRI hegemony:

> The locus of political socialization has shifted from institutions such as the PRI and co-opted unions toward television and other modern mass media that are overwhelmingly in private hands.

At the midpoint of the 1980s even the rare upbeat suggestion of future state-society continuity predicated itself on a complex set of unrealised assumptions:

> ...the safest prediction would be that Mexico will experience further, carefully controlled adaptation of the political system rather than any abrupt shift in regime type. But this projection assumes that sustained economic growth will be restored; that inflation can be reduced to a socially tolerable level; and that the social tensions which have accumulated over the past decade of boom-and-bust in the economy do not erupt into civil disorders that require military intervention or a generalized increase in the level of repression (Cornelius, 1987: 35).

One can infer that, for Cornelius, the structure of Mexican state-society relations remained intact, yet avoiding a future breakdown required this list of propitious conditions. He wrote in early 1986, before inflation peaked in late 1987, economic decline continued, further cuts in public expenditure ensued, elites split within the PRI, and the PRI's disastrous showing in the 1988 presidential election. Had he foreseen the developments to occur in the next two years, perhaps he would have joined the consensus around imminent transformation.

The unusual strength of traditional state-society relations were, according to many, on the wane by the beginning of the 1990s. Political liberalisation, predicted by proponents of economic liberalisation back in the 1980s, now seemed unstoppable as the Democratic Revolutionary Party (PRD) and PAN increasingly contested and captured political space while the PRI coalition appeared to be imploding. Baer (1997: 145) states, 'No force has proved as corrosive to authoritarian regimes or as supportive of economic development as an open economy'.[4] Debates concerning continuity and discontinuity in state-society relations resonated throughout the Salinas years. This gave rise to a particular language and analytic framework that gained near universal acceptance in academia, that is, public sector *technocrats* or the agents of discontinuity seeking to construct a neoliberal development model versus *políticos* or the agents of continuity that sought to preserve old, clientelistic modes of political legitimation. One important scholarly treatment of this conflict is Centeno's (1994) notion of a 'technocratic revolution from above' in which the agents of continuity progressively lost ground to well-equipped, well-educated technocrats, a view shared by many others (Camp, 1993, 1985; Cornelius, 1996; Smith, 1986; Womack, 1997). Regarding the ubiquitous Solidarity (1988-1994) initiative, Dresser's (1994) remarks summarise how many believed that a 'neoliberal' social policy was exerting pressure on state-society relations in the early 1990s:

> By responding to proposals from community organizations and local governments instead of imposing top-down directives, PRONASOL [Solidarity] narrowed an age-old divide between state and society.

Optimism soured concerning neoliberal presupposition of an unavoidable and transformative linkage joining economic and political spheres after the PRI's display of electoral strength in 1991 and 1994; the PRD's electoral misfortune in 1991 and 1994, and rebound in 1997; the PAN's discouraging performance in the 1997 D.F. mayoral contest, internal splits, and the 1998 gubernatorial loss in Chihuahua; the Chiapas rebellion; and the implosion of the neoliberal Salinas project after the 1994-1995 peso crisis and the discovery of widespread corruption in the privatisation of state assets after Salinas left office.

Further, the oversimplified model of technocrats and *políticos* suddenly proved less satisfactory and underwent revision, for, as Lindau (1996) argues, when assessing the Salinas years it is not easy to discern technocrats from *políticos*. Salinas himself proved, of course, decidedly more skilful in the latter rather than the former. Hellman (1988: 143) was an earlier sceptic: '[on the technocratic revolution] ... the development may simply indicate that a new definition of *patronage* is needed'.

Less often mentioned, in some cases the *políticos* displayed a propensity to adjust to Mexico's new environment rather than falling by the wayside under the weight of political modernisation and economic liberalisation. Consider, for example, how the businesses of the Hank González family have thrived under the economics of the de la Madrid-Salinas-Zedillo years, as did traditional PRI financiers from the private sector such as Roberto Barrera González and Alberto Santos (two individuals featuring in the Conasupo case study). PRI *político*, stalwart and ex-governor of Puebla Manuel Bartlett used the neoliberal cover of 'fiscal decentralisation' to redirect state resources from wealthier PAN areas to poorer PRI areas. In 1997 the PRI governors of Tabasco and Campeche (classic *políticos* in profile) accused of flouting electoral spending rules, held on to power at least in part by arguing that these affairs were for state officials to sort out and not the federal government.

In the more recent literature, Cornelius (1996) refers to a 'painfully slow' transition, Smith (1998) to a 'checker board' transition, Heredia (1992) to a 'muddled' transition and Fox (1994) to the 'difficult transition from clientelism to citizenship'. Camp (1993:14) adds that Mexican 'political culture is neither democratic nor authoritarian... It is contradictory: modern and traditional'. The sense of uncertainty prompts Rubin (1996), Fox and Aranda (1996) and Kaufman and Trejo (1997) to deconstruct, 'decentre' and forego macro analysis in favour of a regional framework.

The aforementioned studies confirm that, at different levels of analysis, there is an ongoing struggle to situate Mexican state-society relations along a continuum of continuity and discontinuity. The resultant map appears imprecise. In retrospect, most scholars now concede that the 1970s were probably less managed and stable, the 1980s were undoubtedly less precarious and potentially combustible, and the early 1990s were less neoliberal and innovative than first thought. Some factors that contributed to this outcome include: (1) wedding 'continuity' to a discourse about ossified, 'traditional' state intermediaries; (2) assuming that Mexico would follow the South American experiences of the 1980s or the East European experiences of the 1990s; and (3) exaggerating the dynamic between economic and political liberalisation (by modernisationists and neoliberals), which often led to a debate about 'when' rather than 'why' a state-society breakdown would occur.[5] Today's tacit consensus lies at a more cautious or indeterminate location, recognition that the cohabitation of continuity and discontinuity is stubborn, yet its core determinants are not well understood.

Continuity and Discontinuity in Mexican Social Policy

Having briefly surveyed a sample of the views of continuity and discontinuity in general, let us look more closely at how it applies in the area of social policy.[6] Most accept that there is an intimate relationship between the management of social policy and continuity, something that can be approached from two perspectives. The first, and the preferred choice of scholars, documents in meticulous detail high-profile projects, crisis-inspired policy lurches, and timely patronage. Here researchers probe episodic, impulsive replies to economic and political crises in separate presidential terms.

Analytically, this perspective is based on one conceptualisation of how the government renews its legitimacy; however, it de-emphasises traditional or long-running bureaucracies and social assistance stretching across several administrations. Closer attention to the latter represents a second perspective to continuity that differs though, of course, it is not disconnected from one-off executive management.

Ward (1993: 617) refers to 'social expense expenditures' or handouts delivered under no pretence of productive investment:

> These are lightweight and superficial activities ('bread-and-festivals') which the state promotes in order to sustain its legitimation functions, pacify the workforce, and to obscure ideological bases for class or

cultural solidarity.

For Ward 'lightweight and superficial' denote flexibility and not triviality, where public handouts are mobilised in long-standing social programmes that carry an overt political dimension. Illustrations that one could point to include festivals celebrating mothers, children, labour, the Revolution, and Independence. Traditional social programmes that factor into this present case study include schemes that dispense resources under the auspices of anti-poverty, natural disaster relief, and regional, union, family, and indigenous development. Economist Ramírez de la O (1998) prefers the term leakage:

> When I was attending university we accepted a certain degree of corruption or leakage due to the governing party's obligation to maintain social stability. Everyone accepted this fact of life. Things like Conasupo fit squarely into this general, social calculation.

This study adopts this second perspective, seeking clues toward a better understanding of continuity from public handouts that enter into the expectations of large segments of the population. Likewise, there is an implicit suggestion that in areas of social policy where new executive schemes have not materialised, we carefully examine the evolution of established services, particularly when they factor into a wider legitimation strategy.

Downplaying episodic executive management is not a subtle way to devalue its impact. Subsequent chapters, however, usually refer to the government's 'structural social assistance' and its 'temporary social assistance', to draw what is taken to be a useful empirical distinction. For in either case the institutional, political and bureaucratic arrangements involved are apt to encompass distinct policy arenas at the local, regional and federal level.

Take the well-studied Solidarity initiative, engineered in an environment of economic restructuring and a direct appeal to foster executive legitimacy (Fox and Moguel, 1995; Guevara Sanginés, 1995; Díaz, 1997). Its construction, meticulous attention to procedural detail and overpowering publicity stand in contrast to a concurrent agenda to maintain and reorient traditional programmes and bureaucracies such as Conasupo,

Infonavit, INI, and the Defence of the Family Agency (DIF). Too often the two processes are loosely aggregated, even though bureaucratic constraints, informal negotiations, and inertia 'on the ground' contrast sharply.[7] Bureaucratic inertia in traditional programmes, derived from recruitment, contracts, and other routinised arrangements, sometimes bend or reverse reform packages.[8] This applies to Conasupo and other parastatals. From the 1960s to the present, each Conasupo reform package has aimed at ridding the agency of corruption without noticeable success. Jesús Silva Herzog's aborted reforms at Infonavit in the late 1970s – a project blocked by the corporatist Confederation of Mexican Workers (CTM) – offers another illustration. Observing Conasupo's performance in de la Madrid's National Food Programme (Pronal, 1983-1987), Jusidman de Bialotovsky (1987: 351) remarks,

> There seems to be a large gap between the grand objectives, strategies, and programs proposed, and the concrete work carried out by the multitude of governmental employees. Such a vacuum is seen between the agreements reached at the highest levels of the public, private, and social sectors, and the daily behaviour of individuals or units that make up such sectors.

The large gap or vacuum is, again, typically filled by informal negotiations involving the state and strategic populations.

Although the bending of policy is common at traditional parastatals, the problem often assumes a different profile when the executive formulates a new or parallel bureaucratic initiative, where close policy advisers can monitor policy articulation from conception to recruitment of personnel to final operation. Again, it is instructive to compare Solidarity and Conasupo to clarify this conceptual distinction between parallel and old bureaucracies.

On the one hand, Solidarity's political dimension mostly centred on curtailing resources to non-allies or delivering resources with clear strings attached (Acedo Angulo *et al.*, 1995; Cornelius *et al.*, 1994; Kaufman and Trejo, 1997). Haber's (1994) case study of Solidarity and the CDP in Durango provides a revealing glimpse of this process. Political studies of Solidarity ponder who accessed resources and at what price in a broader context where demand eclipsed supply, granting the executive discretionary latitude.[9] On the other hand, little congruence presents itself in the Conasupo case study between an official blueprint (when there is one) and the reality of programmes in practice; very often resources simply disappeared in Conasupo's informal negotiations.

Grindle (1977c: 525) prefers separating public policy introduced under 'crisis' and 'non-crisis' conditions:

> Policies introduced under noncrisis conditions ... may be more valid indicators of both influences and constraints on the policy process and they may ... provide insight into the more normal, day to day functioning of the political system itself.

There may be room to apply her two-fold distinction to Solidarity ('crisis') and Conasupo ('noncrisis'). There has never been a 'crisis in Conasupo policy management' whereas Solidarity was directly linked to the 1988 legitimacy crisis of Carlos Salinas. This comparison is further supported by the fact that Conasupo survived the collapse of the Salinas project in 1994-1995, while Solidarity was abruptly discontinued.

With respect to parallel structures, scholars such as Dresser (1991) and Moctezuma (1993b) indicate that the Solidarity Committees of the Salinas years often duplicated the traditional function of the PRI's National Confederation of Popular Organisations (CNOP). This entailed directing demands for services from community leaders, on a community by community basis, to representatives of the executive. Additional parallel structures include Salinas' public housing initiative, The National Popular Housing Fund (Fonhapo), which encroached on Infonavit and The State Employees' Housing Fund (Fovisste) (Herrasti Aguirre, 1993). In sum, while observers of the Salinas years effectively evaluate the implications for state-society relations from parallel bureaucracies, in particular the significance of Solidarity, less attention has been forthcoming on the relevance of traditional bureaucracies. Thus a case study of Conasupo offers an opportunity to complement the rich literature on schemes such as Solidarity, to balance episodic executive management and the experience of more entrenched programmes, and to arrive, in the end, at a more accurate map of continuity and discontinuity.

By focusing on a parastatal such as Conasupo that survived the economic crisis of the 1980s, the intention is not to downplay the profound transformations in state-society relations or indeed at Conasupo during this period. That there were transformations during the de la Madrid and Salinas years is not in doubt. But what is less clear, at the level of state-society relations, is the intensity, pace and scope these changes have taken, and whether they are genuinely new tendencies or a continuation of old tendencies (Hellman, 1988). Further, there is disagreement as to how recent transformations have influenced the manner in which Mexicans, in particular lower-income Mexicans and strategic clients of the old system, interact with government structures and vice versa.

Contributing to the Continuity-Discontinuity Map

Against the backdrop of the continuity-discontinuity debate, this book proposes four areas for discussion that aim to sharpen and construct more adequate boundaries. Each area proposes different factors that have a causal relationship regarding continuity and Conasupo policy. They are laid out here and briefly justified; however, final lessons in the light of the evidence from the Conasupo experience and their potential utility for more general theorising about state-society relations are saved for the end of the book.

(1) Policy Making Parameters

In contrast to the view of Centeno and others, it is suggested that a small circle of technocrats cannot impose 'in the field' neoliberal reforms ('discontinuity') that try to put long-term politicised handouts on a needs-based foundation when, and crucially, an executive prescribes 'reform' but prohibits 'privatisation' or 'parallel' operative and administrative structures. To be sure, various examples of discontinued politicised handouts and the formation of parallel structures remind us that political power is concentrated and capable of policy innovation in Mexico.

However, reform under this narrow premise introduces a slightly different challenge to configurations of political power inside the government; that is, when technocrats must impose 'discontinuity' by somehow reorienting the administrative, workplace, and exchange expectations of agents of the status quo both inside and outside parastatals, the results are unlikely to bear much relation to the initial blueprint. This questions the effectiveness of technocrats to reform rather than replace or dismember the public sector through prescribed policies of meritocratic recruitment, liberalisation, decentralisation, retraining, contracting out, and so forth.

If neoliberal reform is unpredictable under these parameters, then this case study will help identify the limitations of policies reliant on technocratic leadership from above. This would also locate one set of conditions that nurture continuity at Conasupo and perhaps at other parastatals and in other areas of the public sector where discontinuing existing institutions is deemed politically or practically off-limits.

(2) Executive Management

A second area for discussion builds on the first: the true objectives of the executive policymaker were not so much neoliberal reform ('discontinuity') as political management and electoral pragmatism ('continuity'). This presumes that continuity staved off the encroachment of discontinuity at the crucial 'executive level' and, moreover, that continuity is perhaps a pre-requisite for neoliberal reform in some circumstances, a situation that is discounted in recent preoccupation with creeping technocracy and neoliberalism in the public sector. Behind this proposition is a belief that conditions animating Conasupo policy before 1982, particularly the acceptance of political exchange relationships among strategic populations and the executive ('local-executive forums'), remained salient thereafter.

(3) Studying Traditional Parastatals

Recently, few analysts have proposed that neoliberal rigour impacts the final character of policy no more, or perhaps less, than perceptions of legitimacy do. In contrast to studies of technocratic ascendancy, focusing on shifts in executive or regime legitimacy recycles a common framework in the literature before 1982. This emphasises the broader impetus for policy innovation: In some policy areas outcomes may be determined more by a familiar political economy calculation than by a neoliberal paradigm shift among policy makers or processes of modernisation. For example, in the area of anti-poverty policies, there was an intellectual shift from universal subsidies to 'targeting' in the 1980s. This shift (discontinuity) and traditional resource commitments (continuity) exerted pressure on Conasupo. Whether the latter eclipsed the former receives careful consideration in the chapters that follow. In Chapter Six a similar scenario arises. Another intellectual shift, this time in favour of 'bundling' different welfare services to overcome the 'structural condition' of poverty, had to contend with familiar political constraints.

(4) Political Culture and Basic Service Provision

A national political culture featuring high levels of clientelism or informal reciprocity coming into contact with the austerity of the 1980s poses a dilemma: when patterns of reciprocity collapse, or are threatened, is this an adequate impulse to transform patterns of state-society interaction? Morris (1991: 81) concludes: 'For the [political] elite, an abundant and perhaps even growing resource base is needed to maintain the accommodation game [with society]'.[10] This assumption that the government needs a growing resource base will be evaluated in this study and shown to be misleading in the context of Conasupo. It is clear from the Conasupo experience that the 'pie' can shrink without causing a breakdown in past patterns of reciprocity, if it is managed in a specific way.[11] Related, should a democratic model of state-society relations, where voters reward good governance with loyalty and political power, supplant resource-oriented reciprocity? These two questions inspire many contemporary studies of Mexican state-society relations. Contrary to much early speculation there are reasons why social norms that are part of a broader clientele-based political culture may survive and adapt to policy changes in lean times. Those reasons require us to investigate the potential pace (incremental or expedient) and dynamics (transformation to *what?*) of continuity and discontinuity in state-society relations.

The Relevance of Conasupo

A case study of Conasupo is well suited to evaluate the issues raised above. It is a parastatal with a long history, solid clientele networks, peculiar inertia (in terms of recruitment, workplace norms and revolutionary/nationalistic premise), strong linkages to the PRI and its corporatist branches, and a sustained presence with large segments of the population. It also offers a unique case of technocratic, 'modern' and neoliberal policy making, both over a sustained period and in the specific context of the Salinas years.

The issue of general and targeted subsidies, and the question why this transition has been so difficult, provide an example that crosscuts each of the four areas for discussion designated above. In 1989 President Salinas instructed the Ministry of Commerce (Secofi) to reform Conasupo according to a neoliberal ethos, aligning agents of the parastatal against administration technocrats. Yet he did so in a context with distinct policymaking parameters. Before articulating his neoliberal agenda in October 1989, Salinas publicly contemplated during his 1988 presidential campaign the discontinuation of the parastatal. But he eventually rejected this option (for reasons discussed in Chapter Two) and prescribed far-reaching reform for the next six years.

Methodological Tools I, Clientelism and State-Society Relations

While the first three areas for discussion propose direct assumptions about continuity and the state, the final consideration encompasses both state and society, calling for a brief discussion of the concepts of clientele norms and political culture; how they are presented in the literature and the types of empirical obstacles they raise. It is important to reiterate that clientelistic norms of reciprocity and informality, and their status in the face of shifting economic and political conditions in post-1982 Mexico, are at the centre of the continuity-discontinuity debate.

Briefly, the academic literature concerning political culture oscillates between two poles that are united by an assumption that political culture and political structure (for example, regime type) are somehow interconnected, either in a determinant or reciprocal type arrangement. At one end, Almond and Verba's (1963) classic approach identifies social attitudes (e.g., efficacy, trust, and civic competence) that are deemed to be conducive to a democratic civic culture and the maintenance of democratic institutions. Among others, Craig and Cornelius (1980), Cornelius (1996), Fagen and Tuohy (1972), and Booth and Seligson (1984) apply (sometimes reluctantly and with some modifications) *The Civic Culture*'s empirical approach to Mexico. At the other end, political sociologists adopt a broader framework and seek to uncover an array of structures in the community that attach meaning to political life.

> Roughly a 'political culture' is the totality of ideas and attitudes toward authority, discipline, governmental responsibilities and entitlements, and associated patterns of cultural transmission, like the education system and even family life. The importance of all these factors, and the reason for linking them together into one portmanteau concept, is that they give an overall profile of how people are likely to react to political matters (Robertson, 1985: 263).

Camp's (1993) discussion of Mexican political culture leans toward this wider approach.

Since the 1960s, putting the term political culture into operation has sparked much debate and controversy. In part, criticism of Almond and Verba generally and the application of their model to Mexico rests on two analytic points. First, there was an immediate reaction that their survey-based methodology captured recent evaluation of government performance, that is, a snapshot rather than enduring, socially embedded orientations concerning political life. Among others, Inglehard's (1988) time-series data overcomes this problem.

Second and related, in the Mexican context societal efficacy, trust, or attitudes toward participation crosscut characteristics of the political system and political life that must be treated with caution. Consider the utility of concepts such as 'trust' and 'participation' in Mexico. Normatively, trust is connected to the stature of the sitting president and less focused on parties, elections, courts or public bureaucracies (i.e., democratic institutions), not only because of the executive's considerable powers and imprint on Mexican political history but also because of the traditional mobility, turnover and six-year divisions that this country's constitutional ban on public office re-election engenders. In Mexico, for example, large segments of society embraced Solidarity's larger-than-life status during the Salinas term, hailing it a watershed, a potential successor to the PRI, and a pillar in a new market-oriented state-society bargain. Much of this was based on trust concerning the executive's economic management and ability to generate a sense of national progress (Guttmen, 1998). Shortly thereafter, following the 1994-1995 economic crisis, the same Solidarity imagery invoked widespread 'distrust' and scepticism. Empirical investigations of trust in Mexican society must somehow clarify such socially embedded orientations before beginning to speculate on a correlation with political structure. This is born out in Inglehard's (1988: 1217) study; Mexico alone registered high levels of life satisfaction overtime despite its non-democratic government that produced 'negative conditions' for society at large.

'Participation' faces similar obstacles. The dominant-party system encouraged significant, albeit vertically and regionally controlled, political mobilisation and participation. It has been part of the corporatist game, part of the process that communities enter in order to secure basic services, part of patron-client bargaining around election time, and, on occasion, an executive tool to check local or regional politicians and bureaucrats. An interesting example of 'participation' is seen in the Conasupo case study. Starting in the early 1970s, the Chamber of Deputies convenes an annual session in which hundreds of housewives from around the country, who represent a community, are transported to Mexico City to report on the operation of Conasupo's consumption programmes. Comments by housewives participating in 1990 indicate that they understood that their role in this annual ritual was important to those who decided whether or not to fund Conasupo services; but they also expected no action on their complaints as a result of their participation (*Excelsior*, 9 January 1990).

Thus attitudes concerning participation and forms that protest in the dominant-party system can take (e.g., signing petitions, attending community groups, strikes, voter abstention, peaceful demonstrations, opposition party development, etc.), offer a host of different meanings across an authoritarian-pluralistic continuum. In which case, *The Civic Culture*'s framework may or may not produce much of a profile of how people are likely to react to political matters or intricacies of 'political life' in Mexico.

However, it is also true that in practice covering an unmanageable number of variables renders 'political culture' a black box and unusable.

Mexican political culture is a time specific complex of overlapping supranational, national, regional, communal, class, ethnic, family, workplace and religious orientations or subcultures that attach divergent and sometimes congruent meaning to complex political life. Nonetheless, our concern is state-society relations in the narrow context of entrenched social services and not the multitude of social structures and processes that sustain or thwart democracy or authoritarianism.

Once this limitation is imposed, it is difficult to deny that the most effective agent shaping norms, expectations and political culture, for the past sixty years, has been the dominant-party state. Social policy on the scale discussed in this book, after all, is a manifestation of the modern state. Only the state, with the possible exception of the Catholic Church, has sustained a presence across Mexico, operating as a constant source of socialisation concerning matters related to the public sphere (in particular social policy) and in the area of state-society relations. A poor corn farmer comments before voting in the 1997 mid-term election: 'This is the party we were born into; its the system we've been accustomed to since the time of our grandfathers' (*New York Times*, 6 July 1997). Its ubiquitous status is a conspicuous feature in studies of socialisation, political attitudes and inevitably political culture by Cornelius (1975) in the D.F., Fagen and Tuohy (1972) in Veracruz, Ugalde (1970) in Baja California and Grindle (1977a) in Puebla. These studies discuss political culture, in particular the embedded social norms related to the provision of basic services, as the composite of descriptive and normative qualities, that is, experience with day-to-day political outputs (local bureaucrats associated with basic services) as well as general orientations toward the political system, both its social output and its core components (the presidency, the PRI, and the revolutionary legacy).

Here the goal is not to advance *The Civic Culture* debate as it relates to Mexico, instead it is to narrow our attention to the formal and informal discourse surrounding the policymaking process and political context that exert strong pressure on official food policy and its final implementation. On the one hand, our interest will be the demand making process that takes place through formal and informal channels locally (descriptive), and, on the other hand, we want to be cognisant of what strategic populations expect more generally (normative) from the dominant-party state and vice versa.

There are of course conceptual obstacles to flag from the outset. How could one falsify the claim that clientele norms around Conasupo policy are as strong as, or perhaps undiminished, before and after 1982 as well as before and after 1988? Likewise, definitional problems intrinsic to discussions of traditional/clientele norms arise. How does one distinguish between pluralistic pork-barrel politics witnessed north of the Río Grande (i.e., in the USA and Canada multiple political parties act as patrons in an arena with transparent and functioning oversight mechanisms) and traditional/clientele politics *a la mexicana* or what Fox (1994) labels 'authoritarian clientelism' – authoritarian because the PRI dominates the delivery of public resources.[12]

To illustrate the resilience of clientele norms around the provision of social assistance, one is tempted to highlight government handouts; for example, housing or consumption subsidies, that were designed to maintain corporatist loyalty. There can be no doubt that a proportion of these resources include a clientele dimension. Additional investment does not, however, necessarily equate to more clientelism or the same level of clientelism. Clientelism and services that aid deserving non-clients are bound to overlap. In Mexico, the corporatist union structure, which has an instrumental role in the Conasupo case study, covers individuals with a low-income or 'deserving' profile.

Likewise, even when lines between clients and non-clients and deserving clients can be demarcated, another problem emerges: what signposts mark the transition away from or a relaxation of clientelism? When loyal clients embrace social mobilisation – after the 1985 earthquake or perhaps voter disloyalty in 1988 and 1997 – does this signal a degeneration of clientelistic norms and structure in Mexico? Or, have clients requested a better deal in moments of patron vulnerability but without seeking or perhaps possessing the opportunity to re-negotiate the norms of state-society relations? What Arce (1999: 213) describes as a 'social contest that pits competing rent seekers against each other over a shrinking pie of revenues'. Similar, consider Hernández's (1991, 1990) discussion of the 'March of the 400 Pueblos' in 1990. He suggests that long-running clientelistic producer associations, often affiliated with the corporatist National Peasant Confederation (CNC) exerted pressure for more control over the state's traditional rural infrastructure but they were not seeking a radical transformation of Mexican agriculture. Research on the Popular Urban Movement (MUP) by Moctezuma (1993a, 1993b), Moreno (1993) and Bohórquez (1989) present comparable conclusions.

A better understanding of this final question is certainly a crucial dimension of the continuity and discontinuity debate. It forces us to ask, as a neoliberal state-society discourse diverts attention, 'agency' and responsibility from the state to individuals, what does the clientele population want or accept as legitimate, and how might the profile of this request or acceptance affect the evolution of specific policies?

The literature provides some indication of how a relaxation of clientelism might unfold in Mexico. Adopting a state-centred institutionalist perspective, Ward (1993) stresses continued technocratic recruitment and administration since the López Portillo public sector reforms of 1977. Morris (1991) posits two primary pressures on governmental corruption (of which clientelism is a meaningful component): that occurring from globalisation pressures (technological and international economic forces) for decentralisation and greater efficiency, and domestic structural transformations. Morris, in the latter, depicts a historically strong state and an equally weak society, a structure that maintained and legitimised Mexican clientelism/corruption. This functionalist account suggests that Mexican corruption 'peaked' between 1978 and 1981, when oil money strengthened the state, while it ebbed after 1982, when the financial crisis sapped the strength of the state.[13] Cornelius (1996: 39-41) asserts that the structure of the Mexican political elite, where upward mobility for elected and non-elected members rests on strict loyalty to one's boss, is crucial, and that changes in party politics and control over rewards strain this established structure. Fox (1994) points to cycles of confrontation between community organisations and middle/lower-tier reformist bureaucrats that have encouraged incremental steps toward pluralistic exchange, partly due to political learning and partly from hard fought gains by communities. Similarly, Foweraker and Craig (1990) focus on the role of so-called popular social movements, or pressure from below, as undermining clientelism and redrawing past state-society boundaries.

One way to proceed is to study developments ('signposts') largely inside society, either from a pluralistic or structural/institutional viewpoint.

One could also look to the actions of new entrants in the political arena, presumably products of a recent political climate. Are there signs of transformation, such as growth of NGOs, rejection of dwindling electorally-oriented handouts, and more pluralistic political party organisation and social participation? Have the clients demanded a different arrangement with the state? Various civil society and state-society studies confirm and shed much light on these issues (Aitken *et al.*, 1996; Barry, 1995; Cornelius *et al.*, 1994; González de la Rocha, 1991; La Botz, 1995; Lomelí *et al.*, 1996).

However, turning our attention in the opposite direction is the enthusiasm with which large segments of society, notably low-income populations, heralded Solidarity and voted for the PRI in 1991 and 1994. Another illustration comes from a case study by Acedo Angulo *et al.* (1995), where in 1992 the PAN Governor of Guanajuato – reacting to Solidarity resources bypassing PAN municipalities between 1989-1991 – spearheaded a rival participatory-oriented scheme called *Barrios y Colonias*. It faced insurmountable obstacles because PAN sympathisers, according to PAN officials, 'expected paternalism and were unwilling to participate' (Acedo Angulo *et al.*, 1995: 48). Martin's (1993) study of educational reforms in Jalisco (1988-1991) presents an interesting and comparable local climate, where local educators, parents and education ministry officials manipulated a federal decentralisation policy to increase patronage, clientelism and partisanship. The Cárdenas administration's insistence on putting the PRD emblem and the DFMA government logo on a new targeted milk scheme in Mexico City (the 'Betty Affair', see *El Universal*, 28/29 January 1999) – a clientelistic PRI-ploy lambasted by the PRD in the past – suggests that the social norms of a clientelistic political culture persists, at least in the eyes of the Cárdenas administration and in the more pluralistic, 'modern' DFMA electorate. Of course other developments such as opposition party expansion, a proliferation of NGOs, demands for clean elections and so forth, affirm that a transformation unfolds in significant segments and at a certain level of political discourse in Mexican society.

The current analysis contributes to the debate on clientelism and political structure by clarifying how far, after 1982, the federal government still recognised the salience and utility of maintaining the norms associated with continuity at Conasupo. No attempt is made to interpret 'what clients want' directly (e.g., a detailed, upward view of life below the state); instead causation for clientele norms and the socialisation process behind it are sought from what life looks like 'from the inside' of the state. It is instructive to examine the developments at parastatals handling social resources, for the reasons stated above and based on the rationale that if the government felt that the old model was exhausted, it would adopt a new approach in order to maintain power. Camp (1993: 13) states:

> ...Mexican politicians, lacking constituent responsibilities, have generally been pragmatic, doing whatever is necessary to remain in office rather than pursuing a committed, ideological platform.

Ames (1987) links management of public policy and general political pragmatism in a similar way, both in Mexico and across Latin America. It will be assumed that his basic argument remains valid.

Methodological Tools II: Integrating Institutions and Actors

At this stage, let us now proceed to discuss some general methodological tools employed in this study. Though we want to correlate structural social assistance and continuity in state-society relations, issues of precise welfare (did Conasupo improve health under Salinas?) or efficiency (did Conasupo lower the cost of delivering subsidies?) are secondary. Instead this research proposes to define and evaluate policy success and failure above all based on whether it continued to generate legitimacy for the executive, within some not very precise budget and distributional constraints. To differentiate a complex process such as 'generating legitimacy' and to decipher authoritarian clientelism from mere pork-barrel handouts will require attention not only to patterns in the distribution of Conasupo goods (rural versus urban, corporate versus non-corporate, individual versus group handouts) but also to the timing, terms, and structure in which transactions take place.

Table 1.0 Mexican Polling Data from 1988 and 1991*

Year	1988				1991				
(%)	PRI	PAN	Card.	*N*	PRI	PAN	PRD	Minor	*N*
Region									
North	59	24	15	479	71	21	5	3	477
Central	56	17	24	474	72	15	6	7	532
South	67	12	20	446	78	6	4	11	421
D.F.	42	25	29	515	56	18	13	14	599
Gender									
Male	53	20	25	973	63	16	10	11	975
Female	58	21	20	941	74	15	5	7	1,054
Union Member?									
Yes	64	14	22	442	74	13	7	5	460
No	53	22	23	1,472	67	16	8	10	1,509
Class									
Prof.	58	21	18	324	71	14	9	6	294
Middle	46	21	29	298	70	14	6	10	272
Working	59	15	24	325	62	17	10	11	386
% of Vote	55	20	22	1,914	68	15	7	9	2,029

*Gallup interviews conducted in May 1988 and July 1991
Source: Domínguez and McCann (1995: 38)

Patterns of electoral behaviour can suggest clues to the loyalty of Conasupo clients. It would be difficult to establish a direct electoral relationship because Mexican voters are influenced by a multitude of factors and because the geographic range of this study is too broad. At a lower level of analysis, moreover, the data that are available on Conasupo are apt to be unreliable and it would not lead to a strong electoral correlation. However this book can show whether patterns in Conasupo distribution parallel electoral support for the PRI, something pursued in similar studies of social policy.

Varley (1996) analyses land-titling and electoral behaviour, a general connection which helps her to understand how the PRI won 41 of 123 municipalities in the State of México in 1988, but turned around and won 121 of 123 municipalities in 1991. This turnaround, for her, is correlated to the delivery of basic services, 'what the poor voter clamoured for'. She calculates that 288,130 plots were regularised between 1974-1988, but the government regularised 1.1 million between 1989-1993, much of which came before the 1992 mid-term election – a distributive pattern that arises in Chapters Three and Four of this book. Bruhn (1996), Domínguez and McCann (1995), and Dresser (1991) produce similar studies that connect provision of social services and electoral behaviour.

Since subsequent chapters concentrate on the Salinas years, it is logical to highlight the 1988 presidential election, when record numbers of Mexicans voted for opposition parties, and the 1991 mid-term election, when the PRI staged a remarkable recovery. From table 1.0 it is possible to generalise that the typical Cardenista (later PRD) sympathiser (often middle or working class, often unionised, and often located in the D.F. or central Mexico) was more likely to access Conasupo than the typical PAN sympathiser (often professional or middle class, often non-unionised, and often located in the D.F. or northern Mexico).[14] Because the Cardenista/PRD profile broadly fits the 'strategic populations' that had preferential access to Conasupo, it is logical to focus on the challenge on the Left. The concurrent PRI recovery and the PRD decline in 1991 crosscut most electoral groups and can be attributed to many factors (a drop in inflation, party organisation, Solidarity, etc.).

Two important electoral groups that were likely to be influenced by Conasupo resources are the D.F. and female voters. Before 1988 Conasupo had been concentrated in the D.F.; it was part of a strategy to supplement the wage-income of public workers and official unions (Hewitt de Alcantara, 1987). Likewise, since it is typical that females of lower-income households have daily contact with Conasupo, females (notably females who voted for the PRD) represents an interesting category. Among females, 1991 marked a major swing for the PRI (58 percent to 74 percent) and away from the PRD (20 percent down to 5 percent), while the PAN's percentage was less volatile (21 down to 15 percent).

The book adopts Ward's general conception of a 'negotiated social policy' (see Introduction) to help assess executive management and shifts in clientele norms (such as informal negotiations and preferential corporatist agreements). This approach invites empirical verification based on policy output and process (sources of political capital), and avoids delving into the motives of certain actors. For experience shows no exact correlation between the stated motives of policy elites and the final character of Conasupo policy. This approach also appeals to historical precedent and logic, connecting developments and tendencies at Conasupo that predate and follow 1982. After examining Conasupo intervention in the basic foods marketplace from the 1930s to the 1980s, economic historian Ochoa (1994: 322) writes,

> ... it was not the purpose of the State Food Agency [Conasupo] to solve Mexico's hunger and nutrition problems. Instead, in participating in the marketplace it has served to increase access to foodstuffs at slightly below the going rate, and in the process has attempted to win political support.

How 'process' relates to political capital deserves further comment. The old model of state-society relations relies on perpetuating a 70-year myth, namely, that the government is pursuing social justice and that it alone can confront the interests that inhibit this process (domestic and foreign capitalists, foreign governments, the Church, large land-owners, etc.). This logic cements the corporatist branches of the PRI, political elites and Mexicans loyal to the old model (i.e., 'shared interests'). It also provides the impetus for policy innovation when social justice appears overtly compromised because the appearance of shared interests (part of the political capital of social policy) must be maintained. However, the absence of social justice in Mexico, despite social programmes promulgated in its name, underscores the fact that perpetuating the local-executive process takes greater precedence over achieving a successful outcome, and in the end produces more continuity and less discontinuity. Indeed, had the government fulfilled its promises, then the logic of a powerful executive, official corporatism and the old, clientele state-society model in general would be seriously compromised, and along with it the tacit bargains that society enters in return for some sense of social justice.

Turning to more general theory, the following analysis incorporates methodological tools from both the institutionalist and pluralist approaches to bureaucracy and public policy. This eclectic approach is a response to the climate one encounters inside Conasupo and the factors that influenced relevant policymaking at the top levels of the government.

To begin, Ames (1999: 222) writes, 'scholars can conceive of institutions as either objects of explanation or as explanatory concepts'. I adopt the latter viewpoint. The institutional hypothesis contends that it is the variation in the institutions or rules of policy making that help account for different patterns with respect to policy formulation and final policy outcomes. Rules imply 'routines, procedures, conventions, roles, strategies, organisational forms, and technologies around which political activity is constructed' (March and Olsen, 1989: 22). Policy studies in this vein try to pinpoint and extrapolate how institutional configurations emit positive and negative incentives concerning the agency of individuals or groups, and, in turn, how these configurations effect a policy's development, implementation, final execution and monitoring. This approach also deduces what passes for 'appropriate behaviour' by illuminating patterned outcomes in a given institutional order, and thus concerns itself with contextual circumstances, linking institutions to individual or collective action. What types of institutions help us understand continuity and discontinuity at Conasupo?

First of all, institutions sometimes encourage dynamism, mobility and innovation, and at other times stagnation, atrophy and the status quo. For example, Mexico's constitutional prohibition against re-election to public office assures cyclical turnover at the federal, state and local level, injecting mobility across the political system. It also detaches politicians from their constituencies. Systemic mobility affects Conasupo policy at the design, execution and monitoring stages. New executives appoint their Conasupo team, in turn these officials operate with the knowledge and expectation that their mandate concludes in six years or less. This exerts strong incentives for short-term planning, for use of the agency as a stepping stone to a future post and for reluctance to tackle long-running issues such as corruption and clientelism. Also, prohibiting the re-election of members of Congress (introduced into the Constitution in 1933) weakens the monitoring of parastatal activities. In Mexico, the Chamber of Deputies (like the US House of Representatives) investigates usage of all public funds.

'No re-election' is one institutional dimension that contributes to the cycles of incomplete and unsuccessful projects in the area of food subsidies. Upon taking office, López Portillo cancelled Echeverría's National Nutrition Programme, de la Madrid cancelled The Mexican Food System (SAM), Salinas cancelled The National Food Programme (Pronal), and Zedillo cancelled Solidarity. It is noteworthy that Conasupo featured prominently in each scheme, and survived as these larger schemes were abandoned.

Institutional dynamics therefore offer clues or a guide as we investigate the parameters for neoliberal technocrats and executive management. Interestingly, interviews with Conasupo bureaucrats reveal that they expect administrative projects to end with the presidential term despite the fact that they are supposedly crafting policy across sexenial boundaries. Today at Conasupo there remains a strong sentiment that policy is in the hands of the executive and dependent on the six-year presidential timetable, a set of expectations that emerges in Chapter Six's discussion of the current Progresa programme.

A complex of norms, conventions and expected accommodations concerning the PRI's corporatist branches regulate recruitment to some parastatals, including Conasupo, and, though strained after 1982, these institutional features help to maintain the corporate-government partnership (see Spalding, 1981; Sloan, 1985). The government also insists on direct negotiation with the corporatist labour and *campesino* leadership, and this, together with aspects of Mexican labour and rural property law, can sometimes paralyse state-society relations across certain policy areas – land distribution, public housing funds, legal mechanisms in Mexican labour law, etc.

An example from this government-corporate sector framework brings Conasupo into this discussion. Although it is not official policy, incoming executives have consistently entered formal corporatist negotiations (*concertación*) with the PRI-affiliated CTM and CNC in order to arrange guidelines for Conasupo policy for the next five years. In part this forum shaped Conasupo policymaking during the 1960s and 1970s, and it became overt during the de la Madrid years when the executive increased the flow of resources to loyal corporate leaders in 1983. Chapter Two examines how this institutional dynamic unfolded at the beginning of the Salinas term.

Discussing the Salinas years, Mexican sociologist Gurza Lavalle (1994: 81) concludes that 'in reality, to restructure Conasupo is to redefine the social dimension of what is understood as *public*'. For him, President Salinas legitimised and repositioned private capitalism into 'public' or what society demarcated as 'strategic' sectors. His reference to the dimensions of the public or what people understood or expected as strategic opens the door to two types of institutionalist observations. On the one hand (and this is his intention) segments of Mexican society expect the government to deliver certain goods and to do otherwise challenges the institutional foundation of state-society relations. This basic contention has been discussed above.

On the other hand, inside the public sphere associated with Conasupo – of course, this is one of many public spheres – there prevailed a set of norms, rules and appropriate behaviour. Examples of its *modus operandi* could be observed in daily interaction around Conasupo services, community dialogue to secure services initially and continued supply or capitalisation later that frequently involved informality and clientelism. Attention to the institutional order where society engages the government is necessary if we want to conceptualise how neoliberal policy prescriptions affected the parastatal's capacity to generate support for the executive or transform state-society relations.

For instance 'community participation' featured in the October 1989 Conasupo agenda. This step was designed to exert pressure on local intermediaries and improve Conasupo's performance. Effective participation had to start with policymakers, who had to formulate a coherent plan to overcome these prevailing institutional configurations, where members from society expected clientelism and abuse. If this did not occur, then it would be hard to imagine meaningful participation taking place.[15] Chapter Three examines whether or not Salinas took coherent steps to transform the prevailing institutions at this intersection of state and society.

However, while the incentives vital to the institutionalist reveal much about everyday Conasupo policymaking, the challenges awaiting reformers, and the general constraints on the agency of actors, they offer an incomplete story. At least in part, imposing neoliberal reforms at Conasupo infers discord between existing institutions and new policy initiatives. Sometimes this clash between old and new does not materialise over a long time horizon, according to an institutionalist, incremental logic, but rather is a product of contemporary configurations of power between interest groups inside and outside the government. Moreover, there were occasions when policymakers 'broke the rules'. Alongside institutional configurations, it is therefore instructive to integrate a pluralist's conception of public policy and bureaucracy.

Pluralism embodies a set of analytical tools and policy prescriptions to the issues of political power and process.[16] It assumes that multiple actors, some more obvious than others, crowd a given policy arena and that actor dynamics bear strongly on the outcome of policymaking. Studies from this perspective give primacy to the efficacy of individual and group strategies in reproducing or transforming patterns of political action.

In addition, at Conasupo one might add that who formulates the rules, their strategies and interaction with a given institutional context, counts alongside the rules, incentives, and norms under observation.[17] Although a handful of actors oversee major Conasupo policy decisions (privatisations, pricing policies, new programmes, etc.), it is also true that private firms, middle and lower-tier bureaucrats, partisan interests and foreign actors are influential. For example, Chapter Two shows that President Salinas did not act independently of the recommendations of a 1986 World Bank report on Mexican food markets, the wishes of private tortilla maker Maseca, and other group interests. Furthermore, inside Conasupo one encounters disparate bureaucratic currents ranging from Marxists to Keynesians to neoliberals.[18]

To combine the rules, norms and structure of the institutionalist and the group dynamics or agency of the pluralist methodology – or 'reciprocal causality' according to Ames (1999: 222) – is not novel for general studies of Mexican politics. Camp (1993: 10), after reviewing the claims made by pluralists, institutionalists and Marxists, expounds a mid-range theoretical alternative,

> An eclectic approach to politics, incorporating culture, history, geography, and external relations, provides the most adequate vision of contemporary political behavior.

Nor is this approach novel for studies of policy making in Mexico. Writing in the 1970s, Grindle (1977c) constructs a mid-range or eclectic model to explain the causes of rural policy change. Her explanatory scheme revolves around (1) institutional features (no re-election and tight executive control of public sector careers), (2) inter-ministerial rivalry (e.g., a pluralistic or multi-actor view of bureaucracy), and (3) broad intellectual currents and mid-level bureaucratic reformism. These factors, together, produced a policy process that led President Echeverría to adopt a favourable stance toward subsistence agriculture.

Following on from these earlier studies, the framework adopted for this present research will be more empirically driven and less theoretically rigid, an admission of a particular climate discovered inside Conasupo. At Conasupo, political 'legitimacy is based upon a system of beliefs, of shared values, that stems from concrete realities and expectations' (Rubio and Newell, 1984: 2), or the intermixing of formal and informal institutions alongside political context that is based on group and power dynamics at a moment in time.

Yet, while methodological eclecticism is a more accurate picture of the Conasupo policy arena, the institutional weight of social inertia around Conasupo in the late 1980s needs to be accented in order to strike the appropriate balance between structure and agency. Indeed, many norms from an era of hegemonic PRI rule are so firmly embedded in the system that they are almost taken for granted. Some Conasupo policymakers do not consider it at all surprising, for example, that they use the words 'us' and 'the PRI' and 'the government' and 'the administration' interchangeably when discussing social policy, Conasupo's past and present, and the parastatal's relationship with opposition governors. Moreover, for over 25 years Conasupo competed with other parastatals (notably the Ministry of Agriculture and Ministry of Water Resources) and with periodic social sector initiatives for resources, partisan recruitment, delivery of services and allocation of contracts that led to a lasting imprint on a number of administrative and operative areas. Outside Conasupo, technocrats formulated policy that relied on social actors, both intermediaries and final beneficiaries, who have operated in a wider political culture that includes pervasive and embedded social orientations concerning the solicitation, the reciprocity and the final provision of basic services. With these factors in mind, this analysis aims to illuminate some ways in which conceptions of the state, 'public philosophies, historical contexts, and elite and public preferences intersect with institutional structures to produce particular policy outcomes' (Thelen and Steinmo, 1992: 27). Thelen and Steinmo (p.27), self-proclaimed mid-range theorists writing from the institutionalist perspective, write,

> Political evolution is a path or branching process and the study of the points of departure from established patterns ('critical junctures' of institutional choice) becomes essential to a broader understanding of political history.

Critical junctures focus on instances when institutional constraints and actor/group dynamics threaten patterns of political activity. The Conasupo *Modernización* Plan (1990-1994), analysed in great detail in the next four chapters, poses a critical juncture at an important Mexican parastatal. What was being proposed was incompatible with past state-society relations. Previously, institutional constraints and a collection of foreign and domestic interests propped up the parastatal or coalesced around its policymakers. Most actors coincided with the pursuit of executive legitimacy and social justice and were consistent with the existing institutional order, while other interest groups, for instance, the World Bank and domestic business associations, propounded another course. Events during the CMP present a window to inspect how a major reform agenda traversed and interacted with a maze of institutions and interest groups and, in the end, either disrupted or maintained a state-society balance predicated on previous institutional configurations and interest group behaviour.

Conclusion

General theorising from the modernisation or neoliberal perspective about continuity and discontinuity has not produced an accurate map of post-1982 state-society relations in Mexico. Consequentially, the dynamics involved are not well understood and require eclectic modes of explanation. Predictions based on processes of modernisation or neoliberal theory have placed Mexico's old model at the brink of collapse at various moments after the 1982-1983 economic crisis. Given the coexistence of continuity and discontinuity, coupled with the tendency towards incremental rather than rapid transformations in state-society relations, this chapter suggests an alternative methodology that is sensitive to institutional constraints and other conceptual tools. Chapter Two starts the Conasupo case study by analysing how institutional constraints influenced the formulation of President Salinas' agenda at the parastatal.

Appendix 1.0: An Overview of Conasupo Development (1961-1988)

On 15 March 1961, rising speculation in domestic food markets impelled the government to merge what had been miscellaneous food programmes into The National Basic Foods Company (Conasupo).[19] Figure 1.0 sketches antecedents prior to the formation of Conasupo. Today Conasupo employees typically refer to the Wheat Market Regulation Committee (1937-1938), a parastatal that intervened throughout the production-consumption chain for wheat, as the main precursor to the modern Conasupo apparatus.

- Wheat Market Regulation Committee (1937-1938)
- Mexican Export and Import Company (Ceimsa, 1938-1961)
- Consultation Committee for Necessary Consumption Items *and* the Marketing Monitoring Committee (1940-1941)
- National Distribution and Regulation Board (Nadyrsa, 1941-1949)
- By presidential decree Nadyrsa became part of Ceimsa (1949-1951)
- Scope of Ceimsa intensified and extended (1959-1961)
- National Basic Foods Company (Conasupo, decreed 15 March 1961)

Source: Secretaria de la Presidencia (1974)

Figure 1.0 Antecedents to Conasupo

During the 1960s the parastatal steadily concentrated its resources in Mexico City, a policy designed to curb wage growth and bolster nonwage income of the working and middle classes. Later, rising rural instability prompted Presidents Echeverría and López Portillo to stretch Conasupo resources into the rural sector, however this did not alter the preferential treatment of Mexico City consumers. By the 1970s, Conasupo's mandate grew to include the regulation of basic food markets, processing activities, a monopoly over all grain imports and exports, a national food reserve system, a national grain storage system, supply of food across public sector institutions (hospitals, schools, the military, etc.), and co-ordination of emergency and natural disaster relief. To perform these multiple tasks, Conasupo developed a number of decentralised, semiautonomous, and task-oriented branches (table 1.1).

Table 1.1 Overview of Conasupo's Decentralised Branches

Branches of Conasupo System	First Year	Function
• Conasupo, Central Branch	1961	Organisation/co-ordination
• Boruconsa, *Bodegas Rurales Conasupo, S.A.*	1971	Grain Storage/collection
• Iconsa, *Industrias Conasupo, S.A.*	1975	Processing
• Triconsa, *Trigo Industrializado Conasupo, S.A.*	1972	Processing bread/wheat flour
• Liconsa, *Leche Industrializada, S.A.*	1972	Processing/distribution milk
• Impecsa, *Impulsora del Pequeño Comercio, S.A.*	1977	Distribution (businesses)
• Diconsa, *Sistema de Distribuidoras Conasupo, S.A.*	1972	Distribution (households)
• Fidelist, *Fideicomiso para la Liquidación al Subsidio de la Tortilla**	1991	Tortilla distribution/Progresa programme
• FIA, *Fondo para la Industria Asociada*	1981	Credit to processors
• Andsa, *Almacenes Nacionales de Depósito, S.A.*	1936	Grain storage/collection

continued..

Infrastructure of Conasupo's Decentralised Branches (1988):

Diconsa	22,669 retail outlets	
	7,222	urban stores
	15,447	rural stores
	352	warehouses

Liconsa   5 industrial plants; 1,477 retail outlets or *lecherías*

Miconsa   5 industrial plants; 37 percent of the domestic corn flour

Boruconsa 1,642 grain collection centres

Iconsa   11 Industrial groups with 19 production plants producing cooking oil, butter, pasta for soup, cookies, soap, detergents, wheat and corn flour and clothing

Impecsa   163 Wholesale Warehouses

* Diconsa operated the government Tortilla Programme before 1991.
Source: Informe de Gobierno 1988, Statistical Annex.

Arguably, one finds layered into Conasupo's infrastructure disparate executive projects as well as the remnants of longer-term economic development strategies. In a way, Conasupo has been constantly 'recreated' to meet the challenges facing new executives. Echeverría's efforts to defuse rural tensions via a celebrated pro-*campesino* agenda provided the impulse for constructing thousands of community Boruconsa grain silos ('*conos*'). Similarly, The Mexican Agricultural System's (SAM, 1978-1982) official concern with structural barriers in the Mexican agricultural sector – viewed as causing Mexico's dependence on imported basic commodities – led López Portillo to construct processing plants and the rapid growth of most Conasupo branches (Austin and Esteva, 1987; Meissner, 1982, 1981; Redclift, 1981). The National Food Programme

(Pronal), de la Madrid's replacement for SAM, shifted attention to consumption subsidies by inflating the Conasupo distribution branch's (Diconsa) retail outlets in number (13,000 rural stores in 1984) and size (first-ever mega-super markets in urban areas).[20] Here de la Madrid 'recreated' Conasupo as a mechanism to secure popular consumption during Mexico's post-1982 economic crisis. The impetus for Conasupo development was also connected to general policies of import-substitution-industrialisation, oil-led growth, corporatism, and low wage and low inflation economic development. This vast public enterprise therefore stood in between millions of consumers and producers, strategically inserting the government in the middle of competing interests: urban and rural, capital (industrial versus agricultural), class (*campesinos* versus manufacturing workers) and regional (south, central and north).

Nonetheless, although Conasupo's activities stemmed from the broad mandate to regulate basic food markets, it is worth underscoring that the government never equipped it to accomplish this function. On average, Conasupo marketed 15 percent of the domestic corn harvest and a lower percentage of other crops between the 1960s and 1980s. It never approached 'controlling' the market *per se*, but instead, as Ochoa's (1994) historical investigation discovers, it delivered palliatives to specific groups of producers, consumers and intermediaries.

Likewise, by 1988 Conasupo imported 4 out of every 5 kilos of corn that it distributed, even though Mexico produced around 12 million tons of corn or roughly enough to cover domestic *human* consumption. In 1983, a good year for corn production, Conasupo imported 72 percent of its corn. In large part, the situation observed by 1988 can be viewed as the end of a pattern dating back to the 1970s. Mexican production has not dipped below domestic human consumption needs since Conasupo's formation in 1961, yet it supplied cheaper imported corn to urban areas in order to lower domestic prices and divert domestic production, increasingly in the 1970s, into the cattle sector as feed grain. Intervening in this way eventually disconnected many producers from their natural markets in urban areas. This dynamic in turn produced an inertia, political economy and logic whereby the government expanded the scope of Conasupo as urbanisation and population growth rates swelled urban centres in the 1960s, 1970s and 1980s. In the mid-1970s, Cornelius (1975: 214) discovered that Conasupo was a common fixture in marginal urban communities around Mexico City.

Nearly two-thirds of the migrants had benefited from the government's marketing of low-cost foodstuffs and other commodities through CONASUPO stores or mobile markets.

By the end of the 1970s, Hall and Price (1982: 310) reported that, across Mexico, an estimated 70 percent of low-income households consumed Conasupo goods.

Table 1.2 Total Nominal Conasupo Spending as a Percentage of Total Parastatal Spending excluding PEMEX ($US million)

Year	Total Conasupo Spending (1)	Total Parastatal Spending (2)	(%) (1)/(2)
1974	465.44	1,731.20	27
1975	636.48	2,890.72	22
1976	165.01	1,438.15	12
1977	241.69	1,809.99	13
1978	485.43	2,300.96	21
1979	603.56	3,229.05	19
1980	1,221.15	5,520.04	22
1981	1,784.97	7,380.74	24
1982	838.41	3,610.08	23
1983	877.07	4,981.77	18
1984	1,806.50	5,504.85	33
1985	1,217.90	4,201.88	29
1986	687.92	2,468.98	28
1987	470.18	1,885.06	25
1988	776.59	2,544.26	31
1989	1,329.16	3,371.68	39

Source: Martín del Campo and Calderón (1990: 92).

These introductory comments indicate, by the 1980s, that Conasupo rivalled or surpassed other parastatals as a reservoir of patronage through its handling of contracts, transportation, public jobs, imports and exports, subsidies for consumers, intermediaries and producers, and so forth. A brief review of the academic literature on Conasupo reveals a political dimension of Conasupo development.

Table 1.3 Ranking according to Total Parastatal Budget

Year	1978-1982	1983-1984	1985-1988
Conasupo Parastatal Ranking	4th	2nd	4th
Order	PEMEX	PEMEX	PEMEX
	CFE	Conasupo	CFE
	IMSS	CFE	IMSS
	Conasupo	IMSS	Conasupo

Source: *Informe de Gobierno* (1988) statistical annex.

Ochoa depicts the period 1970 to 1982 as the parastatal's 'golden years', marking its transformation from mere welfare to a fundamental component in national development. Echoing this view, Lustig and Martín del Campo (1985: 221) furnish data on Conasupo's operating deficit; it climbed 150 percent in real terms on average between 1977-1982, and, in 1981, the height of the SAM programme, it went up a spectacular 1,125 percent in real terms over 1980. Behind the statistics, moreover, Echeverría elevated the parastatal's status by appointing powerful PRI Senator Jorge de la Vega to the post of general director of Conasupo and made ex-Diconsa director (1968-1970) Carlos Torres Manzo Secretary of Commerce. With its heightened stature in the Mexican bureaucracy, by the conclusion of the 1970s Conasupo appeared to many a labyrinth of producers, processors, intermediaries, distributors, final consumers, technical consultants and market analysts. Table 1.3 shows that only PEMEX eclipsed Conasupo spending in 1983 and 1984, indicating that for two years Conasupo outpaced appropriations for health and education. In 1988, as seen in table 1.2, Conasupo represented 31 percent of non-PEMEX parastatal resources, and table 1.3 indicates that it ranked fourth after PEMEX, The National Electricity Company (CFE) and IMSS. Although it does not appear in these tables, in 1988 it also delivered an impressive 45 percent of total public sector subsidies (*Informe de Gobierno*, 1988).

The Political Economy of Conasupo Development

An early case study of Conasupo comes from Alisky (1973: 59), who introduces his subject as a parastatal acclaimed across Latin America, and goes on to endorse the performance of Conasupo Directors *Professor* Carlos Hank González (1965-1968) and later Jorge de la Vega (1970-1974).

> A study of the operations of Conasupo, a probing of its political overtones, indicates that this Basic Commodities Company indeed does achieve the bonus yield of a favorable image among the public it serves, and symbolizes to the lowest-paid or impoverished Mexicans one facet of governmental service, a specific program of social justice.[21]

However, negative repercussions seemed to parallel the parastatal's rapid expansion, and in the 1970s, research on Conasupo turned unmistakably pessimistic. It no longer prompted social justice but nurtured PRI authoritarianism, obstructed popular mobilisation against a faltering regime, and postponed a transition to democracy (Fox and Gordillo, 1989; Fox, 1992; Appendini, 1992; Austin and Esteva, 1987). Rapid expansion coupled with lax administrative controls produced a self-sustaining bureaucracy, captured most convincingly in Grindle's (1977a, 1977b, 1980) seminal work during the mid-1970s. For her, 'policy implementors', that is, local Conasupo agents, operated local clientelistic webs of PRI and/or executive patronage. In turn, a negative political economy pervaded the Conasupo apparatus. Conceptually, Grindle's experience with Echeverría's rural reformism and SAM led her to depict Conasupo clientelism, patronage and sub-performance as stemming from localised partisan contingencies and not reformist policy elites. This is an important distinction that surfaces in later Conasupo case studies.

Tharp Hilger (1980: 491) applied a private-sector-marketing model to Conasupo before SAM injected unprecedented funds into the parastatal.

> Both strategic and operating marketing decisions are impinged upon by the political context in which Conasupo exists...the place Conasupo and its administrators have in the Mexican political hierarchy must also be accounted for when describing the marketing strategies that it pursues... formal organizational structure and decentralization do not mean that decision-making is decentralized. In fact, it appears Conasupo's structure and reward systems contribute to centralization of strategic, administrative, and operating decisions in marketing areas. In addition, such centralization and external influence in decision-making contribute to inconsistencies in organizational purpose, marketing objectives, and tactics and programs designed to meet those goals.

Heath (1985), another economist, drew a similar conclusion. Subsequent studies lament how oil revenue and a burgeoning public sector cultivated obstinate institutional interests. Austin and Fox (1987: 87) write,

> [parastatals such as Conasupo] should not be viewed, as instruments that respond automatically, willingly, or even efficiently. Their responsiveness is shaped by the positive and negative incentives for change that they face. Each SOE [State Owned Enterprises] has its own institutional agenda, and its managers have individual priorities. Any new policy thrust impinges on these institutional and individual agendas and priorities, and the degree of congruence shapes the responsiveness. It should also be recognised that SOEs have a natural tendency to bend the policy in the implementation process toward their own inclinations, which may deviate from the original intentions of the policy makers.

Hall and Price (1982: 313) offer another pessimistic view of the SAM experience:

> Conasupo, which is the institutional mechanism for the implementation of many of the SAM's programmes, may itself be the greatest barrier to

increased domestic production [of food] and its distribution.

Their study also distinguishes a reformist policy elite from a politicised Conasupo bureaucracy adept at defending and advancing its interests.

With the advent of the 1982 economic crisis, Conasupo soon symbolised the populist excesses of the López Portillo administration, and, according to Jusidman de Bialotovsky (1987), it promptly reverted to being an emergency welfare tool lying outside a national development strategy. Fiscal austerity during the 1980s in effect marooned Conasupo between irreconcilable consumer desires for low prices and producer demands for the opposite. Moreover, in 1983-1984, Cox (1985), former British ambassador to Mexico, notes that access to and control over Diconsa retail outlets were instrumental in securing inflation agreements with the CTM. As Conasupo operations increased in the 1980s, de la Madrid supposedly used it to reward supportive unions while punishing disloyal ones. The comments of Raúl Salinas (1988: 11), Director of Diconsa (1983-1988), reveal the political reality that researchers encountered and criticised during the 1980s:

> Diconsa's function is to carry basic products to the classes that most need them. But providing basic products to these classes most in need is never neutral. Nothing in society is politically and socially neutral...Who processes them, who carries them and finally who buys them, remains a decision of political and strategic character. Because of this, each one of our decisions [at Diconsa] is tied to the administrative strategy of President Miguel de la Madrid.

By 1988, Conasupo had defended and advanced its interests vis-à-vis the populist reformers of the Echeverría and López Portillo years as well as the neoliberal, belt-tightening technocrats of the de la Madrid years. It is at this juncture that this current study picks up the Conasupo story.

Notes

[1] The research by Davis (1994) on Mexico City's system of community representatives (*delegados*) and by Grindle (1977) and Ward (1989, 1990) on basic service provision depict informal federal-local dialogue as a crucial factor behind stability in Mexican state-society relations.

[2] The interpretation by Baer (1993: 55) summarises one view in the literature: '...the adoption of a market economy is fundamentally incompatible with corporatism. Corporatist organizations had existed in a symbiotic relationship with parastatal industries, which functioned as politicized economic preserves of labor unions. When efficiency and market forces replaced patronage as employment criteria, reductions in force and a decline in union clout were inevitable consequences'.

[3] Philip (1986: 122-123) was an early scholar to speculate that the post-1982 danger to the system would not come from the economic burden on formerly co-opted peasants and the working class but instead from the 'urban and above all metropolitan middle class which has benefited from subsidized food, subsidized transport, a disproportionate share of public works and, for most of the past fifteen years, a relatively cheap dollar'. With PRD support based in the Mexico City middle class and PAN support based in the northern urban middle class, recent experience seems to confirm Philip's prediction.

[4] Similar viewpoints are offered by Baer and Weintraub (1994), Quezada (1993), Salinas (1991), and Reott (1995).

[5] According to the IDB (1994: 1): 'The 1993 approval of the North American Free Trade Agreement (NAFTA) between Canada, Mexico, and the United States heralds a rediscovery of hemispheric relations based on democracy, economic liberalization, and the freedom to unleash outward growth'. Volumes by Colclough, Manor, *et al.* (1991) and Smith *et al.* (1994) explore the debate on the linkage between political and economic liberalisation.

[6] There is a rich literature on Mexican social policy; among others see Nord (1994), Mesa Lago (1989), Ward (1993), and Friedmann *et al.* (1995).

[7] Varley (1996: 205) makes a good point that often new executive projects soon mean whatever people want them to. Some argue that Solidarity was withheld from opposition districts to punish disloyalty, while others argue that the funds were targeted to such districts to undermine opposition.

[8] The cautionary words of Maier *et al.* (1989: 22) resonate in this case study: 'Not all efforts to reclaim the private from the political yield successful outcomes. We may want the market but end up with the Mafia'.

[9] While the 'Solidarity Committees' were a new feature of Mexican social policy, of course the various Solidarity programmes that paved roads, constructed health clinics, offered education scholarships, delivered regional development funds and sponsored community infrastructure projects were not.

[10] Alternatively, Roniger (1990, Ch.1) argues that Mexican clientelism is more dynamic and capable of innovation as society modernises and passes through periodic crises.

[11] Brachet-Márquez and Sherraden (1994) arrive at a similar conclusion in their general study of welfare changes under de la Madrid and Salinas. In particular, they show that the government responded to economic austerity by cutting public sector wages to avoid discontinuing health and nutrition services.

[12] Fox's (1994) continuum runs from pluralism to semiclientelism to authoritarian clientelism, tying each category to degrees of citizenship: achieved (pluralism), restricted (semiclientelism) and denied (authoritarian clientelism). Optimistically, Baer (1997: 141) claims that, by 1997, Mexican politics struggled with 'lingering pork-barrel politics'; Gershberg (1994) makes a similar argument.

[13] However, corruption during moments of 'state weakness' – related to the privatisation of parastatals and the billions of dollars lost in the importation of grains during the de la Madrid *sexenio* – limit the utility of assuming that a 'financially strong state equals more corruption' in this case study.

[14] This division was actually more overt because the PAN campaign in 1988 supported the liquidation of Conasupo while the PRD supported its expansion. Similar policy positions arose in 1991 and 1994.

[15] Morris (1991: 47) notes an interesting constraint on participation: Mexican courts hold the person who files a corruption complaint financially accountable if the case is not proven.

[16] Dahl (1982, 1961) is a central figure in the development of pluralism; Kimber (1994) and McFarland (1987) provide useful pluralists views on interest groups.

[17] Discussing current approaches to state-society interaction in Mexico, Brachet-Márquez (1995: 164) posits, 'scholars are faced with the relatively new problem of identifying complex networks of actors who, in the course of carrying out their private projects and strategies, may in some circumstances reproduce the established order but transform it in others'.

[18] In the course of this research I have been quizzed on Marxist economics – 'Is it really true that only three universities in the USA still teach Marxist economics?' – the sanctity of free markets and private enterprise, the neutrality of technocratic planning – 'The computer now decides who receives subsidies' – the validity of government intervention, the supposed 'Mafia that actually makes policy' – the evil colossus of the North, the value of social work and redistribution – 'I am here to help the poor' – the ugly side of corruption and other blends of ideological or workplace orientations. The opinion data presented in appendix 6.0 captures the pluralistic employee profile found at Conasupo.

[19] For details on the Mexican government's early intervention in domestic food markets, see Yates (1978: 763-803), Ochoa (1994) and Gamble (1970).

[20] Solís (1984) discusses the arguments for expanding Diconsa under the Pronal. See Moreno (1987) for a general discussion of Pronal.

[21] For a less optimistic view of Conasupo development in the 1960s, see Yates (1978).

2 The Policy Formation Period: Incentives, Actors and Institutional Constraints

Introduction

This chapter covers the period between the 1988 presidential campaign and the announcement (21 October 1989) and immediate reaction to the Conasupo *Modernización* Plan (CMP, 1990-1994) – hereafter the policy formation period (PFP). On the campaign trail candidate Carlos Salinas initiated the PFP by floating the idea of liquidating Conasupo, while as President Salinas marked its conclusion by unveiling an ambitious reform package and declaring Conasupo a 'fundamental right earned by all Mexican workers and *campesinos*' (*El Gobierno Mexicano*, 1994b). Analysing this brief flirtation with sharp policy discontinuity reveals much about the politics of food in Mexico, and more importantly, the constraints and pressures for innovation at Conasupo that ultimately produce significant continuity in state-society relations involving this parastatal, beneficiary groups, and President Salinas.

It is important to emphasise that the PFP overlaps with the transition to a new administration, a strategic juncture in Mexican state-society relations when the incoming president crafts bureaucratic teams, consolidates corporatist backing, and assuages anxiety within the private sector. He must transmit the appropriate signals to foreign lending institutions and the United States government while appearing to defend Mexican sovereignty and popular symbols. During this interlude, the patronage mechanisms endogenous of the traditional state-society model operate to legitimise the new executive, reward loyalty and punish disloyalty. Thus a systemic timetable, with wider constraints and pressures for policy innovation, crosscuts the specific circumstances relevant to the

PFP (i.e., relevant to Conasupo policy). Furthermore, outside Conasupo, the ascendancy of the left-wing *Cardenista* challenge before and after the 1988 election exerted pressure on Salinas to uphold nationalistic symbols of social justice, including Conasupo, or risk more PRI defections. This threat gave greater weight to the general constraints of the Salinas transition period.

This chapter starts with the assumption that candidate Salinas was serious about complete discontinuation of Conasupo. This assumption is based on interviews with Conasupo policy-makers that served during the PFP. The chapter reconstructs the course of policy development, as indicated by the public record and the process emanating from actual sources. It also probes some 'behind the scenes' factors that may have contributed to the eventual choice of strategy, including the pivotal intervention of two key actors – Salinas's Commerce Secretary Jamie Serra Puche and his brother and top-level Conasupo functionary Raúl Salinas de Gortari. While some elements of the explanation inevitably remain open to debate, this conflict of the public and private record generates a reasonably specific context within which to analyse the interplay between factors of continuity and discontinuity in this policy area.

External Pressures – Constraints and Conasupo Reforms

The timing and packaging of Conasupo reforms suggest that to some extent Salinas balanced audiences at home and abroad. Discussing the World Bank, Conasupo and the CMP, Gurza Lavalle (1994: 104-105) writes,

> The final Conasupo *Modernización* Plan adopted a closer resemblance to World Bank loan conditionality and displayed less congruence with the eleven recommendations produced by Conasupo General Director Ignacio Ovalle at Los Pinos [the executive's office] on 22 August 1989.

Arguably, the evidence in this chapter indicates that the crucial dynamic driving the PFP remained domestic and that conceptions of 'external constraints' are exaggerated. However, it is still important to discern how and to what degree foreign actors exerted pressure on Conasupo policy during the PFP.

Foreign Debt Negotiation: Pressure for Public Spending Reform

Mexico's debt burden topped the policy agenda in 1988-1989. Mexican real GDP growth averaged zero percent between 1982-1988, a period when the state paid international banks around ($US) 10 billion annually (World Bank, 1996) and debt payments on interest and principal exceeded fresh loans by ($US) 45.53 billion (Russell, 1994). When Salinas entered office in December 1988 domestic and international debt obligations consumed 60 percent of the public sector budget (Centeno, 1994). Hence lower debt payments were a prerequisite to future economic growth, and in a minor way the fate of Conasupo came to overlap with a negotiating process that eventually ended in the servicing of Mexican debt.

In speeches to business, *campesino* and labour associations during the course of the PFP, Salinas intertwined the debt issue with the difficulties afflicting the country. To one official union he proclaimed that 'renegotiating the foreign debt would lower inflation' and there was 'no better policy to improve the lives of all Mexican workers than cutting inflation' (*El Gobierno Mexicano*, 1994h). In 1988 and 1989 Salinas recycled this argument on multiple occasions in speeches to the General Assembly of the National Agricultural Council (CAP) and the Labour Congress (CT).

The need for structural reform of public sector spending and parastatal activities helped to solidify Salinas' commitment to balance public revenues and expenditures. After de la Madrid's experience, both positive (Mexico continued debt payments) and negative (the government overshot IMF public spending targets), anything less than a full commitment to the public sector deficit jeopardised ongoing debt negotiations. Stoking foreign creditors fears, presidential candidate Cuauhtémoc Cárdenas skilfully wielded the 'debt moratorium card' in the 1988 campaign. By pressing the issue and demanding debt re-negotiation for Mexico, Cárdenas forced Salinas to the left at a time when he preferred to concentrate on the right-wing PAN challenge. However, our concern in this section is the foreign dimension, where cutting producer subsidies, freeing food prices and privatising a sacred patronage institution such as Conasupo built Salinas a bridge to audiences outside Mexico.

Tables 1.2 and 1.3 in Chapter One indicate that an effective programme of public spending reform could hardly overlook Conasupo.

This proposition is also supported by the fact that candidate Salinas pledged spending increases at PEMEX in order to reverse inadequate investment after 1982, at CFE in order to satisfy escalating energy demands associated with export-led growth and at IMSS (part of a 1986 agreement with the IMF and World Bank). These budgetary commitments added pressure to reduce or discontinue Conasupo during the PFP.

Two phases in Mexican debt negotiations merit our attention. Phase one includes the Brady Plan announcement (named after United States Treasury Secretary Nicholas Brady) and subsequent debt negotiations spearheaded by Mexican Finance Minister Pedro Aspe and international banking representatives, running from 10 March to 24 July 1989. Initial negotiations were aimed at forging a general framework; thus, without demarcating firm commitments, the Brady Plan first linked debt forgiveness of major debtor countries to new, pro-market policies favourable to foreign investment (Sachs, 1989; *New York Times*, 11 March 1989). Forging a consensus around Brady Plan objectives required the endorsement and participation of a divided international financial community, and a precise Brady Plan agreement first emerged on 23 July 1989.

In phase two, the Conasupo reform process and debt negotiations overlap after 23 July 1989. This marked a crucial phase in Mexican Brady Plan negotiations. Proposals outlined on 23 July 1989 faced an arduous ratification process in which each individual bank holding Mexican debt – of which there were around 500 – had to be consulted. 'This process was not automatic, for it was still not certain that all banks would participate', notes Kennedy (1994: 235). The CMP, announced on 21 October 1989, coincided with Mexican special negotiator José Ángel Gurría's trip to major financial centres between 19-31 October 1989, when he laboured to persuade individual bankers to endorse Brady Plan relief for Mexico. Conasupo reforms, which included steps to privatise processing factories and deregulate agricultural markets, signalled to the financial community that Salinas was firmly committed to the 'debtor reform' component in the Brady Plan. Of course, Conasupo reform was one of a number of signals: Salinas privatised TELMEX (The National Telecommunications Company) on 18 September 1989 and dismantled many guaranteed agricultural prices on 26 October 1989. By January 1990, initial creditor scepticism had receded, and enough bankers consented to the Brady Plan to reschedule approximately ($US) 48.5 billion of Mexican debt.

To summarise, debt negotiations largely hinged on convincing Mexico's creditors that there would be a reduction in public spending under the incoming Salinas administration. Belt-tightening measures after 1982 failed to placate creditors. Conasupo was the archetypal parastatal that unnerved the international financial community in the late 1980s; indeed, its deficit spending between 1983-1988 was on par with the final years of the López Portillo term (Ochoa, 1994: 290). Thus the announcement of Conasupo reform seems to have offered an opportunity to bolster the image of Salinas at a crucial early juncture in his administration.

The World Bank and the Mexican Foodstuffs Market

Gurza Lavalle's quote above suggests that some saw the World Bank as a source of 'pressure for innovation' during the PFP. In 1989 Mexico secured a World Bank agriculture sector loan that was partly linked to a 1986 World Bank document (World Bank, 1986, 1983). The 1986 document resembled the World Bank's standard package of liberalisation policies, including four recommendations to reorient Conasupo:

1. Channelling all Conasupo consumer subsidies via coupon schemes (i.e., targeting)
2. Liquidation of Triconsa (wheat flour/bread production)
3. Restriction of Conasupo import monopoly to beans and milk
4. Closure of 500 Diconsa stores

Source: Escalante and Rendón (1988: 115-152)

For the World Bank, problems in Mexican food markets were rooted in state intervention in factor and product markets, which distorted domestic prices and sustained inefficient output-income structures throughout the production-to-consumption chain (Solís, 1984; Polanco, 1990). The Mexican Commerce Ministry calculated a 40 percent differential between the purchase price and the final consumer price of basic foodstuffs in 1982; this surpassed the differential of other Latin American markets (Serra Puche and García-Alba, 1983). In the eyes of the World Bank, 30 years of Conasupo operations cultivated an entire middleman sector, which it blamed for agricultural stagnation, for inadequate private investment, and for the fact that subsidies failed to improve living standards in the countryside.

This is not the place to critique the World Bank agricultural model. Interestingly, one finds in World Bank reports on Mexico an admission that past support for 'second best' agricultural projects was due to its general impatience during the transition stages of the Echeverría and López Portillo administrations. The World Bank believes that during presidential transitions it must secure ties to the new administration or risk marginalisation for the next five years (World Bank, 1995: 117-131; World Bank, 1988b: 67-72; World Bank, 1979). Here Mexico's six-year presidential timetable influenced actors outside Mexico and to some extent it relaxed a constraint (i.e., the World Bank) that some observers thought was covertly behind the PFP. One could argue that, among other considerations, advocating the application of the tortilla coupon scheme to other products signalled more 'second best' policymaking. In theory, it is easy to see why targeted schemes appealed to the World Bank, yet there was a gap between practice and theory. Conasupo officials involved with the Tortilla Programme acknowledge enormous corruption and partisan manipulation during the 1980s – an issue taken up in Chapter Four.

In 1989 some observers in the Mexican media levelled harsh criticism against the World Bank. They claimed, inaccurately, that the '1986 World Bank report was not made public' at the time of signing, nor 'before the 21 October 1989 Conasupo reform announcement' (*La Jornada*, 6 November 1989). However, Escalante and Rendón (1988: 115-152) cite the World Bank agreement in an article written before Salinas entered office. Critics noted the congruence between loan conditions and the CMP – something that is evident when we analyse the CMP in Chapter Three – provoking objections to a perceived challenge to national sovereignty, and familiar suspicion with Mexico's northern neighbour (Gurza Lavalle, 1994; Hernández, 1991; Moguel and Bartra, 1995; *Unomásuno*, 13, 16 October 1989; *La Jornada*, 6 November 1989).

It is true that some World Bank recommendations surfaced in the CMP. Prescriptively, some Mexican officials undoubtedly concurred with the World Bank's overall assessment of the situation in Mexican agriculture. Notwithstanding this convergence of interests, other World Bank conditions were implemented partially or not at all – yet the World Bank signed a loan agreement with Mexico in 1989. Mexico did not follow its recommendations concerning the corn market, for instance. Reforms in this area did not include discontinuing producer subsidies or Conasupo's import and export monopoly. In fact, Chapter Three shows that Conasupo corn subsidies climbed in late 1989. Considering the spirit of the World Bank's recommendations, the proposed reform of Conasupo 'did not go far enough' (World Bank, 1996), notably in the area of consumption services, where Salinas envisioned total Conasupo consumers rising from 30 million in 1988 to 50 million in 1994.[1]

The Public Interest Debate: Reaching out to Corporate Actors

Candidate Salinas and several of his confidants, such as Jaime Serra Puche, Ernesto Zedillo, Leopoldo Solís (since the 1970s a prominent Mexican policy-maker in the area of social policy) and Luis Téllez Kuenzler, probably preferred to liquidate Conasupo, viewing the PFP as a chance to axe an institutional and fiscal liability. Resources released by discontinuing Conasupo, likewise, could have fortified the nascent Solidarity scheme, the true social policy passion of Salinas and key figures like Carlos Rojas, Luis Donaldo Colosio and José Córdoba. The Salinas administration calculated that the total debt of Conasupo and its branches (e.g., the financial cost to maintain Conasupo) topped ($US) 2 billion at the conclusion of the de la Madrid term – figure estimated from Conasupo (1991). It should also be mentioned that the government believed that the true total was much higher due to a lack of information concerning Diconsa operations during the de la Madrid *sexenio*. Closer inspection of Conasupo's financial and administrative operations follows in subsequent chapters; here it suffices, that the 'costs to maintain Conasupo' were high in monetary terms. That Salinas officially rejected liquidation of Conasupo in the 'public interest' suggests that this price tag did not transcend a threshold at which the financial costs were simply too high, as they had become with other government policies. What was this public interest? The public interest and Conasupo were controversial topics before the launch of the CMP in January 1990.

Given that the initial part of the PFP unfolded in the context of a highly contested presidential election in which the PRI elite had split and led to a group of ex-*PRIistas* challenging from the left, opinions on public policy among the PRI leadership assumed greater significance than normal, and here views clashed. The Conasupo question converged with the divisive ideological debate reverberating within the PRI over state intervention, which Maxfield (1990) traces back to the 1930s. A loud pro-intervention voice was Demetrio Sodi de la Tijera, PRI Deputy and ex-General Co-ordinator of Food Provision and Distribution in Mexico City. For him and others, Conasupo compensated for the negative side of Mexico's market economy: speculation, poor infrastructure, price instability and a lack of private investment in domestic food markets. He wrote several articles to counter publications by private sector associations and Salinas administration voices (*La Jornada*, 29 September 1989, 24 October 1989 and 9 November 1989; Sodi de la Tijera, 1988). Sodi de la Tijera predicted that eliminating Conasupo would leave low-income producers and consumers, who were the rationale for constructing Conasupo in the 1960s, at the mercy of middlemen and speculators.

Business groups pushed for the rapid dismantling of Conasupo. Cross-party criticism came from the industrial city of Monterrey, notably by way of PRI Deputy Alberto Santos de Hoyos, Eduardo García Suárez (President of the Commercial Chamber of Monterrey, Canaco), Enrique Grajeda Alvarado (President of the Central Employers of Nuevo León, CPNL), and Luis German Carcoba (President of Concamin). The PAN sided with this view. PAN Deputy Jesús Ramírez Núñez remarked, 'privatising Conasupo would be 20 years overdue' (*Excelsior*, 24 October 1989).

One factor that ignited the anger of business was de la Madrid's decision to increase Conasupo retail distribution in the lucrative Mexico City market. During the Salinas presidential campaign, Conasupo's Mexico City distribution branch nearly doubled total distribution from ($US) 44 million in 1987 to ($US) 81 million in 1988 (*La Jornada*, 25 October 1989). Once Conasupo reforms had been announced, García Suárez posited that Conasupo *modernización* failed to go far enough toward market liberalisation. The Director of the Canaco, José Luis Mastreta, underscored Conasupo's dismal record of benefiting the nation's poor, claiming that a mere 15 centavos of each peso in subsidies reached intended beneficiaries in 1988 (*Excelsior*, 27 October 1989).[2]

The PRI's corporatist sector leadership supported Conasupo reform, yet there was no support to discontinue subsidy programmes. Some corporatist unions elected to desert the leadership. In June 1989, State Director of the Cardenista Campesino Central in Michoacán, Ignacio Garnica Márquez, described Conasupo, SARH, Banrural and Andsa as 'Organs working to impede rural development so as to pave the way for private agro-firms to take over the agriculture sector' (*Excelsior*, 11 June 1989).

Individual *PRIistas* with past connections to Conasupo expounded views between these extremes. On 23 August 1988 General Director of Conasupo Ernesto Costemalle Botello recounted to Carlos Salinas that it would be '...unlawful and against the basic rights of Mexicans to sell Conasupo' (*Excelsior*, 23 August 1988). Costemalle Botello was responding to Salinas' comments in the state of Campeche the day before concerning the possible liquidation of Conasupo. However, Conasupo documents underline that Costemalle Botello strongly advocated reforms at the agency. On 4 December 1988 Ignacio Ovalle took over from Costemalle Botello and proclaimed,

> Of the institutions to emerge from the Revolution, the National Basic Foods Company (Conasupo), perhaps is that which best represents what President Carlos Salinas de Gortari denominates as 'the sentiments of the Nation of Morelos'; an institution designed to moderate opulence and indigence (*Excelsior*, 5 December 1988).

In mid-March 1989 Ovalle stated:

> The activities of Conasupo would be revised to convert it into a powerful tool to foment rural development, through subsidy programmes, aid to producers making the transition to the market, and paying a just price to all *campesinos* (*La Jornada*, 17 March 1989).

Ovalle (1990), like his predecessor, acknowledged the public's interest in subsidy programmes yet conceded the inevitability and utility of structural reform:

> In December 1988 we had to establish a budgetary culture at Conasupo [and to stop practices] like the common use of indiscriminate bridging accounts [contracts between Conasupo and private distributors] that

confused our efforts at clarifying accounting records (Conasupo, September 1994).

Director of Diconsa (1983-1988) and Director of Conasupo Planning (1989-1991) Raúl Salinas de Gortari (whose role in this case study is taken up below), ex-Director General of Conasupo Jorge de la Vega, General Co-ordinator of Conasupo Consultation Carlos Alamán Bueno, and Director of Planning and Budget at Conasupo (1983-1988) Enrique Gavaldón Enciso, defended this same reformist yet moderate position. In July 1989, Alamán Bueno explained that Conasupo constituted 'an instrument for redistributing wealth' and an 'important shock absorber against the economic crisis' (*Excelsior*, 18 July 1989) though its rural programmes had caused social instability and required rethinking.[3] Gavaldón Enciso, responding to the argument for eliminating Conasupo advanced by Economists Alfredo Sánchez Daza and Sergio Vargas Velázquez (1986), retorted, 'Conasupo is an instrument for compensating and correcting the forces of disequilibrium in the productive and commercial structure of Mexican agriculture and industry' (Gavaldón Enciso and Pérez Haro, 1987a: 187). This debate in academic journals continued in the media during the PFP. Perhaps Ochoa (1994: 299) best summarises the moderate position:

> Because of its unique role as a catchall social welfare agency [under de la Madrid], it [Conasupo] did not undergo massive restructuring during the early years of the crisis [1982]. Indeed, many government officials publicly proclaimed that the National State Food Agency would be spared privatization [under Salinas] due to its overwhelming social importance.

Actors outside the PRI enriched the debate. PRD Deputy Alberto Barranco Chavarría responded to Eduardo García's critique of state intervention by agreeing that Conasupo had lost its 'innocence', but suggested that the agency remained a 'positive force' in the daily lives of poor Mexicans (*La Jornada*, 25 October 1989). Guaranteed prices offered *campesinos* an alternative to exploitative intermediaries. For him, speculation persisted in poor communities and the private market was a dangerous solution to Mexico's structural dilemma. In a particularly revealing editorial (*La Jornada*, 17 June 1988), Barranco Chavarría reflected on the observations of author Armando Ramírez (in his book *Chin*

Chin El Teporocho), who marvelled at Conasupo's ability to deliver milk, beans and tortillas to Mexican tables:

> It is not a small portion of the people ['la gente del pueblo'] that maintain that Mexico has three tributaries: its faith in the Virgin de Guadelupe, its love for the flag, and the daily visit to the Conasupo.

At this moment, when Salinas was discussing liquidation, Barranco Chavarría also contended that Conasupo could exercise fiscal restraint.

> At the end of this year [1988], without either cancelling programmes or decreasing its function of regulating and supplying the domestic market with basics, the parastatal [Conasupo] will save [$US 52 million]. In the first trimester alone the agency secured savings of [$US 114 thousand] in administrative spending, and liquidated its internal debt for 1987 that reached [$US 72 million]. From this operation it channelled part of its fiscal resources to financial authorities and the rest to current spending for the national grain harvests, seeds, pay guarantee prices, and maintenance of a regulated reserve of basic goods (*La Jornada*, 17 June 1988).

PRD Senator Ifigenia Martínez labelled Conasupo a 'tool in the war to secure social peace' while PRD Deputy Graciela Rojas depicted reforms as a sign of '*PRIismo* and *PANismo* unity' (*Excelsior*, 24 October 1989). Ex-presidential candidate Cuauhtémoc Cárdenas also defended the pro-Conasupo position (*Excelsior*, 24 October 1989).

Mexican academia enhanced the debate. The Director of the Economics Faculty at Mexico's Autonomous National University (UNAM), Eliezar Morales, criticised discussions of agriculture or Conasupo that avoided 'the historical agricultural question' – e.g., Mexico's *ejido* system (annex, *El Financiero*, 30 October 1989).[4] In May 1989, economist Fernando Rello argued that Conasupo was 'dying naturally' and 'with each [harvest] cycle it captures less of the national harvest' (*La Jornada*, 25 May 1989). Rello believed that it was no longer necessary for the government to market crops for *campesinos*, nonetheless, he cautioned against dismantling Conasupo overnight.

Economists Eduardo Pérez Haro (1990; Gavaldón Enciso and Pérez Haro, 1987a, 1987b) painted a more optimistic picture. First, he asserted that Conasupo delivered resources to disadvantaged sections of the population. The question whether subsidising consumption or production was a valid enterprise in Mexico, however, had to be considered at the level of overall economic policy, not Conasupo. Second, he claimed that Conasupo symbolised a tacit acknowledgement that large segments of Mexican society suffered under the industrialisation model of the sixties and seventies as well as the neoliberal model of the eighties. UNAM Professor José Luis Calva dubbed it 'common sense' that scrapping price supports invited cheap imports to flood the Mexican market (*El Financiero*, 31 October 1989). He noted that, in 1988, the average agricultural subsidy in the European Union stood at 48.5 percent and in the USA/Canada 53.6 percent. He cautioned that price liberalisation and reducing producer input subsidies made little sense, in this world market, unless the goal was to raise rural unemployment and increase Mexico's imports.

The President and Concertación

To be sure, the public dialogue alluded to above affected the context and policy arena in which decisions on Conasupo were made. However, perhaps the fundamental barometer was Carlos Salinas. His stance on Conasupo deserves careful examination. On 11 March 1989, in Mexico City's famous market district *La Merced*, he announced that 500 Conasupo milk outlets (*lecherías*), benefiting 2 million Federal District (D.F.) residents, had been constructed in his first 100 days in office (*La Jornada*, 11 March 1989). Furthermore, soon after the CMP announcement, Conasupo's general director retorted to a group of 20 angry PRI deputies:

> [CMP] is a line drawn by President Carlos Salinas in his *Informe Presidencial* [official budget], it will be carried out whether you like it or not; these are decisions made at a superior level, it is not a decision of Conasupo (*La Jornada*, 15 November 1989).

It also needs to be emphasised that a process of *concertación* (or official corporatist-administration negotiation) at the beginning of the six-year timetable had great significance with respect to our broader interest in continuity and discontinuity in state-society relations. It involved most of the parastatal's strategic client groups and it was here that the constraints on Salinas were formidable. If Salinas wanted to 'break with the past' then he had to abandon long-running corporatist commitments.

Salinas was well-versed and passionate about public sector reform in the area of social policy. His Harvard doctoral thesis constructed a political economy model that assessed whether traditional rural outreach programmes generated support for the political system (Salinas, 1984).[5] Salinas observed the *Caminos de Mano de Obra*, President Echeverría's rural road construction/paving programme that experimented with federal finance, community labour and local participation in project planning.[6] To circumvent what Salinas depicted as structural and political barriers, such as monopolistic intermediaries, he called for collective participation at the design and implementation stage of new (for example 'Solidarity') and established (for example 'Conasupo') social programmes (figure 2.0).

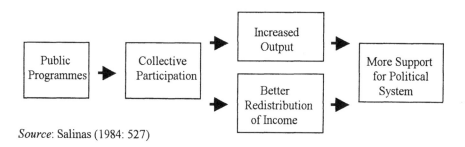

Source: Salinas (1984: 527)

Figure 2.0   Implicit Causal Model in Certain Public Sector Programmes

The rest of this section offers a chronology of executive speeches from April to October 1989. This was a period when President Salinas publicly began defining the direction and scope of Conasupo reform (and consequently state-society relations in this area) to official labour and *campesino* leaders, Commerce Secretary Jaime Serra Puche, Conasupo Director Ovalle, and the other participants in a *concertación* process. Such a process involving corporatist and administrative leaders was not unique in itself, as a comparable *concertación* process unfolded at the beginning of other presidential terms, including in 1983, which culminated in de la Madrid's *modernización* agenda for the parastatal.[7]

Likewise, it is significant that Salinas recycled the language of *modernización* from de la Madrid's *concertación* experience; it signalled to the actors involved a sense of continuity from the old to the new administration. Conasupo summarises the key elements of *modernización* in 1983 as 'enhancing co-participation between state and society' as well as 'decentralisation towards civil society to improve Conasupo's capacity to respond to the objective population' (Conasupo, 1987a: 35-37). Without detailing the de la Madrid years, it suffices that, based on this earlier experience, the term *modernización* implied no obvious threat to corporatist access to Conasupo. In 1986, for example, a campaign of decentralisation at Conasupo in practice delegated control of large Mexico City retail stores to the PRI and the CTM. Furthermore, in the rural sector, from 1983 to 1986, decentralisation delegated control of 13,000 rural stores via the CNC. Thus, in 1989, to embrace the *modernización* label, and avoiding reference to *neoliberalismo*, Salinas recycled a well-known set of expectations among core client groups.

23 April 1989: The Concept of Modernización and Reforms at Infonavit

To the General Assembly of Infonavit, Salinas proclaimed that this institution 'owes its success to its founder and permanent institutional motor; one of the most honoured labour leaders in contemporary history, my friend Don Fidel Velázquez' (*El Gobierno Mexicano*, 1994l). He went on to rationalise Infonavit's future role under a future Salinas administration. Workers in the Labour Congress (CT) had earned Infonavit benefits by participation in *concertación*. Infonavit was also tied to the Mexican Revolution and the PRI's commitment to social justice. Here the term *modernización*, explained Salinas, implied administrative decentralisation under the supervision of official unions as well as a larger budget; in other words, a relaxation of Infonavit's budgetary and distributional constraints.

Conasupo and Infonavit can be grouped together as sources of structural social assistance in Mexico, over time dispensing valued state resources to strategic client groups of the PRI – notably in and around Mexico City. Both parastatals are anchored by constitutional safeguards and during the PFP experienced similar *concertación* processes that led to similar *modernización* agendas. Thus, President Salinas' comments on Infonavit in late April 1989 informed corporatist leaders on what the new executive meant by *modernización* in this area of the public sector.

23 May 1989: Continuity in Government – CNC Relations

The President reiterated to an audience of CNC leaders at Los Pinos that the 'origins of the CNC are linked to the Mexican Revolution', and pledged to refortify the CNC – State alliance (*El Gobierno Mexicano*, 1994k). He followed his predecessors and challenged the CNC leadership 'to play a serious role in the *modernización* of the Mexican rural sector' with respect to its control over rural credit and marketing infrastructure (*El Gobierno Mexicano*, 1994k). The national CNC leadership, in a response witnessed before at the start of a six-year cycle, noted:

> We understand that *modernización* is to liberate the extraordinary potential of the *campesino* communities, to further social justice as well as the general interest of the nation (*El Gobierno Mexicano*, 1994k).

Here *modernización* paralleled the 1983 *concertación* process, and it also stood as a reconfirmation of a shared interest between the government and the CNC in achieving social justice through familiar types of policy innovations. Indeed, greater efficiency in the rural sector demanded more, not less, resources for the CNC. No evidence indicated that Salinas planned or desired to end CNC influence in Mexican food markets.

26 May 1989: Continuity in Rural Producer Group – Government Relations

To the General Assembly of the National Agricultural Council (CAP), Salinas proclaimed that 'Agrarian reform had provided *campesinos* with opportunity' (*El Gobierno Mexicano*, 1994j).[8] He added that 'The National Fertiliser Company (Fertimex), the National Seed Company, Conasupo, and Andsa converge on the countryside to provide opportunity for *campesinos*' and that these institutions would 'continue complying with their task of raising production and productivity' (*El Gobierno Mexicano*, 1994j).

The CAP's conference manifesto outlined eleven demands, including guaranteed price increases to reflect the true cost of production; securing basic foodstuffs for rural communities; decentralisation to bypass corrupt intermediaries; and organising producers to circumvent intermediaries. Nothing suggested that the CAP anticipated a radical transformation of the parastatals mentioned by Salinas.

23 June 1989: The Government and Rural Producers, Co-partners in Modernización

In a moment of great continuity with past government policy, Salinas delivered the following words to the Ordinary Assembly of the National Agricultural Council:

> As recognised in the *Pacto* [a national corporatist anti-inflationary agreement], we are going to protect guaranteed prices in the Mexican countryside. We also recognise that we cannot use the guaranteed price as the only policy instrument and pretend to resolve all the production and marketing problems because many of them have structural origins (*El Gobierno Mexicano*, 1994h).

On price guarantees he remarked, 'We ought to consider varieties and product quality levels to determine flexible guaranteed prices' (*El Gobierno Mexicano*, 1994h). Discussing the road ahead and *modernización*, Salinas deemed government and society 'co-partners in this grand task' and reconfirmed his commitment to devolve resources to *campesino* groups to 'recuperate the dynamism of the Mexican countryside'. The President of the Ordinary Assembly of the National Agricultural Council responded,

> We propose, Mr. President, that they [new reforms] be distinguished in a clear manner, separating the policies for raising agricultural production from the policies of support for popular consumption, and that these are refined to benefit, effectively, the objective population. Bear in mind that the part of the population with the least income can be found, coincidentally, in the rural sector of the country (*El Gobierno Mexicano*, 1994h).

22 August 1989: The Force of Concertación Producing Continuity

At Los Pinos, Jaime Serra Puche told assembled Conasupo policymakers, the Secretary of Social Work and Provision, Ovalle and Salinas, that the 'force of *concertación*' joining workers, *campesinos* and the government to realise *modernización* of Conasupo had run its course (*El Gobierno Mexicano*, 1994e). It was a marked illustration of continuity that this process unfolded where it did and that Serra Puche credited the president of the CT, the secretary general of the CNC and Ovalle, for its success. This particular scene of state-society management could have transpired in 1971, 1977, and 1983. Serra Puche also outlined this group's eleven recommendations, and amid the predictable rhetoric we can underscore: guaranteed supply and a just price for basic foodstuffs and a commitment that the parastatal should 'bolster the democratic process'. The first recommendation suggests that Conasupo's historic mandate in Mexican food markets remained intact, and the second appeared to imply some form of client participation (presumably the meaning of 'democratic process' in this context).

After Serra Puche's comments, Ovalle informed the audience that on 16 March 1989 Conasupo signed *concertación* agreements to maintain current resource commitments to the CT, CNC, Independent Central *Campesina* and the National Confederation of Small Owners. To promote the cause of social justice, the *concertación* process developed two 'mixed committees'; the first analysed the problems of labour while the second examined rural problems. These committees conducted weekly meetings chaired by either Ovalle or the president's brother Raúl Salinas from 5 April 1989 to 26 July 1989.[9] The Ovalle-Salinas Conasupo team signed 200 *concertación* agreements (*convenios de concertación*) with corporatist groups by 23 August 1989. Moreover, on the same date, in a move depicted as 'bolstering the democratic process' the government admitted corporate sector labour and *campesino* leaders to the Administrative Councils of Conasupo branches (*La Jornada*, 23/24 August 1989; *Excelsior*, 24 October 1989). Hence in August 1989 the situation seemed to resemble traditional state-society management involving Conasupo and familiar PRI clients; what seemed like a continuation of de la Madrid's policy of offering strategic PRI clients greater access to decision making as overall budgetary constraints tightened.

13 October 1989: New Grain Policy

The Mexican President outlined a new initiative to the Inter-American Confederation of Grain and Agriculture Producers, The Programme of National *Modernización* of Production, Exportation and Supply of Grain. The initiative conceived of Mexican producers amid competitive world grain markets, but stressed a need for 'even distribution' and 'just prices' for domestic grain producers (*El Gobierno Mexicano*, 1994d).

The President mentioned SARH, SHCP, Secofi, and the Ministry of Communication and Transport as key components in the 'strategy to reactivate grain production'. This initiative also advocated tariff cuts and export-promotion by way of credit, price and infrastructure incentives. Yet there was no reference to Conasupo, an odd development considering that this was 'the strategy for the grain sector for the next six years' and that these presidential comments came eight days before many support prices were dismantled. Recall that, at this point, Conasupo still guaranteed grain prices, suggesting one of two things: either the president was merely balancing his audiences at home and abroad or at this stage the issue of Conasupo remained unsettled.

19 October 1989: Modernización and Executive Legitimacy

On 19 and 20 of October, Salinas conducted a two-day trip around the State of México in which he discussed his vision of *modernización* with community leaders such as those in the municipality of Chalco.

> We are going to construct here [along with other promised resources] a Conasupo store to supply subsidised basics for the families of Chalco. Also, we are opening Solidarity *Lecherías* to attend to community needs, above all for the children...(*El Gobierno Mexicano*, 1994c). [10]

In his interaction with municipalities across the State of México, Salinas pledged Conasupo programmes as his predecessors had always done. The routine was familiar enough: communities aired demands, which regularly mentioned Diconsa and Liconsa infrastructure, and thereafter the executive committed to deliver services. In many respects, here, two days before the announcement of the CMP, we see the customary political economy of executive legitimacy in practice and the continued manipulation of Conasupo resources in a way that prolonged the old model of state-society interaction.

21 October 1989: Announcing the Conasupo Modernización Plan (CMP)

At Los Pinos President Salinas announced the CMP. The substance of the CMP is the subject of Chapter Three; it suffices to mention here that proposals such as limited privatisation, reducing the number of subsidised grains and the closure of Conasupo's largest retail stores bore no resemblance to the recommendations of the *concertación* process revealed on 22 August 1989. The CMP announcement sent a clear signal to many that Conasupo was about to be the latest conquest of the neoliberal reformers crafting public policy for the Salinas administration. The PRI's official corporate sector allies were furious. 'This [the CMP] was not what we planned in the 17 *concertación* meetings on Conasupo with Serra Puche and Ignacio Ovalle', remarked one member of the CNC's Executive Committee (*La Jornada*, 7 November 1989).

25 October 1989: Returning to Familiar Arrangements

Days after appearing to tighten constraints on Conasupo via the CMP, Salinas seemed to relax them before the CT. In this forum, members from labour, the private sector and the administration signed the second anti-inflationary *Pacto*. Salinas argued that union self-sacrifice secured the drop in inflation from a high of 200 percent in 1987 to 17 percent in late 1989:

> For this, recognising the importance of an institution created by the Mexican Revolution, Conasupo, whose task it is to supply Mexicans that have less (*tienen menos*), I wish to ratify emphatically before you today that Conasupo will not be privatised nor weakened (*ni se privatiza ni se debilita*). It will be fortified to protect the standard of living of our compatriots (*El Gobierno Mexicano*, 1994a).

Although the President of the CT requested that fair salaries factor into any notion of *modernización*, nonetheless, he retraced familiar footsteps, signed the *Pacto* and made the following official statement:

...the CT affirms the need to fortify the policies that channel financial resources into production and combating speculation; amplify programmes of Conasupo, housing, health care; fortify the leadership of the State; place priority on the production of basic foodstuffs; and create social businesses for workers, and finally, increase working-class participation in social programmes (*El Gobierno Mexicano*, 1994a).

He also hinted that bolstering Conasupo programmes under labour control formed part of the CT's deal regarding the second *Pacto*.[11]

25 October 1989: Modernización and Reproaching Rural Groups

After consulting the CT, Salinas turned to campesino groups. At Los Pinos, he framed agricultural modernización within a global context, an environment recognised as both dangerous and brimming with opportunity.

> Conasupo, this institution fundamental to the Mexican Revolution... protects the income levels of producers in the Mexican countryside and the level of consumption of urban habitants... I wish to reiterate here, as I did before the Labour Congress, that Conasupo is not being privatised nor weakened. Conasupo will be fortified to attend better to those in greatest need. Conasupo will conserve its fundamental priority, that is, to avoid speculation in the countryside, fix prices and reduce abuse of workers. Conasupo will be transformed so that those who need resources can receive them at a reasonable price...these reforms are based on nationalistic and popular principles (*El Gobierno Mexicano*, 1994b).

Chronicling the *concertación* period that culminated with the quote above suggests that Salinas' public position on Conasupo and the theme of *modernización* fluctuated by audience and phase in the policy formation process. Earlier on, *concertación* and notions of *modernización* resembled measures taken under de la Madrid. This was exemplified in speeches to Infonavit and the CNC. He also assured audiences regarding his intention to guarantee agricultural prices. Jaime Serra Puche's comments on 22 August 1989 at Los Pinos reaffirmed a strong sense of continuity; above all, he spoke of *concertación* agreements to sustain existing arrangements with the corporatist sector. The message was clear: innovation is on the cards, but traditional resource commitments that linked the state to strategic PRI clients would be renewed. The announcement of 21 October 1989 marked a second, largely unexpected, phase that ties in the discussion above regarding Mexican debt negotiations because this marked the critical interlude (19-31 October 1989) when José Ángel Gurría visited financial capitals to sell Brady Plan debt reduction for Mexico. Again, the CMP surprised the corporatist sector and did not closely coincide with the eleven points announced by Serra Puche on 22 August 1989. Finally, speeches to the CT and *campesino* leaders on 25 October 1989 represented a third phase. Here Salinas back-pedalled, relaxing the constraints that some may have perceived when the CMP was unveiled.

The Backroom Debate

Few are privy to the closed-door settlements in Mexican politics, least of all when emotionally charged subsidy programmes are involved. However, the balance of constraints and pressures for innovation in the PFP cannot be entirely understood in terms of a public interest debate or *concertación* process, so it is helpful to examine the backroom debate concerning Conasupo. In particular, it is useful to focus on what might be seen as potential constraints on Conasupo policy innovation during the PFP.

One figure deserving further comment is Jaime Serra Puche. The Commerce Secretary co-ordinated the Conasupo *concertación* process, and later oversaw the privatisation of Conasupo industrial plants and the liberalisation of agricultural prices. Serra Puche held the position of President of the Administrative Council of Conasupo, a body including the Ministries of Treasury (SHCP), Budgeting and Planning (SPP), Social Welfare (Sedesol), Agriculture (SARH), and the executive Chief of Staff. The Council presided over Conasupo affairs and major agency decisions were subject to its approval (Conasupo, 1994a, Articles 5-19). On the one hand, the director general of Conasupo furnished information to the Council but was not a member: 'The General Director will attend the sessions of the Administrative Council with a voice but without a vote' (*con voz sin voto*) (Conasupo, 1994a, Article 10). On the other hand, the Council's power was concentrated in its Presidency, permitting Serra Puche to shape the debate in the Council and to craft specific reforms. The Council President's primary functions included: (1) representing the Council to the executive, (2) submitting to the Council and executive an annual programme of activities, (3) organising, presiding and executing Council sessions, (4) directing and moderating Council debates, (5) deferring or suspending a session when justified, (6) resolving cases where the Council is divided with a decisive vote, and (7) signing all acts emerging from Council sessions (Conasupo, June 1994, Article 14).

It was significant that Salinas preferred a high-powered technocrat over a *politico* to craft reform measures and run the Council. In other areas, for example, at the Agricultural Ministry, Salinas selected two political stalwarts: Jorge de la Vega (1988-1989) and later Carlos Hank González (1990-1994). In terms of strengths, Serra Puche had direct access to Salinas, and enjoyed credibility with both the private sector and multilateral lending institutions – Serra Puche is best known as President Salinas' point-man on NAFTA. Likewise, his parents were not born in Mexico, which barred him from the presidency and 'reduced his ties to the political class' (Centeno, 1994: 96). In other words, in Serra Puche, Salinas had a person with little loyalty to the traditional interests surrounding Conasupo. We find while President Salinas addressed and assured corporatist sector leaders during the PFP, Serra Puche stretched the Conasupo issue beyond the boundaries of corporatist patronage in separate negotiations with private firms. Moreover, his ability to talk in the technical language that generated credibility among people like World Bank policy advisors secured financial support for Conasupo reform.[12] However, some assert that Serra Puche pursued a private agenda alongside his official or public capacity.

An administrator at the government Tortilla Programme – a 22-year Conasupo veteran – credits Serra Puche with the decision to privatise Conasupo in 1988. He alleges that Serra Puche acted in part on behalf of private tortilla processor *Molinos Aztecas* (Maseca).[13] 'Maseca came to Conasupo requesting that the Diconsa (rural) corn programme be discontinued' (Interview, Mexico City, Office of Fidelist, 22 April 1997). Maseca and other domestic firms involved in corn flour, corn starch, and other derivatives wanted to end Conasupo's import monopoly to gain access to cheap USA grain. In 1988 Diconsa supplied subsidised, unprocessed Conasupo corn to *tortillerías*, or local tortilla makers, across rural Mexico (6 percent, graph 2.0). In urban areas Diconsa distributed subsidised Miconsa tortillas and corn flour through an urban network of US-style supermarkets and a range of smaller points-of-sale and *tortillerías*. In 1989, according to Appendini (1991), 41,533 *tortillerías* across Mexico depended on subsidised Conasupo corn. Maseca and Miconsa split the urban tortilla market. Together their production covered Nixtamal corn flour (34 percent) and Miconsa corn flour (21 percent) on graph 2.0. Forty-five percent of tortilla consumption in Mexico occurred outside Maseca/Miconsa distribution – 39 percent in rural self consumption and 6 percent in small rural *tortillerías*.

Maseca's concern about Miconsa in 1988 was well founded. In the 1980s de la Madrid had employed Conasupo to alleviate social pressure caused by the ongoing economic crisis, which encroached on private retailers like Maseca. The volume that Diconsa distributed grew four-fold while small/medium businesses accepting subsidised goods via Impecsa increased 34 percent (11,918 to 16,056 stores) between 1983 and 1986. Furthermore, Miconsa's participation in the corn flour market (besides tortillas) increased 29 percent in 1982, 37 percent in 1986 and 46 percent in 1988 (Ochoa, 1994; *Excelsior*, 18 July 1989). By 1986 Gavaldón Enciso and Pérez Haro (1987b) calculated that Miconsa supplied enough corn flour to satisfy the demand of six million urban consumers. Perhaps equally troubling for Maseca, Conasupo announced in May 1988 its intention to expand urban distribution by constructing 24 US-style supermarket stores before 1989 (*Excelsior*, 3 May 1988). Of course, if we assess the situation from the view of Serra Puche rather than Maseca, he merely wanted to expand high quality flour/tortillas to rural Mexico, and only Maseca could perform this task.

Graph 2.0 Tortilla Consumption in Mexico

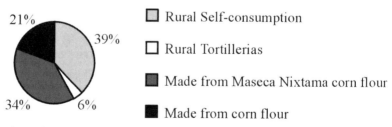

21%

39%

34%   6%

☐ Rural Self-consumption

☐ Rural Tortillerias

■ Made from Maseca Nixtama corn flour

■ Made from corn flour

* These data reflect the tortilla market before the privatisation of Miconsa
Source: Ferrer Pujol (1996: 39)

At Diconsa 'everyone knew' who advanced reforms in 1989. 'Serra Puche said let's change all that [Diconsa rural corn programme]...No more corn, only corn flour... And they [Secofi] pushed, pushed, pushed, to send only corn flour and not corn [to the rural sector]... But they could not do it' (Interview, Mexico City, Office of Fidelist, 4 April 1997). From one perspective, Maseca exerted pressure on Conasupo to stop distributing unprocessed corn to rural areas in order to duplicate the dominance of its Nixtamal flour in this sector. From another perspective, the Maseca representative in charge of Fidelist relations responded that his firm deserved the right to compete for rural consumers (Interview, Mexico City, Office of Fidelist, 22 April 1997).

Serra Puche's alleged proposal on behalf of Maseca encountered institutional obstacles. 'In the Administrative Council the general director [Ovalle] said we cannot stop sending corn and only sell corn flour' (Interview, Mexico City, Office of Fidelist, 22 April 1997) – that is, if the administration wanted to avoid more rural protests. Here the implicit responsibilities of Ovalle and Serra Puche conflicted. Research by Fox (1992), Grindle (1977a, 1977b) and Tharp Hilger (1980) suggest it is the duty of the general director to preserve the executive's image among beneficiaries. President Salinas, however, instructed Serra Puche to reorient Conasupo. Meanwhile, at this initial stage, the Diconsa rural corn policy split into two individual programmes: one sold corn and the other sold corn flour. Serra Puche's ambition to restructure Diconsa's rural sector position was short-lived; soon the two programmes merged and 'it was back to the same as before' (Interview, Mexico City, Office of Fidelist, 22 April 1997).

In an investigation of inflated Conasupo subsidy payments to Maseca, *The New York Times* reporter Anthony DePalma and others depict Serra Puche as the catalyst within the Conasupo Administrative Council (*The New York Times*, 5 July 1996; *La Jornada*, 5 July 1996).[14] DePalma's review of Administrative Council transcripts – furnished by the former advisor to President Echeverría and current PRD Deputy Adolfo Aguilar Zinser – concludes that Serra Puche coerced the Council into authorising a ($US) 7 million payment to Maseca. In October 1989, the matter fell into the lap of Ernesto Zedillo, then Secretary of SPP and Administrative Council member. He branded the payment potentially illegal, but eventually left the final decision to Serra Puche, who later overrode the Council's rejection of Maseca's case (in fact, the Council rejected it on three earlier occasions). Later, Zedillo blamed the affair on Serra Puche, announcing that on the Council, Serra Puche alone sanctioned the payment and personally discarded two internal agency reports that sided against Maseca.

All of the above leaves the impression that Serra Puche advanced Maseca's cause. It points to the types of political settlements that the transition period encourages. Here an ally of the PRI saw its interests compromised under de la Madrid and President Salinas wanted to reconcile the situation. It should be emphasised that neither Zínser nor DePalma suggests that Serra Puche or Zedillo profited from transactions with Maseca (Raúl Salinas is another matter). More generally, during the PFP Serra Puche reassured groups outside the corporatist *concertación* process that there would be innovation at Conasupo.

General Links to the Private Sector

Transactions linking Conasupo and the private sector need to be evaluated prudently. Gibson's (1997: 357) assertion of a neoliberal business-PRI coalition in which 'ties to domestically oriented industrialists and nondiversified, single-sector firms – the traditional business supporters of populist coalitions – were weakened' requires further qualification when discussing Conasupo. The public comments of business leaders listed above illustrate the general pressure for innovation that business imposes on Conasupo, namely, entrepreneurs prefer limited state intervention in the marketplace.

This spirit of entrepreneurialism, while not to be dismissed, sometimes fades upon closer inspection. Large, medium and small-scale firms profited from the agency by reselling Conasupo products at inflated prices or utilising Conasupo goods as inputs in the production process.[15] Observers of Mexican politics continue to encounter the PRI ritual of distributing tortillas and other basics to restaurants, street food vendors and poor communities in exchange for votes. For years domestic cheese and candy firms profited from cheap Liconsa milk (*El Financiero*, 9 May 1990). Conasupo distributed milk to five private firms and a few minor firms based on past quotas through 1991. A Conasupo study concludes that this 'barred new entrants into the market' (Conasupo, 8 August 1995). In the cattle sector, ranchers, especially in the 1970s and 1980s, profited from cheap Conasupo sorghum.

Finally, to stock the shelves of 20,000 Diconsa stores that distribute 10,000 products, Conasupo has had to buy significant quantities of processed and unprocessed goods from domestic and foreign firms. At the local level, it was the job of a state Conasupo director to exchange these types of contracts for political support (Grindle, 1980). Two of Mexico's largest food processors, Maseca and Gamesa, have been significant Diconsa suppliers. 'Maseca and Conasupo go way back', comments Maseca's representative to Conasupo (Interview, Mexico City, Office of Fidelist, 22 April 1997). No one disputes that political influence peddling, corruption and greed entered into Conasupo's commercial agreements. Director of Diconsa Raúl Salinas (1988: 11), summarising his tenure (1982-1988), acknowledged,

> Diconsa's function is to carry basic products to the classes that most need it. But providing basic products to these classes most in need is never neutral. Nothing in society is politically and socially neutral...Who processes it, who carries it and finally who buys it, remains a decision of political and strategic character. Because of this, each one of our decisions (at Diconsa) is tied to the administrative strategy of President Miguel de la Madrid.

Appendini (1992: 13) adds that the 'politics of food' in Mexico incorporate actors from production, distribution and consumption; and at each stop in the chain there are 'political economy as well as state-society questions'. In sum, the Conasupo-business nexus has witnessed both formal and informal, efficient and inefficient transactions.

Perhaps the turning point in private sector impatience with Conasupo can be traced to the decision in 1975 by President Echeverría to develop Iconsa, Conasupo's processing branch. President López Portillo later authorised nine Iconsa factories, criticising the private sector for ignoring opportunities to process basic agricultural goods and adding to the country's import bill. De la Madrid tabled the same criticism in 1986 (Gavaldón Enciso and Pérez Haro, 1987b). It was not, however, until the de la Madrid presidency that Iconsa captured a significant share of the domestic market. By 1988, Iconsa secured on average 14 percent of the market for any particular good. But rather than market share, Iconsa's relevance is that it united business interests against Conasupo.

In the Monterrey business community, Barranco Chavarría explains that López Portillo crossed the line in 1982 by constructing an Iconsa cookie factory in the backyard of Alberto Santos de Hoyos, owner of *Galletera Mexicana S.A.* (Gamesa) (*La Jornada*, 25 October 1989).[16] Barranco Chavarría's story unfolds with Santos as a federal PRI deputy from Monterrey in 1982. Thereafter, Santos embarked on a personal crusade to uproot Iconsa. From the point of view of Santos, Conasupo and Iconsa pursued divergent targets. The first could be justified; it was a commitment to social justice. But the second, public sector competition with private processors could not. The deputy from Monterrey organised a bloc of like-minded party members to protest against the expansion of Iconsa, before and during the PFP.[17]

Raúl Salinas and the PFP

Raúl Salinas, the President's elder brother, is accused of personal enrichment during his tenure at Conasupo (1983-1992). For our purposes, his impact on the PFP merits prudent elaboration because it goes to the question of bureaucratic constraints on Conasupo innovation. As regards this interval, the current administration's official position that 'Raúl and his cronies' hijacked the Conasupo agenda is misleading.[18] In fact, there is little evidence to suggest that he constituted a bureaucratic obstacle during the PFP; the label is more suitably given to Jorge de la Vega, Ernesto Costemalle Botello, and Hank González. These high-ranking officials argued that removing Conasupo would inflame social instability. In particular, de la Vega lambasted proposed reforms. His aversion centred on the selection of Ignacio Ovalle to direct reforms, a person he characterised as 'the enemy of the people' based upon his performance in López Portillo's expensive National Plan for Deprived Zones and Marginal Groups (Coplamar) (*Proceso*, 6 November 1989).

By contrast, Raúl Salinas was apt to exploit the financial opportunities typically accorded to the Mexican President's family, either at Conasupo or elsewhere. Interestingly, Raúl Salinas' legal team embraced this argument to counter alleged drug trafficking (e.g., Raúl did not need to get involved with drugs to benefit financially from his brother's position). Mindful of the above, it is useful to highlight his views on Conasupo before 1988 and to explore the institutional context in which he operated.

Raúl Salinas studied law at the UNAM. Centeno (1994: 152, ft.27), discussing the Salinas brothers' connection to the 1968 student movement, writes:

> Carlos Salinas' brother Raúl (a mid-level bureaucrat) was very involved in the student movement, but apparently Carlos, while he did attend some meetings, never participated actively.

In December 1982 Raúl Salinas entered the Conasupo bureaucracy as director of Diconsa, a job he owed to his brother, then Minister of SPP. Diconsa received significant executive attention under de la Madrid and was used as a mechanism to secure the loyalty of the CTM and CNC after 1982. In his National Development Plan (NDP), de la Madrid outlined that the new ('modern') Diconsa would thereafter 'undergo *modernización* to meet the challenges associated with the new macroeconomic reality' (Salinas, 1988: 9). Discussing his leadership at Diconsa, Raúl Salinas explained that his decisions were aimed at achieving NDP targets, 'particularly the goal of increasing popular participation in the process of development' (p.9).[19] His review of Diconsa policies (1983-1987) affirmed that it was the public sector's duty to regulate and organise society – 'to give a service to society, society must be organised to receive it' (p.18). He criticised the prevailing neoliberal approach to public policy.

> Yes, it is true that our administrative efficiency is important, but what is more important is social efficiency; that is to say, the capacity that Mexican producers will have to market their goods and the capacity that the consumers will have to organise (p.25).

If we move ahead to late 1989, his views on rural sector reforms surfaced in CNC documents when he addressed the CNC's Technical Consulting Council. Conasupo's October 1989 reforms helped to instigate a new round of negotiations over the structure of rural property rights and here a CNC report written by Raúl Salinas forecast a 'pulverisation in the countryside' (*Proceso*, 1 January 1990). He pointed to a clash of structures, one modern and efficient, the other backward and isolated from the market. This depiction is noteworthy, though unoriginal, for it recommended that progress entailed privatising the *ejido* and ending state intervention. During

16-19 October 1989, he participated in a conference at Cornell University on rural sector development and submitted a paper supporting a Malthusian argument. On this occasion, he blamed rural stagnation on several factors, notably inefficient public sector enterprises.

> The efficiency of pubic institutions tied to rural development suffers duplication of functions, inefficient co-ordination and excessive bureaucracy. Total employees of these institutions in the rural sector surpass 198,000 in 1987 or 8 bureaucrats per *ejido* (Salinas, 1990: 822).

From 1987 to 1989, a picture emerges of a perplexed person, confused about the correct place of the state in the economy. He initially praises the public sector's capacity to organise society and two years later calls on it to abandon interventionist activities. Did he convert to the market logic associated with his brother?

Policy orientations aside, it does seem conceivable that in 1989 the executive utilised his brother's 'transition experience', gained at Diconsa during de la Madrid's transition and corporatist bargaining, to renew corporatist arrangements. Raúl Salinas understood how to play this game. He enlarged Diconsa (1983-1984) as reforms to Article 115 of the Mexican Constitution devolved Conasupo resources to municipal presidents, local unions and popular groups. Moreover, he implemented the Community Food Council Programme, which necessitated direct negotiations with *campesino* unions. By 1986, according to Fox (1991), he negotiated deals to delegate resources and administrative control over new Diconsa stores in 13,000 rural communities.[20] For Raúl Salinas, therefore, managing corporate sector negotiation, notably at the local level, was familiar territory.

Interestingly, cries of nepotism did not trail his appointment in December 1988. Apart from Miguel Ángel Granados Chapa's allusion to 'similarities of presidential abuse from former *sexenios*' (*La Jornada*, 7 April 1989), the issue generated little interest.[21] For instance, *Proceso*'s (6 November 1989) attack on proposed innovations at Conasupo never mentioned Raúl Salinas.

Lack of interest can be partly attributed to the reputation of Ignacio Ovalle who arrived at Conasupo with an impressive resume – Secretary to the President under Echeverría, General Co-ordinator of Coplamar and Director of the National Indigenous Institute (INI) under López Portillo, and

Ambassador to Cuba and Argentina under de la Madrid. Commenting on the selection of Ovalle, Dresser (1991) concluded that his bureaucratic experience and stature within the PRI indicated that Salinas desired to safeguard Conasupo reforms. Moreover, parallels can be drawn between Ovalle's earlier Coplamar experience and Carlos Salinas' plans to incorporate local activists into the administration of Conasupo services. No evidence, however, indicates that Ovalle or Raúl Salinas influenced the decision not to discontinue Conasupo in 1988.

Finally, to round off this discussion of Raúl Salinas, it is useful to demarcate the boundaries of Conasupo's Office of Planning, his post under his brother. In 1988, this included (i) import contracts, (ii) budget development, (iii) infrastructure investment and (iv) *concertación* with beneficiary groups and other government agencies (Conasupo, 1994a). It occupied a third-tier location in the Conasupo organisational pyramid, below the Administrative Council and the general director of Conasupo. At this third tier, Conasupo's decentralised structure is visible and responsibility is parcelled out among six directors: Planning, Operations, Delegation (state office co-ordination), Finance, Industry, and Agricultural Marketing.

Although the president's brother was not a 'typical mid-level bureaucrat' as Centeno contends, accusations levied against him should be balanced against the bureaucratic activities under his authority. Coverage of the Conasupo story can misrepresent his sphere of influence and the Conasupo issue in general.

> During the time that Raúl Salinas was the *Director of Conasupo*, the organization was involved in illegal imports of contaminated food and the disappearance of millions of dollars in cash and products (*Washington Post*, 14 May 1997 ... emphasis added).

> [Jorge] Madrazo Cuéller [Attorney General] told a congressional committee that his office is investigating the case [of Conasupo leasing trucks to drug dealers], which deepens a scandal involving the agency, which had been *headed by* Raúl Salinas, the imprisoned brother of former president Carlos Salinas... Raúl Salinas, *former head of the Conasupo agency* during his brother's administration, is in a maximum security prison facing charges of homicide and corruption (*The News*, 31 May 1997 ... emphasis added).

In the first, much discussed case (contaminated food), perhaps 'blaming Raúl' is too simplistic. It involved him but also transcended him. Conasupo and Ministry of Agriculture health inspectors at the port of Veracruz and in the state of Tamaulipas oversaw and facilitated the entire affair. Likewise, Ovalle, a powerful bureaucrat in his own right, not Raúl Salinas, ran Conasupo.

However, the Ovalle/Raúl Salinas partnership deserves further exploration. In order to restructure Mexican food markets, Carlos Salinas had to formulate a strategy to circumvent well-known obstacles that had bent antecedent reforms. Appendix 1.0 refers to several studies that found Conasupo ill-suited to implement executive projects, be they relatively 'populist' (Echeverría or López Portillo) or 'neoliberal' (de la Madrid). Past experiences demonstrated that executive encouragement was necessary but not sufficient to ensure success. Salinas approached the problem by empowering a specific team. Jaime Serra Puche's status as a high-powered and influential technocrat has been mentioned. Likewise, Ovalle arrived at the PFP with considerable experience and clout. However, other powerful figures from the Mexican political elite had been placed in the same situation – for example, Echeverría entrusted ex-CNC leader Jorge de la Vega to guide Conasupo. Ovalle required protection from groups which might stand to lose from the executive's agenda. Salinas apparently anticipated this development. Serra Puche handled potential fallout with domestic processors that relied on subsidised Conasupo inputs – the dairy, cattle, and candy sectors. It was Serra Puche, for example, who addressed angry sugar unions after Conasupo discontinued its marketing subsidy in 1989; he also addressed Diconsa unions after announcing the privatisation of some outlets in November 1989. Equally importantly, he shielded Ovalle from World Bank criticism when accommodations with certain groups had to be made, such as special agreements with labour unions. In effect, Serra Puche sheltered Ovalle from potential obstacles outside Conasupo and outside (and sometimes inside) the corporatist sector.

A central task of Raúl Salinas during the PFP was to deal with official unions. In a period of great uncertainty about the traditional rules of the game, he enjoyed a measure of legitimacy; he was capable of explaining to traditional clients what the administration was offering and the irrationality of disloyalty. For instance, Carlos Salinas wanted to privatise or hand over some small and medium-sized Diconsa stores to their managers, potentially a highly political and selective process. Indeed, this was the purpose of the *concertación* process, both in 1989 and at the beginning of other presidential terms. Discussing this topic, La Botz (1995: 229) remarks:

> Raúl Salinas had been his brother Carlos's right-hand man. He had worked closely with the president to create Pronasol [Solidarity] and to rebuild the power of the PRI in the late 1980s.

His comments exaggerate the relationship and mistake Solidarity for Conasupo reforms; nonetheless, the basic point that Raúl served as a prominent executive envoy seems valid.

In December 1988, the assembled Conasupo team also enlisted allies of Raúl Salinas. His brother-in-law, Juan Manuel Pasalagua Branch became director of agricultural marketing, which controlled Conasupo's rural operations. Salvador Giordano, perhaps Raúl Salinas's closest ally at Conasupo (Interview, Mexico City, Office of Fidelist, 22 April 1997), assumed control of Miconsa, while other confidants, Ignacio Herrejón and Carlos Alamán Bueno took over at Iconsa and at Conasupo's legal council. Likewise, Fernando Peón Escalante, a former Diconsa employee of Raúl Salinas, became the director of Diconsa.

Together this team secured the Ovalle-Salinas axis. Chapter Five argues in greater detail, moreover, that the 'team' was formed especially to push the executive's agenda through the critical early phase, but not to see it realised. Once the reform process survived an initial phase, the members of the team were promoted to new positions outside Conasupo.

Raúl Salinas' influence emanated from his relationship with the President. This became increasingly evident during the *concertación* process, when 26 separate analysis groups convened 126 meetings over a six-month period. Either Ovalle or Raúl Salinas chaired meetings and it was in these closed-door gatherings that political settlements were forged between the new administration and the corporatist sector. Gurza Lavalle (1994: 105) writes that an 'extraordinary aspect' of the October 1989 announcement was the 'early co-ordination of corporate support'. Certainly, the presence of the executive's brother at the table expedited corporate support.

Summary – Actors, Institutions and the PFP

In an environment where the left posed a threat to PRI rule, initially at the ballot box and later in terms of party competition, the political costs of liquidating Conasupo during the PFP were too high. Liquidation risked conceding further ground to the PRD on the theme of social justice as well as additional PRI defections to the opposition. It is worth mentioning that the events of the PFP drove the PRI's most vocal Conasupo supporter, Demetrio Sodi de la Tijera, to the PRD. Assessing external actors and the public interest debate delineated the general constraints and pressures for innovation at Conasupo during the PFP, while a 'backroom debate' adopted a more micro-view. The overall result reveals a complex policy arena encompassing disparate actors with a stake in the future of Conasupo.

Discussing miscellaneous actors can only carry us so far. Implicitly, by prioritising processes of negotiation, both private and public, there is an assumption that such institutional features of the Mexican political system were crucial for the decision to maintain Conasupo. Likewise, the institutional order, in particular, the norms and tacit rules of the transition period, had to be introduced to fully understand this policy choice. The logic and inertia driving this critical juncture in Mexican politics are the expectations among relevant actors. Historical experience with *modernización* and *concertación*, plus well-known patterns of regime-corporate sector and regime-firm interaction, cultivated a set of expectations. Together, an intricate convergence of executive demand for legitimacy vis-à-vis the PRD and the expectations of potential and traditional allies combined to insure that Conasupo survived the PFP. Chapter Three shifts the analysis from the survival of Conasupo to the articulation of the CMP.

Notes

[1] World Bank (1990a, 1990b) note that an agricultural model based on world prices 'eluded' Mexico. Producer subsidies for corn and other basic grains reached ($US) 10 billion in 1997.

[2] For details on the welfare implications of maize subsidies in Mexico, see Lustig (1991) and Solís (1984).

[3] Consult R. Salinas (1988) and Knockenbauer (1990), Director of Iconsa from 1990-1992, for different institutional views on reforming Conasupo.

[4] Two common views emerged from Mexican universities during the PFP. One perspective supports economist Ramón Fernández y Fernández who maintained that the *ejido* had lost its historic significance and should be disbanded. A second perspective points the finger at the resources deficit and not the *ejido per se*. Grindle (1995: 48) suggests that the 1989 intra-government debate on the *ejido* "boiled down to those who wanted the magic of the marketplace and those who said, 'Do not abandon them'."

[5] Salinas' research acknowledged that the work of Leopoldo Solís, especially the belief in a historic bias in public policy toward industrialisation and urban interest groups, inspired his own thinking. Both individuals argue that past rural initiatives funnelled significant resources to the rural sector, but too often assistance never reached targeted populations, a suggestion that Mexican development problems were often distributional in nature.

[6] Salinas formulated his ideas in the late 1970s in the United States, when US President Carter advocated targeted programmes such as the Community Development Block Grant. Later, President Reagan would also embrace targeted programmes. See Weir, Orloff and Skocpol (1988) and Anagnoson (1980).

[7] Consult Salinas (1988), Appendini (1991), de la Madrid (1984) and Gavaldón Enciso and Pérez Haro (1987a, 1987b) for discussions of de la Madrid's Conasupo *modernización* agenda.

[8] Knochenhauer (1990: 837), a ex-Conasupo policymaker, argues that the CAP symbolises 'the [Salinas] Administration's commitment to placing the government/*campesino* relationship on a pluralistic foundation'. For in this May 1989 meeting, the government officially engaged non-CNC unions for the first time, an innovation of the traditional *concertación* framework. However, it should be emphasised that CNC President Maximiliano Silerio was the only *campesino* representative consulted on Conasupo reforms by Jaime Serra Puche after August 1989.

[9] Miguel Ángel Granados Chapa (*La Jornada*, 7 April 1989) offers another interpretation in which Raúl Salinas basically orchestrated *concertación* with corporate leaders months before April 1989.

[10] Chalco, 20 miles Southeast of Mexico City, became a showcase for participatory welfare programmes under Salinas. Traditionally, Conasupo resources have been concentrated in the populous communities around Mexico City. According to one observer, 'Thanks to Don Hank [González], you see Diconsa stores and Boruconsa warehouses in all the communities surrounding the Capital' (personal correspondence with Francisco Zapata, El Colegio de México).

[11] Aside from this official response, labour's response to Conasupo reforms varied considerably. Fidel Velázquez threatened to reject minimum wage agreements. Lorenzo Duarte, President of the CT, claimed that when negotiating the *Pacto*, Salinas assured him that the living standards of workers were a priority in future Conasupo services. The President of the National Association of Industrial Transportation Workers emphasised that citizens, not just workers, should be angry because liberalisation would foment monopolies. Conversely, the Director of the National Union of Public Sector Social

Security Workers and Social Services Workers believed that Conasupo was no longer affordable.

[12] Serra Puche's earlier statistical analysis of consumption subsidies, including work for the World Bank, found that subsidies (1973-1982) for wheat and sorghum hurt the poor while tortilla subsidies helped; a view that factored into Conasupo reforms under Salinas. See Serra Puche and García-Alba (1983).

[13] Maseca, part of the conglomerate Gruma, represented Mexico's sixteenth largest private firm in 1997. It captured around 80 percent of the private tortilla market (i.e., tortillas sold outside Conasupo) and also operated abroad (known as 'Mission Foods' in the USA). Maseca specialises in the Nixtamal process, which extracts a poisonous substance from corn flour (see graph 2.1). Later in the Salinas presidency, various scandals tied Serra Puche, Ernesto Zedillo, the President and his brother (with many others) to Maseca owner Roberto González Barrera.

[14] Columnist Emilio Zedabúa's article (*La Jornada*, 7 July 1996) quotes the congressional committee investigating Conasupo in the various instances where it claims that Serra Puche performed 'illegitimate and corrupt acts'. However, DePalma's rare glimpse of elite politics warrants criticism. Suggesting that Maseca's dominance coincided with Salinas' rise to power is simply wrong. Furthermore, DePalma's parallel between González Barrera and Carlos Slim is misleading. Carlos Slim appeared from nowhere to acquire TELMEX in 1991, a useful illustration of the 'political economy of privatisation' under Salinas that DePalma wants to expose. Maseca owner González Barrera's success in the tortilla market predates the 1980s, and illustrates the entrenched political/private-sector accommodation that developed in Mexico's protected economy. Finally, DePalma would have incited less partisan tension had he consulted sources beyond Adolfo Aguilar Zínser; in all likelihood, approaching a few past and current Conasupo employees would have validated Zínser's assertions.

[15] See comments by PAN Deputy Jesús Ramírez Núñez (*Excelsior*, 24 October 1989 and 26 October 1989) on politicised Conasupo deals with restaurants, bakeries and chocolate factories. Barranco Chavarría notes that Concanaco functionaries simultaneously criticise Conasupo while benefiting from its subsidised goods in *La Jornada* (25 October 1989).

[16] Alberto Santos is now the ex-owner of Gamesa (sold to Pepsico in 1990) and co-owner of Banco Norte with Roberto González Barrera and member of the group that controls the bank Confía. In 1998 he was elected as PRI Senator from Nuevo León (*Proceso*, 16 August 1998).

[17] In her research on the contours of the Mexican private sector, Salas-Porras (1996: 46) categorises González Barrera and Santos in a category known as the Monterrey branch of the 'Alemán Fraction': 'Most of these [business] groups depend greatly on concessions, contracts, infrastructure projects and government spending. Contract and auction results usually favor entrepreneurs who have developed personal ties with public officials and agencies or have become closely articulated to the governing bloc. For this reason entrepreneurs arising in this context have cultivated personal relations with the government, penetrating and virtually 'capturing' certain agencies'. González Barrera and Santos are also members of the 'Group of Ten Businessmen in Monterrey' (p.256) that

raised millions for PRI candidates. *Proceso* (16 August 1998) reports that Santos invested with the Salinas family and other prominent Monterrey businessmen to form the firms *Inmobiliaria Mesopotamia* (a transaction that landed *Confía* Bank director Jorge Lankenau Rocha in jail) and *Cítricos*.

[18] See comments by Zedillo's General Director of Conasupo Humberto Mosconi in *El Universal* (12 October 1996); inside Conasupo 'blaming Raúl' was often heard in interviews.

[19] A sample of his views are also found in a series of Conasupo policy reports (1988a, 1985a, 1985b, 1985c, 1985d, 1984, July 1984, and 1983).

[20] His interlocutory experience actually predated the 1980s. Raúl Salinas, states Fox (1991: 225, ft.36), 'was a rising star in the bureaucracy who had experience promoting rural reform in the rural road-building programme during the early 1970s'.

[21] The Salinas Conasupo team was announced in *Excelsior* (5 December 1988). Toward the end of the Salinas presidency, Raúl Salinas' reputation led the U.S.-Mexican Centre in La Jolla, California, to offer him a research fellowship.

3 Neoliberal Objectives, Policy Responses and Political Constraints

'They pretend to make many things occur at once so that things do not change' -
PAN Deputy Jesús Ramírez Núñez, *La Jornada*, 23 October 1989

Introduction

Ingram and Mann (1980: 7) write: 'A fundamental distinction in public policy analysis is the distinction between policy formation and policy implementation, or the distinction between policy causes and policy effects'. Chapter Two analysed the policy formation period (PFP); this chapter, and the two chapters that follow, examine the effects or output of Salinas's Conasupo policy. In particular, they consider whether and to what degree the Conasupo *Modernización* Plan (CMP, 1990-1994) fell victim to the inertia, logic and expectations that hitherto surrounded and produced continuity at Conasupo.

Conasupo's history of unsuccessful reforms leads to an inevitable query 'why should it be different this time'? Section one starts by situating the CMP within the context of President Salinas' larger neoliberal agenda, before turning to specific innovations imposed at Conasupo. This is intended to show that, like earlier recreations of Conasupo (see appendix 1.0), the CMP's neoliberal or innovative packaging concealed a more traditional political entity. For example, it proposed price liberalisation and limited privatisation in order to decrease government intervention in Mexican agricultural markets, yet it also committed itself to increase the number of consumers 'targeted' by Conasupo from 30 million to 50 million by 1994. Section two evaluates how the CMP influenced Conasupo-producer arrangements, notably, whether Conasupo had to abandon its old clients. Section three turns to a selective privatisation campaign, in particular, it demonstrates that the privatisation of Conasupo's processing branch (Iconsa) reflected a 'continuity formula' in which decisions were more responsive to political considerations than to a coherent neoliberal strategy.

Finally, this chapter reaches the conclusion that there were good reasons why in many regards 'this time around' resembled earlier experiences.

The Conasupo Modernización Plan, Radical Reform?

On 23 October 1989 an executive statement – 'President Salinas de Gortari Orders Increased Services for the Population that most Needs Them' – accompanied the unveiling of the Conasupo *Modernización* Plan (CMP) in twenty-six newspapers across Mexico. Two days before (21 October) Carlos Salinas and Ignacio Ovalle had announced reforms to the public in a press conference that lasted over four hours. Prescriptively, the CMP focused on needs-based and targeted delivery of public resources to the most disadvantaged segments of the population and the removal of Conasupo from 'non-priority' activities.

But Conasupo reform should be understood as just one component (or a lower level) in President Salinas' neoliberal state restructuring agenda:

- The National Development Plan 1989-1994 (NDP)   (more neoliberal)

- The National Programme for the *Modernización* of Supply and the Domestic Market 1990-1994 (NPMSDM)

- The Programme for the *Modernización* of Public Enterprises 1990-1994 (PMPE)

- Agreement for the Structural *Modernización* and the Financial Rehabilitation of Conasupo 1990-1994 (SMFRC)

- The Conasupo *Modernización* Plan 1990-1994 (CMP)   (less neoliberal)

The National Development Plan 1989-1994 (NDP) synthesises the six-year objectives of the new administration across all major policy areas. In the area of food markets, the NDP sought to liberalise domestic markets by reversing an urban bias in public resource allocation, re-capitalising Mexican agriculture with private and public investment, modernising public enterprises, increasing grain production and securing just prices for producers and consumers through efficiency gains (*Plan Nacional de Desarrollo 1989-1994*). One can draw parallels between this general liberalisation agenda and the shift toward a market-oriented development model that was at the centre of de la Madrid's NDP (Conasupo, 1987a, 1987b, 1984b, 1984c).

At a lower level of policymaking, the Secretary of Commerce (Secofi) crafted the objectives of the National Programme for the *Modernización* of Supply and the Domestic Market (NPMSDM): (i) deregulation of the economy, (ii) promotion of commercial infrastructure and support services for marketing, (iii) provision of market information, (iv) promotion of credit and purchasing associations, and (v) most importantly for our purposes, targeting of subsidies to low-income consumers (Secofi, 1990). Innovation at Conasupo would be a cornerstone of this broadly neoliberal agenda. However, we will discover below that sometimes this broad neoliberal, technocratic logic was compromised as NPMSDM objectives were translated into policy under the CMP (notably concerning the issue of targeting). Secofi also developed the Programme for the *Modernización* of Public Enterprises (PMPE), a broad mandate intended to reduce public intervention in the economy. PMPE included provisions concerning basic foodstuff security. It also stipulated that 'non-strategic activities will be disincorporated'; however, among others, IMSS, ISSSTE, Infonavit and Conasupo fell under the category of 'strategic enterprises' (*Diaro Oficial de la Federación*, 16 April 1990). Therefore, while the PMPE may have constituted a pillar of the Salinas neoliberal agenda, it did not mark a radical reformulation of existing Conasupo policy.

Although Secofi played an instrumental role in crafting food policy, the Administrative Council of Conasupo authorised major policy decisions involving Conasupo – as we saw in Chapter Two. In early October 1989, before the announcement of the CMP, Serra Puche, as President of the Council, tabled the following deal to Conasupo officials – what was later called the Agreement for the Structural *Modernización* and the Financial Rehabilitation of Conasupo 1990-1994 (SMFRC). The federal government would agree to assume the agency's external debt and individual branch debts in exchange 'for a profound strategy of *modernización*' (Conasupo,

1991). 'External debt' equalled the import price minus the price at which goods were sold domestically along with 'domestic costs' for transport, storage and marketing, and accumulated debt. Debt figures by 30 September 1990 stood at ($US) 1.3 billion for Conasupo, ($US) 26.7 million for Miconsa, ($US) 30.6 million for Liconsa, and ($US) 23.4 million for Impecsa. A lack of information precluded a figure for Diconsa. The deal would not be a one-off payment and, in 1993, the Council renewed the pledge to assume Conasupo debt.

It was with the SMFRC, the decision had been made to 'recreate' rather than liquidate Conasupo that the government addressed the costs of maintaining the parastatal in a way that assured at least incremental innovation over the *sexenio*. An itemised list accompanied the SMFRC to clarify the types of innovations that Serra Puche had in mind:

- Limit guaranteed prices to corn and beans but participate in other agricultural markets when Secofi deemed it necessary.
- Eliminate general subsidies except when advocated by Secofi
- Pay agricultural producers within 24 hours of receiving goods
- Design an inventory control system
- Improve the transparency of Conasupo's accounting practices
- Construct a mechanism to analyse and revise the agency's financial status
- Restructure the agency's social programmes

Source: Conasupo (September 1994)

The agreement advanced no precise policy initiatives, and recommendations like 'restructuring social programmes' invited multiple interpretations and prescriptive responses. The Council, however, requested that Conasupo take immediate action to clarify its financial status and to address its incapacity to generate reliable statistical information. There was less room for debate or interpretation on these issues and the Council itself spearheaded an overhaul of the Conasupo administrative apparatus. Two trends stood out in the SMFRC and would resurface in the CMP and more generally in Conasupo policy throughout the Salinas years: (1) a centralisation of administrative decision-making in the hands of the Council, which exerted pressure for innovation, alongside (2) a reluctance to reform the bureaucratic channels that distributed Conasupo subsidies.

With regard to the first trend, by late 1989 the parastatal's loose budgetary constraints and decentralised administrative structure had caused serious financial irregularities, to the point where its information system produced 'useless data' according to the Council (Conasupo, 1990). It lacked both an inventory control system and also records of individual accounts, (that is, who paid what, to whom, and when) a clear illustration of Conasupo's loose 'distributional' constraints as well. Diconsa posed a particularly problematic situation in this area. Finally, no accounting or planning system integrated the national Conasupo apparatus, which meant that there were few monitoring mechanisms in place to impede abuse across the parastatal (Conasupo, September 1994). Attesting to the climate in December 1988, Conasupo officials, in the first Council meeting of the Salinas term, admitted to angry Council members that it was not feasible to calculate the 'real balances or debts of Conasupo branches because no records existed to document the status of private accounts' (Conasupo, September 1994).[1] Although the Council prioritised Conasupo's budgeting, planning and operating systems, few concrete reforms materialised before 1992, a point explored at length in Chapter Five. With regard to the second trend, the Council also tabled few measures to address the acknowledged 'culture of corruption' at the local level where intermediaries delivered subsidies to households (Conasupo, 1990).[2] Hence, though the Council's initial effort to reform Conasupo may have been packaged as part of a larger neoliberal agenda (NDP, NPMSDM, and PMPE), it is not clear to what extent this resulted in a comprehensive solution or an explicit reformulation of the constraints on Conasupo.

The Conasupo *Modernización* Plan (CMP): President Salinas's Blueprint

Arguably, the CMP represented another recreation of Conasupo and this time around, as before, the final profile reflected the constraints and pressure for innovation that had always influenced Conasupo development. Affixing the Solidarity label to traditional Conasupo services was one element of this reinvention process. It needs to be stipulated that this chapter provides an overview of the CMP's reforms at Conasupo and its decentralised branches as announced to the public on 23 October 1989. At this point the CMP defined 'non-priority activities' as Iconsa factories and selected urban Diconsa stores. Internal Conasupo documents, however, reveal an unpublicised and broader interpretation that stretched to all processing activities (Conasupo, 1992).

Reforms at the Main Conasupo Office

The CMP did not alter Conasupo's official function, that is, it would continue to regulate the market for basic products. But as of 1 January 1990, Conasupo would cut its purchases from 12 grains to corn and beans alone or the 'essential parts of the lower-income diet' (*El Financiero*, 23 October 1989). Import and export controls were also cut to corn and beans, although the timing of import liberalisation varied. Rice had taken place back in October 1988, soybeans would occur in April 1990, and wheat would follow in 1994. Likewise, the domestic wheat chain fell under direct Secofi control after January 1991 (Conasupo, September 1994). The savings generated from reducing producer subsidies and Conasupo grain imports would approximate half of the total subsidies delivered by Conasupo programmes in 1988 (*Informe de Gobierno*, 1989). Future savings, key to the CMP, would be reinvested in Conasupo.

Beneficiaries of Conasupo's Programme of Support for Rural Commercialisation (PACE), a SAM-era scheme that channelled subsidies to low-income producers, would increase from 300,000 in 1989 to 1,500,000 by 1994. The CMP also liberalised animal feed imports, exposing the heavily subsidised sorghum sector to immediate competition. This action could have harmed the strategic domestic corn sector, as cheap corn-based animal feed entered Mexico; however, the CMP prohibited the import of corn for animal feed purposes.

With regard to consumption subsidies, the CMP called for additional tortilla and milk subsidies, and more important, it identified no fewer than 55 million Mexicans (half of the active population!) as low-income and eligible for consumption subsidies; the CMP, by 1994, aimed to reach 90 percent or 50 million people (up from 30 million in 1988). The policy objectives of the NPMSDM (a response to the NDP) may have advocated market deregulation and the 'targeting' of subsidies as part of a larger neoliberal agenda, however the fact remained that half of the population was eligible for Conasupo benefits.[3] Indeed, if the CMP unfolded according to plan, more consumers would receive Conasupo goods under the CMP than before.

Processing Activities: Iconsa, Miconsa and Triconsa

Iconsa's eleven industrial plants were labelled 'non-priority' activities and slated for privatisation, with the proceeds recycled into Conasupo subsidy programmes. However, Miconsa would continue to produce tortillas and corn flour at five factories. In 1986 the privatisation of Triconsa factories began; there was a pledge in the CMP to finish the process (a condition imposed in a 1989 World Bank loan).

Reforms Involving Grain Producers: Boruconsa

There were no plans to alter the size of Boruconsa's infrastructure, though the same Boruconsa warehouses were renamed Solidarity Warehouses. The CMP, in response to the objectives of the NPMSDM, sanctioned the creation of Regional Committees of Rural Organisation, Production and Marketing. These were regular monthly forums that integrated small-scale producers, community leaders and small businesses around Boruconsa's 1,371 warehouses. Secofi, SARH, SRA and Banrural representatives would attend all meetings, with the aim of integrating regional producers into potential markets and breaking down information barriers. Local committee members would also participate in the administration of Boruconsa warehouses.[4] Finally, Conasupo pledged to pay corn and bean producers within 24 hours after depositing products at Boruconsa and Andsa warehouses (part of the SMFRC).[5]

The Distribution of Subsidised Food: Diconsa

To remove benefits from middle-income neighbourhoods, the CMP privatised 589 urban Conasupers (i.e., large supermarkets), transferred all Diconsa urban warehouses to Andsa, eliminated 2,631 concessions to private retail outlets, and transferred the largest 25 Conasupers to Impecsa. Ignacio Ovalle stressed that the 589 Conasupers generated 80 percent of complaints against Diconsa and were 'overtly corrupt and open to the general public' (*La Jornada*, 23 October 1989). Diconsa employees had the first opportunity to purchase Conasupers, followed by official unions and finally private firms. Furthermore, the remaining Diconsa stores would stop purchasing unjustified items such as wine, televisions, clothes, shoes, and, around Christmas time, imported chocolates and toys; thus lowering Diconsa commodities from 10,000 to 5,000.

Hereafter, Diconsa would construct Solidarity Community Stores in rural and marginal urban areas with less than 5,000 inhabitants. Dubbed the 'participatory model', housewives, the community members that encountered Conasupo each day, would be asked to co-administer new stores with Diconsa officials. Local residents would organise Committees for Community Supply before entering a *concertación* dialogue with Diconsa. In October 1989, Ignacio Ovalle predicted the annual construction of 1,500 new Community Stores throughout the Salinas term (*Excelsior*, 26 October 1989). Shortly thereafter, he increased the expected total from 1,500 to 2,000 (1,000 urban and 1,000 rural) per year until 1994 (*Excelsior*, 5 November 1989).

Solidarity Infonavit Stores would be installed at all Infonavit housing projects with more than 1,000 residents. Infonavit would determine the location of new stores, however *concertación* committees of *colonia*, union, Diconsa and Infonavit representatives would handle the organisation and administration. Two hundred and fifty new stores would be constructed annually to 'support the lives of organised workers' (*La Jornada*, 23 October 1989). By 1994, 600 new cafeterias, producing 4,500,000 meals per month, would enlarge the Popular Kitchens (PK) Programme. PKs operated in the following manner: an urban *colonia* organised a Social Committee (usually composed of 12 to 50 women) to solicit a social credit award from Diconsa. The wives of union workers often organised and operated PKs. Typically, a Social Committee could expect around ($US) 5,200. Diconsa delivered subsidised food and Conasupo fixed a low price per meal, which only official union members could buy. Finally, the CMP requested 200 Mobile Diconsa Units (MUs) or vehicles that distributed Diconsa goods directly. In the past, MUs distributed resources in isolated rural and marginal urban communities, yet these would operate in Mexico City.[6]

The changes that the CMP made to Conasupo's distribution activities again contained innovations as well as strong continuity. Privatisations threatened the clientele arrangements that de la Madrid forged with official labour unions when Conasupers were first built, yet Infonavit Stores and PKs created the opportunity to enter new deals.

Retail Operations: Impecsa

Reforms to Impecsa called for constructing new and converting old warehouses (163 medium-sized and 8 large-sized) into Conasupo Solidarity Warehouses. The largest 25 Conasupers, previously administered by Diconsa, would be renamed Purchasing Unions (PUs). These new Solidarity Warehouses and PUs, similar to the old Impecsa warehouses, subsidised private retail businesses. Yet, under the CMP, Impecsa would have to manage its services in partnership with labour, *campesino* and *colonia* unions.

Distribution of Milk: Liconsa

Construction of new *lecherías* – renamed Community *Lecherías* in 1990 and Solidarity *Lecherías* in 1991 – would enlarge the Social Milk Programme, by adding 7.9 million children (for a total of 12.9 million) by 1994. In the states of Chiapas, México and Oaxaca, Liconsa would test a pilot programme that previously operated in the mountains of Guerrero, to supply milk to isolated indigenous communities.

The CMP: Implications and Oversights

Examining the CMP switches the analysis from the general policy orientations of the Salinas administration to a more specific level of analysis. Hellman (1988: 134) cautions,

> Discerning what is genuinely new in the Mexican system has always been made more difficult by official party rhetoric, which is designed to dress up small adjustments, minimalist reforms, and palliatives as major policy breakthroughs.

In this particular instance no one should question that the CMP included meaningful steps (privatisation, price liberalisation, targeting) toward official objectives and a wider neoliberal agenda. Whether or not it also had other consequences beyond limiting Conasupo to priority areas requires examination. Some observers misunderstand the continuity-discontinuity balance of the CMP. Some view it as less of a 'recreation' and more of a 'liquidation'.[7] While others conclude that the CMP amounts to 'business as usual' according to the observation made by Hellman. However, three components of the CMP stand out as radical innovations: (1) limiting Conasupo's grain monopoly to corn and beans, (2) discontinuing or privatising 'non-priority' activities, and (3) the participation model. The first two objectives are examined below in separate sections. The remainder of this section turns to the issue of the participation model.

The Participation Model

The CMP authorised 'community participation' at warehouses, stores and *lecherías*, through a two-step process: communities would be asked to organise and then enter a *concertación* dialogue with Conasupo. Scholars examine this two-step procedure in the context of the Solidarity initiative, and for some it signalled a new mode of state-society mediation. However, it is worth restating that Conasupo and not Solidarity agents conducted *concertación* dialogues for Conasupo resources, and that the parastatal had been experimenting with community participation since the 1970s.[8] Fox found that the Conasupo/Coplamar agreement of the late 1970s promoted local participation at Diconsa warehouses. However, his conclusions are somewhat mixed:

> Conasupo-Coplamar's community participation procedures ... were primarily intended to make the bureaucratic apparatus itself more accountable to its ostensible clients, that is, to devolve power over policy. The existing staff was too committed to bureaucratic and private interests to implement this policy change; a whole new network of promoters would need to be hired (Fox, 1991: 215).

Raúl Salinas pioneered the participation model from 1983 to 1987, as Diconsa (not to be confused as a 'new network of promoters') negotiated control of 13,000 rural outlets. *Campesino* unions told Raúl Salinas that in order to coerce public intermediaries, he could either transport *campesinos* directly to markets or put locals in charge of public infrastructure (Salinas, 1988). He opted for the latter during the 1980s and the CMP essentially adapted this approach to other Conasupo operations.[9]

On one level, building on Fox's comment, participation under the CMP was a policy to coerce public and corporatist intermediaries so that where these channels continued to distribute Conasupo resources, community participation would in theory realign power relations between intermediary and beneficiary. It is important to recount the prevailing academic discourse of the late 1980s concerning community participation. Observers sometimes misconstrued community participation in Mexico as a 'new right', neoliberal, or pro-market policy that emerged from a conflation of Latin America's *The Other Path* and Ronald Reagan's federalist revolution in the United States. Yet in Mexico, groups on the left have advocated similar policy prescriptions. While the PAN and business groups continued to view participation as a method to curb an inefficient public bureaucracy, left-wing groups rejected the paternalistic state bent on 'demobilising' local communities by co-opting leaders and general clientelism.[10]

Under de la Madrid and Salinas, community participation became virtually synonymous with *concertación* agreements, which had less to do with either North American neoliberalism or traditional Latin American left-wing discourse and more to do with the demands of the old state-society model for certain modes of social organisation.[11] Community participation according to *concertación* presupposed a specific mode of community organisation before any 'participation' could take place.

Emphasising organisation rather than right- or left-wing ideology is useful, for *concertación* agreements were brokered across the ideological spectrum. Moreover, traditional left-wing references to 'demobilisation' misread an important dynamic in the Conasupo/Mexican case: *Concertación* sometimes centred on mobilising allies to pressure parastatals, local government and corporatist allies, a mechanism to channel the pressure for innovation that drives the old state-society model. It is therefore equally true that to pressurise intermediaries through community mobilisation did not necessarily signal an alternative to the government's customary preference for vertical integration and resistance to horizontal social organisation (Escobar Latapi and Roberts, 1991). Indeed, the CMP was clear in this area. After communities organised themselves, it instructed them to negotiate directly with the Salinas administration, which in practice implied negotiations with Ovalle and Raúl Salinas.

The discussion so far indicates that two types of obstacles impeded effective community participation: first, resource issues associated with community organisation, and second, concerns connected to the monitoring of intermediaries. For, as White (1996: 6) suggests,

> Participation must be seen as political. There are always tensions underlying issues such as who is involved, how, and on whose terms. While participation has the potential to challenge patterns of dominance, it may also be the means through which existing power relations are entrenched and reproduced. The arenas in which people perceive their interests and judge whether they can express them are not neutral. Participation may take place for a whole range of unfree reasons.

Encouraging poor Mexicans to participate in the politicised context around Conasupo services encountered well-known obstacles. The literature on interest groups reminds us that initial organisation and subsequent participation entails immediate financial, opportunity and other costs. How did the CMP lower the resource burden of the poor? The CMP solicited women in particular to participate, which represented a segment of society that entered local politics with a clear resource disadvantage (Craske, 1994b; González de la Rocha, 1991). Likewise, if the participation model was to gain any legitimacy in the community – and avoid what Cornelius (1995: 149) describes as the 'cannibalization of federal government programs (by local elites)…when they reach the local level' – presumably policy-makers had to place a premium on low-cost schemes to regulate local officials.

Before and after October 1989, two mechanisms monitored the delivery of food subsidies and, indirectly, the cost of organisation. First, beneficiaries could file complaints at Conasupo. In practice, beneficiaries seldom chose this option because of a low follow-up rate. Second, the Federal Consumer Office (Profeco) served as the main mechanism to enforce official price controls.

The CMP and other Secofi initiatives ignored the Profeco. In October 1989, Director of Profeco Emilio Chuayffet commanded a force of 900 inspectors in 51 branches located across Mexico as well as eight offices in Mexico City. Poorly paid and asked to do a job requiring additional resources, Profeco inspectors, not surprisingly, developed a reputation for corruption (*La Jornada*, 28 October 1989).[12] On 27 October 1989, as he lobbied the Mexico City Representative Assembly for more resources, Chuayffet explained that in the previous month Profeco received 28,000 consumer complaints, gave 40,000 court statements and mediated local conflicts with 21,622 distributors. Further, he warned that the social burden of the anti-inflationary *Pacto* signed in October 1989, together with the government's continued failure to monitor food prices, was a recipe for 'popular restlessness' in Mexico City (*La Jornada*, 28 October 1989).

Therefore, while the CMP sanctioned more Diconsa stores, *lecherías* and tortilla coupons, no additional inspectors or new controls over current inspectors would be forthcoming. Since 80 percent of the complaints against Diconsa originated at its soon to be privatised Conasupers, one might argue that Profeco's job would be more manageable. Unfortunately, by discontinuing 589 Conasupers in central urban areas while constructing over 1,500 stores per year in rural and marginal zones and increasing both tortilla and milk subsidies, the CMP made a bad situation worse. In response to Chuayffet's warnings, the very next day the government, in an absurd statement, solicited the help of 400 housewives to 'organise in order to end price fraud in Mexico City' (*La Jornada*, 29 October 1989). It is inconceivable that a committed policy-maker would have endorsed this proposal. But more interesting is the fact that the immediate response to the Profeco issue was to shift the monitoring costs to poor women.

The CMP, by ignoring the monitoring apparatus, side-stepped the variable most important to its success, namely, reorienting the traditional expectations and incentives to local intermediaries and potential community participants. Ward (1989: 145) writes on local political leadership in Mexico,

> Perhaps the most important role of leadership is that of intermediary between local residents and supra-local institutions, be they governmental, political, or private. Leadership structures do not emerge

in a vacuum, but are created out of the particular political economy in which they are set.

The political economy that he has in mind lists the nature of the commitment (i.e., required skills or knowledge) and endowments (i.e., material resources) necessary to succeed in the job. The CMP did not lower a preexisting resource threshold attached to participation, which would be needed to assure that new community intermediaries could challenge those that already 'participated' via old schemes. Such individuals gained access or the right to participate precisely because they could satisfy the resource requirements.

In other words, to redistribute income or power such as that envisioned for successful community participation, the government had to address local economic and political power relationships, and not simply craft unenforceable rules and regulations. It is not evident that the CMP was a suitable vehicle for this.[13] The government's ludicrous '400 housewife policy' surely sent the message that the CMP was not serious about tackling local power structures.

There is some evidence that the situation was actually worse. Anthropologist Jorge Hernández Díaz, a specialist in indigenous and coffee-producing regions of Oaxaca, explains that the Diconsa participation model under Salinas renewed existing power relations. He explains that 'typically the local food outlet was handed over to the community *cacique*' (Interview, La Jolla, California, 11 May 1998). Local participants controlled store operations or perhaps became the new owners, but Diconsa continued to fill the shelves as it had always done.[14] Hernández's observations are significant, for Oaxaca received a disproportionate number of Community Solidarity Stores under Salinas – Diconsa constructed 667 stores in 1991 alone, amounting to 25 percent of the year's national total (*Informe de Gobierno*, 1996).

Producer Subsidies and Renewing Old Political Alliances

This section switches from the general policy orientations of the Salinas administration to a more specific level of analysis. For many, innovating Conasupo's grain pricing regime was perhaps the most neoliberal and controversial component in the CMP because Salinas was depicted as abandoning grain producers.[15] Sticking with our definition of policy success from Chapter One and general interest in state-society relations, two significant questions are whether the number of producers selling to Conasupo dropped and whether the Conasupo-producer relationship in general became less informal, arbitrary and clientelistic.

Logically, one would anticipate a steep decline in clients as well as a new type of state-society relationship, as Conasupo's mandate fell from 12 grains to corn and beans. After all, in 1989, sorghum, wheat, rice and soybeans comprised 47 percent of Conasupo's total domestic grain purchases (measured in tonnes) (*Informe de Gobierno*, 1994). However, this section shows that under the CMP Conasupo intervention *increased* markedly in terms of total domestic grain purchases. In fact, Conasupo's traditional infrastructure purchased more grain from domestic producers than at any time in history. Hence there is evidence that instead of a coherent neoliberal programme of market liberalisation, the final outcome produced significant continuity and 'recreated' rather than abandoned traditional Conasupo-producer arrangements.

Yet the data on total producers connected to Conasupo are incomplete so I propose to estimate this figure. The reader should also note that this discussion concerns the status of Conasupo as an intermediary between state and a specific section of Mexican agricultural society and there is no attempt to assess broader questions of state-producer relations or conditions for Mexican grain producers.

Conceptually, the decision to discontinue general producer subsidies implies either the exclusion of entire crops (e.g., wheat or sorghum) or re-evaluation within sectors according to a designated criterion, such as rich versus poor, irrigated versus non-irrigated or exporters versus non-exporters. The CMP embraced the exclusion option so that twelve grains equated to a 'general subsidy' regime while restricted access to corn and bean producers signified a 'targeted subsidy' regime. The scope of reform essentially stopped here; for example, there was little attention to the delivery of subsidies within sectors or operations at Boruconsa/Andsa warehouses, besides delivering subsidies in a more timely fashion. The CMP bolstered CNC control of warehouses, a development consistent with the *concertación* agreement of 22 August 1989. One illustration of this is that, as of 1990, a tripartite panel of Secofi, Boruconsa and CNC determined the quantity and price levels in the PACE initiative. In the past, Boruconsa performed this task alone.

There was never a period when Conasupo actually controlled grain markets; in fact, on average it marketed around 15 percent of the domestic corn harvest, and less with regard to other grains (*Informe de Gobierno*, 1989; *Excelsior*, 26 October 1989). It was just one player in a complex domestic grain market. Conasupo's storage infrastructure of Boruconsa and Andsa warehouses stretched across rural Mexico in an *ad hoc* manner, and according to the parastatal, access was 'confined to a specific geographic area' (Conasupo, 8 August 1995).[16] Over time, this area corresponded to the government-funded irrigation system. Often, high transport costs outweighed potential gain for many grain producers, effectively excluding them from Conasupo.[17] Remarking on Conasupo purchases through the 1970s, Hall and Price (1982: 310) note,

> Due to inadequate collection, transportation, storage facilities and staff on the part of the governmental purchasing organisation [Conasupo], it was uneconomical to make purchases from scattered producers. Most purchases were made from commercial growers or merchants. *Because the big growers and merchants benefited most from the food purchasing programme, they appeared to be devices for transfers of wealth to these groups* (... emphasis added)

There was no provision in the CMP for the enlargement or reduction of the Boruconsa/Andsa infrastructure or any attempt at addressing the issue of transportation. From 1989 to 1994, the number of Boruconsa warehouses registered a minimal increase from 1,651 to 1,729, and its storage capacity dropped from 5.9 to 5.8 million tonnes; the number of Andsa warehouses remained stable and its storage capacity increased slightly from 5.5 to 5.8 million tonnes (*Informe de Gobierno*, 1994). It is therefore reasonable to assume a degree of stability in the geographic pool of clients with access to Conasupo.

But whom would this infrastructure continue to serve? Did the CMP abandon the former clients mentioned by Hall and Price? On the one hand, it potentially did abandon producers of wheat, sorghum, rice and soybeans. On the other hand, the aggregate decline was bound to be small, since corn and bean producers represented a large percentage of traditional

Conasupo clients (although their percentage of total Conasupo purchases of corn and beans was eclipsed by purchases from abroad). Graph 3.0 displays Conasupo's total *domestic* grain purchases over three presidential terms. What is striking is the volatility before 1991. Conasupo purchased more wheat than corn from Mexican producers in 1983, while the year 1987 seems exceptional as sorghum surpassed both corn and bean purchases. By 1991, corn and beans more than replaced previous purchases of other grains. Overall, total domestic purchases decreased with the 1982 economic crisis and experienced a partial recovery in 1985. Finally, the decline resumed from 1986-1989 under the weight of lower oil prices, anti-inflationary measures and public spending cuts. Graph 3.0 shows that once the CMP's producer-state reforms started in January 1990, Conasupo intervention *increased* markedly with respect to total domestic grain purchases. Conasupo under Salinas purchased more grain from domestic producers than at any time in history. Equally important, given its infrastructure in 1989, Conasupo purchased more grain from a fixed geographic clientele through 1994.

We can confine 'excluded producers' to sorghum, wheat, rice and soybeans, for other grains which lost subsidies under the CMP encompassed an insignificant pool of producers that had previously sold to Conasupo. Graph 3.1 indicates that an overwhelming number of producers remained eligible for subsidies under the CMP. In fact, limiting subsidies to corn and beans still left 70 percent of total domestic producers eligible in 1989. After January 1990, moreover, numerous producers switched from other grains to corn and beans to avoid the adjustment costs in the competitive export sector (fruits, vegetables and unprotected grains) (Appendini and Liverman, 1994; Barry, 1995). One indication of this is that, comparing 1988 and 1991, the total surface area for sorghum and wheat cultivation declined 16 percent and 15 percent, while corn and beans increased 5 percent and 27 percent. In fact, graph 3.2 shows that gains in corn and beans offset lost surface area for sorghum, soybeans, rice and wheat through 1993.

Data on the average plot size is also instructive. Graph 3.3 compares the size of producer plots for separate grains. Shifts in surface area combined with the small plot sizes for corn and bean production lend evidence against the idea that Conasupo 'lost clients' after January 1990. Another factor that supports this proposition is that Conasupo significantly reduced corn and bean imports after 1990.[18] Previously Conasupo had satisfied domestic demand by purchasing at home and abroad. By the de la Madrid years, Conasupo occasionally bought more corn from foreign than domestic producers (table 3.0). The fiscal dilemma facing Mexico, and a new attitude to imports that abandoned the protectionism of Echeverría's 'food security' and López Portillo's 'food self-sufficiency' campaigns, fuelled the inflow of cheap imported grain. After 1985, the agency also imported large quantities of beans to satisfy domestic consumption. Table 3.0 shows that around 1991 Conasupo corn imports nearly stopped. Moreover, we see that domestic production accelerated as of 1990. Bean purchases experienced a similar pattern. Obeying an 'import-substitution-development' logic, Conasupo exchanged cheap foreign for expensive domestic producers under the CMP. The decision to 'buy locally' (CMP) in record numbers amid a scheme to liberalise grain markets (NDP and NPMSDM) is one of the clearest illustrations of the political settlements, compromises or 'Mexican solutions' that surfaced in the CMP.

Graph 3.0 National Conasupo Grain Purchases (1976-1994)

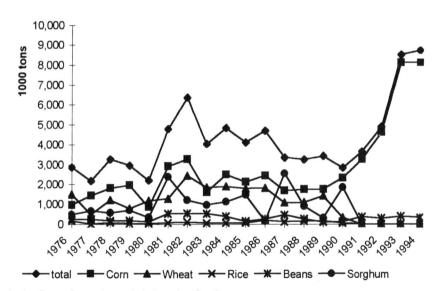

* The figure for soybeans is below that for rice.
Source: Informe de Gobierno (1994, 1996)

Graph 3.1 Total Number of Mexican Producers by Sector (1990)

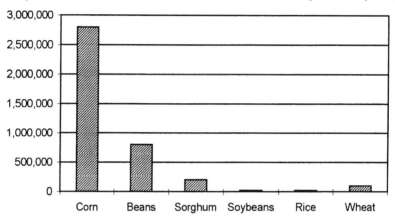

Source: Conasupo (15 September 1994)

Graph 3.2 Total Surface Area

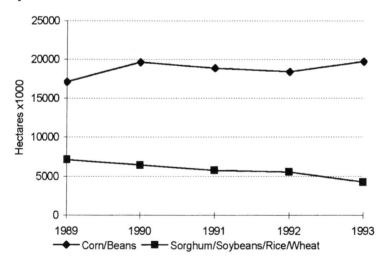

Source: Informe de Gobierno (1996)

Graph 3.3 Average Number of Hectares per Producer (1990)

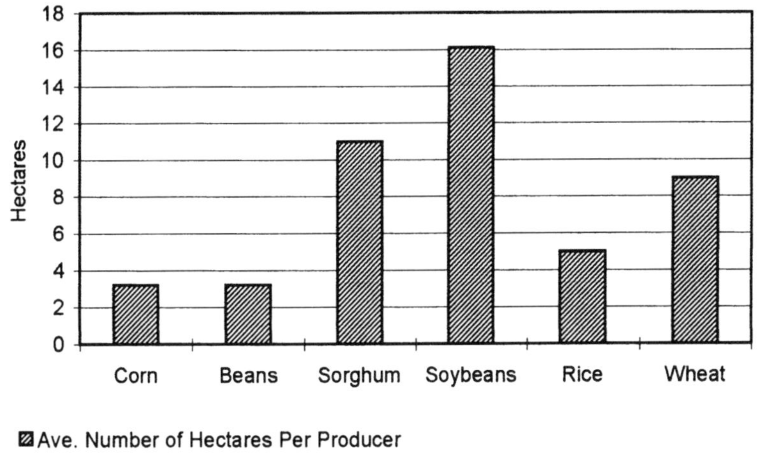

Ave. Number of Hectares Per Producer

Source: Informe de Gobierno (1994)

The Mexican agricultural sector is usually conceived of as bimodal due to its distinct 'traditional' and 'modern' sectors. Corn production continues to dominate the former while crops such as wheat, rice, tomatoes and fruits have typified the latter. Appendini (1991: 980) found that 48 percent of total corn production in 1985 came from producers cultivating less than 5 hectares. This group consumes between 50 and 76 percent of their own production. In particular, one factor accounts for the bimodal structure: irrigation investment absorbed between 70 and 99.2 percent of the government's annual agricultural budget from 1940 to 1979 (DeWalt and DeWalt, 1991: 193). By default, non-irrigated or traditional production obtained scant investment. The bimodal structure exhibits clear regional dimensions by 1990 – see table 3.1. In 1990 corn production predominated in the heavily populated and relatively poor states in central and southern Mexico, aside from the affluent State of México. In contrast, agriculture in the higher-income and less populated northern states has shown more crop diversity.

Table 3.0 Conasupo Purchases of Corn and Beans (tonnes 1,000)

Year	Corn			Beans		
	Domestic	Imports	Total	Domestic	Imports	Total
1983	1,607	4,129	5,736	530	0	530
1984	2,493	2,393	4,886	392	0	392
1985	2,121	1,629	3,750	144	117	261
1986	2,437	1,204	3,641	259	167	426
1987	1,679	2,124	3,803	465	38	503
1988	1,742	2,329	4,068	261	3	264
1989	1,753	2,004	3,757	103	106	209
1990	2,321	1,873	4,194	124	362	486
1991	3,319	**41**	3,360	367	**12**	379
1992	4,628	**15**	4,643	295	**0**	295
1993	8,115	**80**	8,195	393	**0**	393
1994	8,089	**0**	8,089	331	**0**	331

Source: Conasupo (15 September 1994)

Dismantling the old Conasupo subsidy regime reconfigured the incentive structure for grain production in certain areas and altered production patterns during the Salinas years. Between the beginning of 1989 and the final harvest of 1993, total production declined for sorghum (52 percent), wheat (19 percent), rice (45 percent) and soybeans (50 percent). Conversely, total production increased for corn (40 percent) and beans (54 percent).[19] Table 3.2 shows developments at the state level. Notice that Conasupo purchases jumped in locations associated with capital-intensive production. In 1993 and 1994 Conasupo purchased 8 million tonnes of corn in the domestic market, 62 percent of which originated in Sonora, Sinaloa, Chihuahua, Guanajuato, and Jalisco.   However, in 1989 Conasupo purchased around half this total, and roughly 25 percent came from this group of states (Conasupo, 8 August 1995). Conasupo's *1992 Annual Report* acknowledges that spending on grain exceeded its original budget by 45.5 percent, citing unexpected purchases in Jalisco, Tamaulipas and Sinaloa, or areas that previously sold wheat, soybeans and rice to Conasupo

(Conasupo, 1992). This again indicates that some modern producers switched to corn and bean production.[20]

Table 3.1 Total Agricultural Surface Area in 1990 (hectares)

	Non-Corn Production*	Corn Production
Central & Southern States		
State of México	95,285	674,210
Chiapas	115,035	705,112
Puebla	132,432	625,341
Guerrero	33,594	465,612
Oaxaca	74,394	485,359
Campeche	35,287	75,599
Northern States:		
Sinaloa	799,327	121,458
Sonora	406,943	38,323
Nayarit	112,920	58,156
Guanajuato	547,696	415,738
B. California	115,442	2,703
Chihuahua	347,754	239,591
Tamaulipas	1,073,244	277,796

* Non-corn crops include beans, barley, soybeans, sorghum, rice, chilli, sunflower, tomato and wheat.
Source: Conasupo (15 September 1994)

However, production decisions depend on a long list of factors, such as the structure of demand, climate patterns, export markets and input markets. According to Appendini and Liverman (1994: 151), a mere 16 percent of Mexican land is suitable for agriculture while 80 percent of corn and bean producers cultivate non-irrigated plots. This combination means that, for the majority of Mexican grain producers, climate conditions top the list of factors that affect production. Yet, cost/price structures also shape their production decisions. DeWalt and DeWalt (1991: 199) note that in 1984, a record year for rainfall, 9 million hectares of arable land in rain-fed regions were idle because the return on basic grains was so low. They also recall that between 1954-1964 the Mexican Agricultural Programme, a scheme of subsidised machinery, fertiliser, pesticides and high guaranteed prices, improved the rate of wheat per hectare annually. Yet, the end of this scheme in 1965 corresponded with a precipitous decline in wheat production. Later, price inducements in the SAM prompted record grain production in 1982 and 1983, while burgeoning sorghum production in the 1980s followed Conasupo price hikes. All of the above indicate a clear correlation between cost/price structures and Mexican grain production.

From the beginning of 1989 to the end of 1990, the price of corn climbed 45 percent and the price of beans rose 47 percent, while other grains registered smaller price rises: sorghum 17 percent, rice 19 percent, wheat 23 percent, while soybeans actually dropped 14 percent in price (*Informe de Gobierno*, 1994). Sosa (1990: 41) calculates that Mexican corn prices surpassed international prices by 33 percent in December 1989 (i.e., the month before the CMP reforms); and, interestingly, Salcedo *et al.* (1993: 303) calculate that Mexican prices surpassed the price of international corn arriving at the port of Veracruz by 69 percent between January-August 1992. So the price gap essentially doubled in the first two years of the CMP.

Thus, even though the initial impetus may have been to liberalise grain markets, the CMP furnished price incentives to reorient production into protected crops. It is hard to conceive how policy makers – after the mass movement of corn producers into sorghum production in the 1980s due to Conasupo price changes – could have expected anything but a similar response in January 1990. Thus, as climatic conditions encouraged agricultural production in general, price incentives and the security of a fixed Conasupo regime, alongside the decision to bar imports, shifted grain production towards corn and beans. We find in Conasupo's *1991 Annual Report* that as early as July 1990 corn and bean purchases exhausted the expected budgetary appropriation for the entire year, requiring an additional loan from the government of ($US) 130 million (Conasupo, 1991).

Moreover, in 1993 Conasupo's producer subsidy total surpassed both the figure for 1992 (by 100 percent in real terms) and the figure for 1989, that is, before the CMP (*Informe de Gobierno*, 1994). Finally, it is also noteworthy that, according to Appendini and Liverman (1994), 1991 marked the onset of an advantageous climatic cycle in Mexico, thus the clear signs of a shift as early as mid-1990 preceded this development.

Table 3.2 Conasupo Corn Purchases (1989-1994)

Year	1989	1990	1991	1992	1993	1994
Measured in Tonnes						
Sinaloa	26,565	158,722	541,079	854,195	2,345,248	2,645,510
Sonora	26,808	14,187	175,029	163,772	383,002	412,219
Coahuila	396	1,411	13,668	26,768	83,151	78,888
Hidalgo	225	5,299	8,004	8,511	30,106	39,468
Tamaulipas	391,277	469,508	176,207	483,296	920,591	1,098,652
Baja Cal.	273	0	71	7,519	61,076	54,811
Baja Cal. Sur	9,772	21,854	76,890	91,764	89,598	91,963
Nuevo León	2,370	9,979	32,856	35,947	56,074	52,744
Total Purchases	1,773,637	2,321,115	3,318,873	4,570,289	8,115,474	8,088,743

Source: Conasupo (15 September 1994)

The evidence suggests that the CMP amplified the number of producers who sold crops to Conasupo's geographically confined infrastructure. The implication is that state-society interaction concerning Conasupo and grain producers, by 1994, resembled that of 1989. Whether shifting into corn and beans represented a viable long-term development or short-term transitional accommodation is another issue. Furthermore, whether another Mexican president will decide to reformulate the government's subsidy regime in such a way that would end its established relationship with the strategic grain producer sector remains a question for the future.

Neoliberal Reform, Meeting the Left-wing Challenge, and the CMP

Grain policy also responded to political challenges in the first half of the Salinas term. Retiring agricultural subsidies and a general policy of market liberalisation weakened a pillar of popular conceptions of 'social justice' and threatened to push *campesino* unions to the less neoliberal PRD. To begin, the analysis and findings above generally concur with Brachet-Marquez and Sherraden's (1994) contention that, at a general level, Salinas dismantled general price subsidies in favour of a new policy that channelled resources to traditional government allies. I have mentioned the basic characteristics of Mexican corn and bean producers. Over the years demographic and climatic pressures, and irregular access to production inputs, encouraged dependence on parastatals and exchange arrangements with corporatist *campesino* unions. In addition to the analysis above, there is further evidence that the CMP reproduced these types of corporatist exchange arrangements, but in a different guise.

A Conasupo scheme, PACE, which was designed under the SAM initiative to cater to low-income corn and bean producers, offered subsidies for marketing, transportation and threshing.[21] Although the CMP described PACE as an example of successful targeting in the 1980s, the programme also delivered significant resources to official *campesino* unions. Graph 3.4 provides data on the PACE programme. The number of low-income producers increased 43 percent from the end of 1989 to the conclusion of 1991. Before 1990 PACE served *ejidos* alone, however, eligibility stretched to all non-irrigated corn and bean producers thereafter (Conasupo, 1994b).

New guidelines for PACE under the CMP did nothing to address past problems of resource management that had faced planners in Mexico City in the 1980s. For instance, weak monitoring arrangements, the central problem with PACE in the past, impeded their capacity to regulate and control the delivery of PACE resources as the CMP increased the scheme rapidly. In practice, planners allocated PACE resources to state Boruconsa officials, who co-ordinated with state governors. However, the selection of beneficiaries occurred on a regional, individual basis, a process that planners in Mexico City had little influence over, both before and after

1990. However, it was they who set the price and a quantitative limit in PACE's general allocation formula. Indeed a committee composed of Secofi, Boruconsa and the CNC designated the number of subsidised tonnes per producer and the value of subsidies covered by PACE. In 1992 and 1993 Conasupo estimated the average output per producer participating in PACE at 17 tonnes, an average higher than traditional non-irrigated *campesino* production, suggesting that benefits generally flowed to medium-scale producers.

Graph 3.4   Corn and Bean Producers in PACE Programme

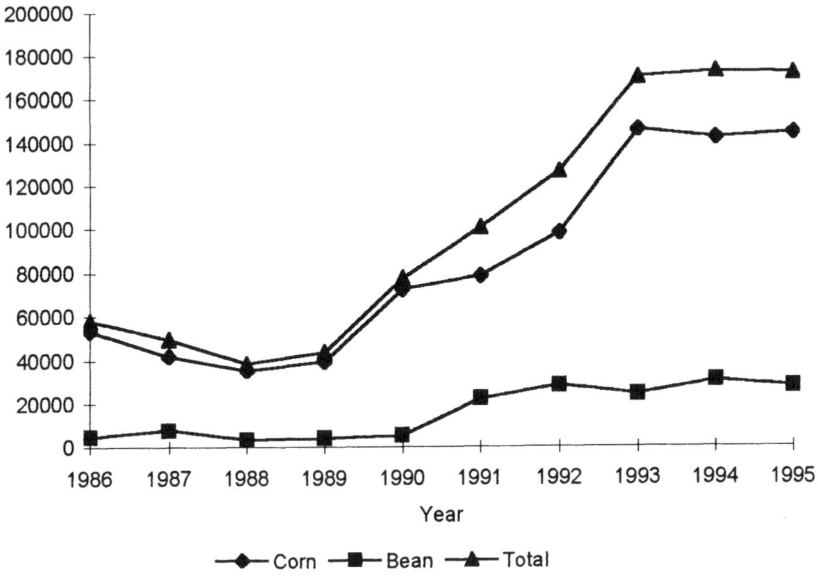

Source: Informe de Gobierno (1996)

Table 3.3 shows that, by 1993, PACE no longer resembled its 1989 profile. However, Conasupo's *1992 Annual Report* asserts that PACE's rapid growth from 1989 to 1991 caused rampant abuse in the local delivery of resources. The report concluded: 'A more rigorous criterion for distribution in the future was required' (Conasupo, 1992). Candid recognition of abuse by planners in Mexico City captures the dilemma they encountered when translating neoliberal objectives into policy via local Conasupo and corporatist intermediaries.

Table 3.3 Agricultural Regions Covered by PACE

Year	1986	1987	1988	1989	1990	1991	1992	1993
Total	4,687	3,712	2,512	2,838	4,110	7,342	5,409	8,257

Source: Informe de Gobierno (1994)

Likewise, PACE reveals a case in which a programme appeared broadly neoliberal but soon evolved into something more politicised. Here the government delivered more resources to the CNC and in a way that was acknowledged to be arbitrary, informal and inefficient. It is also interesting that the government decreased PACE in 1992, following a decision to allow independent investigators to survey the programme. In a pattern that will become familiar, the Salinas administration elected to 'deliver resources' recklessly during its legitimacy crisis from 1989-1991 (in this case, adding 4,504 new agricultural communities via the old clientelistic arrangements), while postponing initial steps toward 'reform' of Conasupo programmes until after the PRI defeated the left-wing challenge of the PRD in the 1991 mid-term election.

Why Privatise Iconsa?

This final section also switches from the general policy orientations outlined at the beginning of the chapter to more specific policy outcomes. Privatising Iconsa was at the centre of the CMP, a 'non-priority' activity that was no longer consistent with the neoliberal agenda in Mexican food markets. However the issue of Iconsa privatisation deserves close attention because under the CMP revenue generated, along with money derived from other cost-cutting measures, would be recycled to expand and maintain other

Conasupo services. In this sense, privatisation under the CMP presented a general 'continuity formula' – but only if the government followed through with reinvestment.[22] Iconsa also offers an instance where one mode of intervention was exchanged for another and where privatising public resources in fact enlarged the overall scope for government intervention. Kiewiet and McCubbins, in *The Logic of Delegation* (1991), argue that, in certain circumstances, politicians delegate power or resources as a strategy to bolster their own status or influence. The same rationale exerts pressure on private firms to 'contract out' specific tasks to improve their profitability. Arguably, the CMP delegated or contracted out processing functions to multinationals and to political allies as a strategy to increase the delivery of final consumption subsidies (i.e., the 'continuity formula').[23]

The Logic of Delegation: Privatising Iconsa

In 1990 and 1991 public perception was sceptical about Iconsa privatisations being anything more than the liquidation of another parastatal.[24] Columnist Juan Antonio Zúñiga summarises a prevalent view:

> It took the government of Carlos Salinas exactly 45 months to dismantle a structure that took 29 years to construct, from the founding of Conasupo in March 1961 until the privatisation of the first Iconsa plants in February 1990 (*La Jornada*, 13 May 1997).[25]

Therefore some observers saw Iconsa's fate as parallel with the dismantling of Conasupo. Though not completely inaccurate, this view fails to mention that more Mexicans consumed Conasupo products in the 1990-1991 period than at any time in the parastatal's history. In fact, in 1990 and 1991, Conasupo constructed 3,186 Solidarity (Diconsa) Stores. Meanwhile, at the same time, Liconsa *lecherías* witnessed spectacular growth, expanding from 300 to 1,370 municipalities.

A thorough analysis of Conasupo consumption services is the subject of the next chapter. The relevant point here is that, in 1990 and 1991, the privatisation of Iconsa occurred as record numbers of Mexicans accessed Conasupo subsidies. There is sufficient evidence to confirm that Iconsa's privatisation, as the CMP intended, financed the rapid growth of consumption subsidies.[26] Secofi put Iconsa factories on the auction block under the Structural *Modernización* Programme of the Conasupo System (SMPCS). The same format was later used to privatise other Conasupo assets.

The Iconsa privatisation process concluded on 21 February 1992. Table 3.4 shows where Iconsa concessions went in 1991. Data corresponds to both infrastructure spending and the operating budgets of Diconsa and Impecsa, while the data for Liconsa is for infrastructure spending alone. The operating budgets for Liconsa, Diconsa and Impecsa increased in 1989, 1990 and 1991. Table 3.4 does not cover the cost of food distributed by these branches; this expenditure appears in the main Conasupo budget. Further, Iconsa proceeds did not benefit Boruconsa because the SMPCS stipulated that revenue from Iconsa privatisation should go to consumer subsidies.[27]

Table 3.4 Branch Budget and Source of Financing 1991 ($US million)

Sources of Finance	Total Branch Budget	Diconsa	Impecsa	Liconsa
(Total)	177	107	60	9
Iconsa*	107	37	60	9
Savings from Iconsa**	70	70	0	0
Budget***	0	0	0	0

* Total raised from privatisation
** Savings accrued from no longer subsidising Iconsa factories
*** The resources received from Conasupo.
Source: Conasupo (1992)

Iconsa concessions and savings (once these factories stopped consuming Conasupo resources) generated sufficient revenue to cover the 1991 budgetary requirements of Diconsa, Liconsa and Impecsa at a time when each programme, along with the Tortilla Programme (part of the

Diconsa budget at this time), experienced rapid growth in its infrastructure. In effect, privatisation made this possible.

Table 3.5 Diconsa Total Budget for 1991

	($US million)	(Units)
Total	107.5	
Operations*	73.4	
Investment	34.1	
Urban Stores	0.166	(490 new stores)
Rural Stores	0.194	(870 new stores)
Infonavit Stores	14.600	(234 new stores)
Re-capitalise Rural Warehouses	7.600	(264 warehouses)
Other**	11.500	

*Operations consist largely of transport equipment and salaries
**Includes large purchases of computers
Source: Conasupo (1992)

Table 3.5 categorises Diconsa spending in 1991. Two activities account for the lion's share of Diconsa investment in 1991: constructing 234 new Infonavit stores (43 percent of total investment) and re-capitalising 264 rural warehouses (22 percent). Expenditure on rural warehouses attests to the infrastructure demands associated with supplying roughly 4,000 new small-sized rural stores built between 1989 and 1991. Table 3.6 verifies that, as with Diconsa, Iconsa revenue constructed and equipped new *lecherías*. In fact, Liconsa constructed an unprecedented annual total of 3,453 *lecherías* across Mexico in 1991.

Iconsa was the first in a series of privatisations (table 3.7) in which Conasupo redirected revenue into consumption subsidies under Salinas. Zúñiga (*La Jornada*, 13 May 1997) estimates that the privatisation of Diconsa, Liconsa and Miconsa netted ($US) 340 million for the government by 1995. This figure corresponds to the total listed in Conasupo documents. In late 1991, Secofi auctioned the first Liconsa factory (*Productos Alimenticios La Campiña* to *Nam Inversiones*) and soon transferred two other factories for ($US) 51.5 million. Additional Liconsa assets raised another ($US) 69.8 million by 1994. The privatisation process moved to Impecsa and Miconsa in 1992. In 1993 Impecsa concessions generated ($US) 9.6 million, and in 1994 the sale of 18 Impecsa warehouses raised another ($US) 14.9 million. Finally, Miconsa's five plants generated ($US) 140 million (Conasupo, 1993, 1994b).

Table 3.6 Liconsa Investment Budget for 1991 ($US million)

Investment Budget	**9.45**
Modernise Fresh Milk Factories	0.886
Construction and Equipment for *Lecherías*	**6.530**
Modernisation of Processing Plants	0.415
Information Services	1.301

Source: Conasupo (1992)

Table 3.7 Conasupo Privatisations from 1989 to 1994

Branch	Assets	Timing
Iconsa	9 plants	October 1989 to February 1992
Liconsa	5 plants	October 1991 to March 1993
Miconsa	5 plants	September 1992 to January 1994
Impecsa	18 warehouses	At the end of 1994 there were 110 warehouses in operation

Source: Conasupo (1992), Conasupo (1993), Conasupo (1994) and Conasupo (1995)

The Hidden Agenda of Privatisation at Conasupo

In addition to the 'continuity formula' whereby resources were switched from processing to final consumption subsidies, Conasupo privatisations in part involved a hidden agenda as well. Salinas sometimes used Iconsa and other assets to reward select business leaders and political allies.[28] Furthermore, removing Conasupo from processing activities muted intra-PRI criticism by Alberto Santos and Roberto González Barrera. Indeed, Maseca acquired a Miconsa plant in Guerrero, a dubious transaction still under investigation in the Mexican courts, which so far has produced three formal corruption charges against ex-Conasupo functionaries Salvador Giordano Gómez, Carlos Alamán Bueno and Víctor Gómez (*El Universal,* 12 October 1996).[29] The CTM and a partner purchased the Iconsa factory in Monterrey that first mobilised Alberto Santos – whose own bid was rejected by Secofi. The CTM-affiliated Association of Dairy Operators as well as the Union of 800 Small Grain Producers of Chihuahua acquired Liconsa factories (Conasupo, 1992).[30] Assets also switched hands inside the public sector. Iconsa factories in Ciudad Obregón and in Tlaxcala were transferred to the Central Conasupo Office while Liconsa devolved its plant in Guerrero to the state government. Finally, strings were attached to the sale of Iconsa factories. Privatisation agreements, according to Ignacio Ovalle, bound new owners to supply up to 50 percent of the factory production back to Conasupo at a price determined by Secofi (*La Jornada,* 21 May 1990).

The domestic dairy sector also follows this pattern. Traditionally, five large private co-operatives dominated the dairy sector (Alpura, Boreal, Gilsa, Lala, and Ultralácteos) and each controlled a region of Mexico and usually avoided head-to-head competition (Nicholson, 1995). As with Maseca, subsidy schemes in the dairy sector brought co-operatives into regular contact with the government. In transferring Liconsa's Veracruz plant to Lala and its Tabasco plant to Ultralácteos, the geographic bases for these groups, the government reduced an already low level of regional competition. It also preserved its relationship with co-operatives as the government began lifting producer and consumer subsidies and encouraging foreign competition in the dairy sector in 1992.

As for Miconsa, Secofi's decision to privatise its plants incited disharmony within the Administrative Council of Conasupo. On 21 October

1991, the secretaries of SHCP and SPP agreed to discontinue Miconsa's public financing (Conasupo, 1993). In March 1992 Secofi in turn elected to transfer the five Miconsa factories individually without any new guidelines for a domestic market that Maseca would now effectively monopolise. Secofi's plan met opposition in the Council, suggesting some members preferred a market where Maseca faced at least partial competition (Conasupo, 1993). A compromise emerged on 13 October 1992 that permitted Maseca to purchased one factory and stipulated that new owners of the other four factories could operate under one label or what would eventually become Minsa. Minsa thereafter captured around 15 percent of the domestic market and Maseca the remainder, a significantly different market distribution from 1988, when Miconsa captured 46 percent.[31]

Apparently the chief motive in the privatisation of Miconsa was neither 'liberalisation' nor developing a competitive market. Chapter Two commented on the intimate relationship that joined the PRI and Maseca financially, and Carlos Salinas and Roberto González Barrera politically. Thus the pivotal domestic corn flour market was in no way delegated to an unknown entity. Indeed, personal linkages transcend the Salinas-González Barrera relationship and continue to the present.[32]

The hidden agenda also stretched to the issue of Mexico's foreign creditors. Consciously or not, the announcement on 21 October 1989 that Iconsa factories would be sold coincided with a critical phase in Mexico's negotiations with multilateral lending institutions. In 1990, as mentioned in Chapter Two, the World Bank justified fresh lending to Mexico as a reward for encouraging private ownership throughout the domestic food chain in 1989. In effect, the World Bank's approval rested on the Iconsa issue, since subsequent privatisations had not been announced.

Summary

Ingram and Mann (1980: 21) write:

> Wholehearted accomplishment of goals can scarcely be expected when a policy is directly in conflict with other policies, or if it is internally inconsistent.

This chapter sketched the Salinas administration's general policy orientations concerning domestic food markets, before turning to a more specific level of analysis. By moving from the general to the specific, it was shown that the articulation of official goals of market liberalisation were less 'neoliberal' in practice than they appear. Evidence of this pattern surfaced in each of the three specific issues analysed above.

By examining the (i) participation model, (ii) Conasupo-producer arrangements and (iii) privatisation, it appears that the CMP, through a series of half-way solutions and trade-offs, attempted to balance a broad neoliberal agenda ('market liberalisation') and the political objectives of the government ('deliver the goods to populations that might support the PRI'). Community participation under the CMP avoided the necessary steps that would have addressed the existing resource asymmetry between local patron and client; in fact, to some degree the CMP exacerbated the gulf (at least in Mexico City) by shifting the monitoring costs to potential participants. Under Salinas, Conasupo's rural infrastructure purchased more grain from Mexican producers than at any time in history. The CMP channelled unprecedented resources to official *campesino* unions through PACE, while it also incorporated the CNC into management of programmes. Finally, privatisation achieved less market intervention in one area (in processing) yet it enabled the government to expand intervention in another area (final consumption subsidies). Privatising a handful of Iconsa factories only to use the proceeds to expand Conasupo's consumer infrastructure (*lecherías*, community stores, etc.) to millions of additional households, blended neoliberalism and traditional populism in a way that was both politically rational and favourable to incremental policy innovation. In the end, this combination of discontinuity and continuity 'recreated' Conasupo and should not be mistaken for (as many have done) either a coherent neoliberal alternative or a dismantling of the parastatal. In this manner, we have come across good reasons why in many regards 'this time around' resembled previous episodes of incremental change under the guise of sweeping reform at Conasupo.

This chapter mentioned that the CMP set out to extend Conasupo subsidies to 50 rather than 30 million Mexican consumers. Undoubtedly, this goal of subsidising the consumption of half the Mexican population represented the crucial feature of the CMP with respect to general patterns of state-society relations. Chapter Four examines Conasupo's three main consumption programmes, showing how a process of expansion coupled with specific neoliberal reforms followed the same pattern of continuity and discontinuity witnessed above.

Notes

[1] The reader should be aware of the continuity here; de la Madrid's *Sistema de Comunicación Integral Diconsa 1983-88* outlined measures to reduce corruption and the serious financial mess bequeathed by López Portillo's Conasupo team (Conasupo, 1987a).

[2] Columnist John Saxe-Fernández (*Excelsior,* 24 October 1989) wrote that the Conasupo reforms 'freed up prices' however without tackling the political problems such as coupon distribution or Boruconsa corruption.

[3] The private sector picked up on this immediately. One business spokesman asked Ovalle, 'why should the private sector approve a policy that ... expects to deliver benefits to an additional 20 million consumers'? (*La Jornada*, 27 October 1989).

[4] The official CMP statement notes: 'The Committees will serve as a channel for market information between producers, based on information generated by Secofi and other institutions, contributing as such to more certain, opportune, and conscious decision-making in the rural sector'.

[5] Producers sometimes waited for months to collect payment from Conasupo, amounting to a tax on producers in Mexico's inflationary environment of the 1980s. To implement this policy, Conasupo capitalised 1,329 Boruconsa and all 938 Andsa warehouses, and constructed 600 payment centres for the spring-summer harvest of 1990.

[6] In the 1970s Cornelius (1975: 213-225) describes the manner in which MUs rolled into a *colonia* the day before President Echeverría gave a speech as 'circus like'. Under the CMP, the first 100 MUs were in use by February 1990. Director of Diconsa for Mexico City Ignacio Barrón Carmona, calculated that they would service 700 locations per week around the D.F. (*Excelsior*, 9 January 1990).

[7] Economists Torres Torres and Delgadillo Macías (1991: 141) assert, 'The new policy for supply [CMP] proposes mechanisms that guarantee a major infusion of private capital, retiring systematically the State from playing any active role in regulating the [basic food] market'. Furthermore, Ochoa (1994, ch.10), after depicting Conasupo as a tool for presidential legitimisation since the 1960s, argues that the parastatal was essentially 'dead' as of October 1989.

[8] Varley (1996, 1993) found the same to be true in Solidarity's land-titling component; Solidarity might be involved in the handing over of titles but the thorny, deeply corrupt matter of land expropriation was handled by a long-serving bureaucracy.

[9] One *campesino* unionist, commenting on his experience during the 1980s with Diconsa's participation model, depicted the reappearance of participation under the CMP as a 'white elephant' for continued PRI patronage (*La Jornada*, 7 November 1989).

[10] Mitastein (1996) shows in the D.F. that President Salinas devolved control over tortilla coupons, Popular Kitchens and Diconsa stores to mobilised popular groups that worked

through Popular Co-ordination Councils. Of the roughly 400 D.F. Diconsa stores, official popular groups administered around 100. Likewise, leaving a Labour Congress (CT) meeting on 26 October 1989, Ovalle commented that the population with the fewest resources that 'deserved to run new Conasupo stores' were official labour, *campesino* and popular unions and that 'restructuring Conasupo is for workers and not for bureaucrats out to cut costs' (*Excelsior*, 26 October 1989).

[11] PAN Deputy Jesús Ramírez Núñez argued that CMP *concertación* reflected 'intra-PRI politics' and not public sector reform (*La Jornada*, 24 October 1989). PRD Deputy Ifigenia Martínez deplored the CMP as the renewing of 'historic corporate sector alliances' (*La Jornada*, 10 November 1989). A Popular Socialist Party (PPS) Deputy compared the CMP *concertación* process to norms under Porfirio Díaz: 'peace and progress; growth and *concertación*, but, the question remains, *for whom*'? (*La Jornada*, 24 October 1989). Also see Herrasti Aguirre (1993) and Hernández (1991).

[12] At Diconsa outlets, Profeco inspectors encountered price violations in 20,000 out of 90,000 inspections from January to October 1989. With respect to milk prices, Nicholson (1995: 21) calculates 41 percent of total raw milk is distributed informally in Mexico; he blames the Profeco for parallel markets.

[13] One Diconsa policy-maker indicated that the participatory model was designed for isolated rural communities and ill-suited for urban communities. 'Diconsa already had a good operation in the cities and it should not have been changed' (Interview, Mexico City, Office of Fidelist, 22 April 1997).

[14] That government officials should dispense privileged access to public resources was not without precedent. For example, Hansen (1971: 12) describes the allocation of Pemex gas stations to a handful of 'revolutionary politicians'.

[15] Following the CMP announcement (i) The National Union of Autonomous Regional *Campesino* Organisation, (ii) the Independent *Campesino* Central, and (iii) the National Confederation of Small Land Owners predicted more exploitation of *campesinos*. During their *concertación* dialogue, the government explained to these groups that 'greater social participation' meant participation in the evaluation of guarantee prices, not their elimination (*Excelsior*, 24 October 1989). An ex-Boruconsa policy analyst suggests that the CMP represented the 'government's exit from supporting Mexican agriculture, a process that began in 1982' (electronic correspondence, 1 April 1997).

[16] The World Bank (1986) argued in its 1986 report that insufficient Boruconsa/Andsa infrastructure cultivated intermediaries, corruption and politicisation of Conasupo resources. In 1989 it advocated private investment, which the CMP did not pursue (World Bank, 1990c).

[17] Geographic exclusion was not the limit of Conasupo's influence. Conasupo, by purchasing these grains at an artificially high price and limiting imports, created a loose price floor for corn and beans. In general, the same did not hold for wheat, soybeans, rice and sorghum, where producers typically sold to private processors at higher prices. Here Conasupo was a 'buyer of last resort'.

[18] Secofi permitted private industry (corn starch, flour, tortillas, etc.) to import some cheap foreign corn after 1988. However, Secofi withheld private sector import permits in 1991,

increasing domestic corn purchases in the starch industry by 251,700 tonnes, in the corn flour industry by 280,200 tonnes and in the small business sector by 535,200 tonnes. A Conasupo analyst proclaims: 'Conasupo intervention in the importation of grains seems only to obstruct fixing prices in the free market and prejudices the true Mexican *campesinos* while only benefiting the organised Mafia of supposed producers' (appendix 6.1, respondent #2).

[19] To put these statistics in perspective, Mexico produced 18,125,000 tonnes of corn and 1,288,000 tonnes of beans in 1993 compared to 3,582,000 tonnes of wheat, 288,000 tonnes of rice and 496,000 tonnes of soybeans in 1989. The former exceeded the latter by a substantial margin (*Informe de Gobierno*, 1996).

[20] Barry (1995: 101) observed that Conasupo subsidies 'even encouraged commercial growers with irrigated land to cultivate corn instead of less profitable cash crops'. Interestingly, railroad tariffs increased 9.9 percent for agriculture products in 1993, but Conasupo producers incurred a smaller hike of 5 percent. Since commercial producers customarily utilised the railway system, it is noteworthy that in 1992 and 1993 Conasupo's tonnage transported via rail increased significantly while tonnage transported by road decreased (Conasupo, 1993, 1994b).

[21] In 1992 PACE subsidies were valued at around ($US) 18 per tonne of corn and ($US) 31 per tonne of beans (Conasupo, 1992).

[22] The PAN was the only voice in the debate that immediately understood this. For example, Victor Bernal Sahagun commented that privatising nine Iconsa plants and 589 Conasupers while at the same time planning to construct between 5,000 and 6,000 new Conasupo stores by 1994 raises the question 'is this renewed *populismo* or *neoliberalismo*'? (*Excelsior*, 24 October 1989).

[23] The repercussions of privatising Iconsa for the 30 million Mexicans partaking in Conasupo consumption schemes were minimal. One Conasupo policy-maker admits that 'the poor don't care if Unilever or Iconsa supplies their cooking oil, as long as it is cheap' (Interview, Mexico City, Office of Fidelist, 22 April 1997).

[24] Demetrio Sodi de la Tijera cautioned: 'It is as if we are going to cut off our foot to run faster' (*La Jornada*, 24 October 1989). Later Augusto Gómez Villanueva, Sodi de la Tijera and Eloy García Aguilar spoke for 20 PRI deputies who condemned the CMP, notably the privatisation of Iconsa. Ovalle cautioned this group: 'Conasupo decisions were an executive order... whoever is against the measure, be careful, the doors of Conasupo and the party are wide open for those who wish to leave or to enter' (*La Jornada*, 15 November 1989).

[25] A joint PRD-PPS statement concurred that the CMP signalled a 'continuation of the destruction of the Mexican Revolution by the current government' (*La Jornada*, 24 October 1989). Alberto Barranco Chavarría suggested 'it signalled an irreversible triumph for the business sector' (*La Jornada*, 25 October 1989). The PARM, PPS and PRD forecast the CMP foreshadowed a future PAN-PRI alliance (*La Jornada*, 24 October 1989).

[26] See *Crónica del Gobierno de Carlos Salinas de Gortari 1988-1994* (1994). Public statements by President Salinas on 30 September 1991 (see year 1991: 334) and by SHCP

on 4 March 1993 (see year 1993: 118) clarified that this had been the policy. In a SHCP report ('Results from the Modernisation of Conasupo'), it is argued that privatisations enabled Liconsa to increase milk beneficiaries by 50.4 percent between 1988 and 1993.

[27] Note that Zúñiga (*La Jornada* 13 May 1997) calculates total Iconsa concessions at ($US) 85.2 million while the *Diario Oficial de la Federación* (18 May 1992) reports that, at its conclusion, Iconsa assets generated a mere ($US) 17.2 million for Conasupo consumption programmes. The disparity can be attributed to the fact that Iconsa revenue also settled branch debts at Liconsa, Diconsa and Impecsa. In this manner, Iconsa concessions not only boosted consumption subsidies, but also erased the debts and momentarily concealed the profound corruption that had occurred in the de la Madrid years.

[28] In *La Jornada* (13 May 1997), David Márquez Ayala contends that Conasupo privatisations raised ($US) 400 million between 1990-1993, a sum that he alleges undervalues these assets. He argues that regime politics plagued Conasupo transfers. *Mexico Business* (edition, March 1998) offers one case of presidential patronage and a privatised Iconsa asset.

[29] In late May 1997, the Mexican Attorney General (PGR) submitted a report to the Chamber of Deputies in which it claimed that fraud was involved in the sale, along with the sale of two additional Miconsa plants and the Liconsa plant in Atlacomulco, State of México. As of 1998, the PGR continues to investigate all Liconsa privatisations.

[30] In the 1980s, the Association of Dairy Operators urged the Mexican government to pursue self-sufficiency and protect the domestic dairy market. This group gained control of the largest Mexican reformulation plant, a move that co-opted a potential critic of liberalisation (Nicholson, 1995).

[31] By 1995, the corn flour sector listed 19 Maseca plants, 6 Minsa plants and 2 Agorinsa plants (a new entrant in the market).

[32] Juan Mora has managed Conasupo's Tortilla Programme since 1993. He previously worked for many years at Diconsa in Guadalajara. Efren González Flores, a cousin of Roberto González Barrera and Maseca's representative to Conasupo since 1992, worked for Mora at Diconsa in Guadalajara, a relationship that dates back to their university days in Guadalajara (Interviews, Mexico City, Office of Fidelist, 4, 7 & 22 April 1997).

4 The Switch from General to Targeted Consumer Subsidies: Three Case Studies of Programmes under the CMP

'Is this [CMP] renewed *populismo* or *neoliberalismo*?'
- PAN Deputy Victor Bernal Sahagun, *Excelsior*, 24 October 1989

Introduction

The critical element of the Conasupo *Modernización* Plan (CMP) was replacing Mexico's traditional policy of general consumption subsidies for basic foodstuffs with targeted schemes. It was unavoidable that scrapping general subsidies would impact state-society relations, as overall consumption of basic foodstuffs declined. However, because the new subsidy policy of 'targeting' envisioned an additional 20 million Mexicans (for a total of 50 million) consuming Conasupo goods by 1994, it is an open question how far the CMP encouraged greater market liberalisation (neoliberalism and 'discontinuity') rather than intervention (populism, clientelism and 'continuity'). To evaluate this situation, this chapter analyses Conasupo's three core consumption schemes: the Tortilla Programme, the Milk Programme and the Community Supply Programme.

Given that the switch to targeting had been official policy since 1983, why should it be different this time around? On this topic Fox questions

> Why it takes the Mexican government so long to switch from general to targeted subsidies; a process that began in 1983, if that has indeed been the objective? (...personal correspondence)[1]

Despite the fact that the CMP intended to expand Conasupo consumption services considerably, the fact remained that the supply of such services

122

could not satisfy the demand, even if the CMP unfolded according to plan. Thus the Salinas administration had to formulate a policy of needs-based targeting in such a way that lower-income consumers had priority access to limited resources, as opposed to middle- and higher-income consumers. How this distributional issue was resolved is crucial to our interest in continuity and discontinuity in state-society relations, because transparent and accountable needs-based distribution was both difficult to achieve and incompatible with Conasupo's old (arbitrary, informal, corporatist) patterns of distribution, particularly with consumers in the Mexico City Metropolitan Area (DFMA). There are certain conceptual problems inherent to needs-based targeting schemes that the CMP had to manage. First, such schemes typically assume a world where life among the 'poor' population is predictable; that is, where technocrats can identify eligible and non-eligible households, where households have the information to participate according to neoliberal guidelines, and where intermediaries are organised in a way that encourage the goal of needs-based targeting over other considerations. In the analysis that follows, it is often discovered that the assumption of predictability was unrealistic in the context of this case study.

In earlier chapters the threat of the PRD had a significant influence on the design and the execution of the CMP. This factor resurfaces with respect to consumption subsidies. Adding 20 million lower-income Mexicans to Conasupo can be interpreted as an attempt to win back many former PRI supporters that Cárdenas captured in 1988. A crucial constituency that responded to the Cárdenas message was the urban poor in the DFMA (29 percent of urban poor DFMA voters supported Cárdenas in 1988). In the past, Conasupo had concentrated its consumption services in the DFMA, thus policy in this area merits close attention. Formulating a coherent policy of 'targeting the poor' implied that Conasupo would have to transfer resources from and reform services in the DFMA. Yet to do so risked more defections to the PRD, and here lay the dilemma for the government in the DFMA: how to renew relationships with the urban poor that had supported Cárdenas, without abandoning past Conasupo distribution arrangements with governmental allies?

Finally, before proceeding, it is important to bear in mind the unusual region-wide context around the issue of general subsidies in 1989-1990. Other Latin American countries were contemplating and attempting the same general-to-target transition as Mexico, with different degrees of success. It is certainly the case that food riots in the capitals of Venezuela and Argentina during 1988 and 1989, themselves stark reminders of the delicate social balance around basic food markets, projected powerful and frightening images that Mexican policymakers could hardly ignore.

The Government Tortilla Programme

Antecedents. It is difficult to overestimate the political, cultural, and nutritional significance of corn-based tortillas in Mexico. 'From ancient times to the present day, Mexico's rulers have kept the cost of tortillas deliberately low to buy social peace' (*Financial Times*, 28 December 1996). Mexicans consume around 10 million tonnes of corn tortillas per year and they are a primary cause of excess carbohydrates in the diet of poor Mexicans (Casanueva, 1996). Tortillas are a national symbol and a component of the Mexican identity; the country's literature, paintings, artisan crafts, and modern *telenovelas* preserve the image of women preparing tortillas for the traditional afternoon meal. Through the Salinas years, social unrest threatened to surface whenever the public suspected cuts in the general tortilla subsidy.

Conasupo documents trace government intervention in food markets to the pre-*Porfiriato* era, usually the congressional debate over Article 28 of the 1857 Constitution that covered domestic commerce (Conasupo, 1984c, 1987b). Ochoa (1994) traces government intervention in the tortilla chain to the 1930s, a period when urban shortages animated lawmakers to act to stave off market speculators.[2] Martín del Campo and Calderón (1990) isolate Article 28 of the current Mexican Constitution and the Law of Attribution of Executive Power in Economic Material, written in 1950. It established a legal framework for price controls and subsidies to counter urban speculation. Another view highlights the year 1937 and Cárdenas era Committee to Regulate the Wheat Market as Conasupo's original blueprint (Gavaldón Enciso and Pérez Haro, 1987b). The Committee fixed retail prices for wheat, regulated imports and exports, and constructed a national reserve system to assuage slumps in domestic production. Turning to the particular issue of tortillas, the formation of *Maíz Industrializado, S.A.* (Miconsa) in 1950 marked a key juncture for government intervention, as it introduced modern technology, equipment, and distribution infrastructure throughout the tortilla production chain.

An interventionist trajectory continued through the 1980s; had Mexico not experienced the 1982 debt crisis, one could speculate that liberalising tortilla prices would have remained inconceivable. However, as the Mexican economy deteriorated, first de la Madrid and later Salinas pledged to dismantle general tortilla subsidies, that is, the price at which all Mexicans can consume tortillas, but not the price Conasupo (starting in the 1980s) sets for its beneficiaries. After ignoring a promise to do so in 1983, de la Madrid – when oil prices dropped again in 1986 – reintroduced an end to general subsidies only to reverse course in 1987. In the early 1990s, the government fixed two tortilla prices, one inside and another outside the DFMA. Technical Director of Miconsa Ferrer Pujol (1996: 40-41) writes,

> The government policy during the last five years [1990-1995] has maintained different prices for the D.F. Metro Area and the interior of the country, and raised the price of tortillas at a rate less than inflation so that there has been a reduction in real terms of 39 percent in D.F. Metro Area and 44 percent in the interior of the country.

However, alongside Secofi's management of general tortilla subsidies, graph 4.0 identifies three stages in Conasupo's targeted tortilla policy that operated in urban areas: (i) the Diconsa Programme, (ii) *Tortibonos*, and (iii) the *Programa de Subsidio al Consumo de Tortilla* (PSCT). Analysing these different schemes reveals once again a process of policy 'recreation' that provided a degree of continuity in state-society relations.

A report by the office of social programmes at Conasupo (Conasupo, November 1994b) notes that 'The 1984 Diconsa Tortilla Programme was, without doubt, the first attempt by Conasupo to target the transference of tortilla subsidies'. According to official records the Diconsa Programme subsidised 750,000 households from June 1984 to December 1986. 'Targeting' at this stage implied that Diconsa stores located in 31 cities sold tortillas at a 50 percent discount to the public at large; therefore, targeting was limited to geographic rather than socioeconomic considerations. Diconsa's centralised, DFMA-oriented infrastructure channelled subsidies to public employees and official labour unions disproportionately, a shortcoming acknowledged inside Conasupo as early as 1987 (Conasupo, 1987a). Less often acknowledged, however, was the fact that the Diconsa Programme discarded any notion of procedural guidelines or monitoring; in fact, no one at Diconsa or Conasupo could identify who exactly benefited from the subsidy. Despite a 1983 pledge by then Diconsa Director Raúl Salinas to generate this data, surveying only started in 1992 (Conasupo, 1983). In hindsight, the Diconsa Programme neither helped to relieve the government's fiscal burden nor assured benefits to the poor.

In April 1986 a coupon scheme entitled *Programa de racionalización en el manejo del subsidio de la tortilla* (henceforth *tortibonos*) replaced the ill-conceived Diconsa Programme. *Tortibonos* resembled the food stamp programme in the United States; that is, a targeted public assistance scheme that supplemented the consumption of the urban poor. At this moment, Secofi announced the imminent liberalisation of general prices in the next six months, first in northern states and gradually to the rest of the country (*El Cotidiano*, 1986, ft. 11: 37).

Graph 4.0   The Number of Cities and Families Covered in Conasupo's Target Tortilla Programmes (1984-1994)

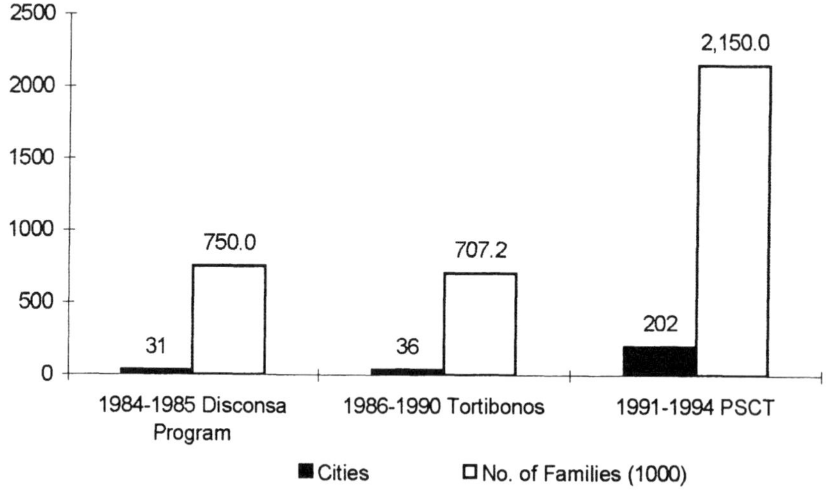

Source: Conasupo (1994)

The two initial targeted schemes incorporated approximately the same number of households (graph 4.0); however, with *tortibonos,* recipients exchanged coupons at local *tortillerías* (community tortilla makers) in 36 cities in 16 states. At first glance *tortibonos* constituted an advance upon their predecessor. They circumvented dependence on Diconsa infrastructure with *tortillerías* and, equally importantly, formulated the first ever National List of Conasupo Beneficiaries (NLCB). To be eligible households had to earn below two times the national minimum wage, the same income ceiling as the earlier Diconsa Programme. In 1987 Director of Planning and Budget at Conasupo Gavaldón Enciso (Gavaldón Enciso and Pérez Haro, 1987a: 183) wrote,

> ...in the current administration, the subsidy policy [of Conasupo] has been modified substantially, avoiding the transfer of resources towards sectors that should not have obtained access...in the case of tortillas, *tortibonos* permit direct distribution exclusively to the low-income population.

In practice, however, the NLCB and *tortibonos* succumbed to familiar noncompliance with procedures and monitoring. It is important to note that critics at this time such as Sánchez Daza and Vargas Velázquez (1986) – perhaps misinterpreting the scheme – painted it as assisting an export development model based on low-wage labour and as a case where neoliberalism inflamed class divisions and where Conasupo's survival (in 1987) was predicated on its ability to placate international capitalism.

Instead, *tortibonos* often served as a palliative to official labour unions as wage and price freezes took hold in 1986. Diconsa supervisors in Mexico City distributed coupons along with the CT, CNOP and the PRI (Conasupo, 1985d, 1983). At this moment 'targeting' meant delivery of *tortibonos* (i) to Diconsa stores that signed *concertación* agreements (i.e., union stores and the CNOP), (ii) to stores with *concertación* agreements with the CTM and CROC (PRI-affiliated unions), and (iii) via the Liconsa infrastructure (over 50 percent of which was located in the DFMA). It should be stressed that, for Conasupo, access to *tortibonos* formulated a response to the demands of the CT, and Diconsa signed 250 *concertación* agreements, benefiting 500,000 union households, in 1986 alone (Conasupo, 1987a). Thus, the impetus for the policy was domestic corporatism and political alliances and not international capitalism, illustrated by the fact that CTM boss Fidel Velázquez unveiled and sanctioned *tortibonos* in 1986.[3]

Perhaps *Tortibono* abuse was rife. In one case during August 1989, Secofi arrested PRI *colonia* leaders across the state of Veracruz. In a subsequent report to congress, Secofi indicated that 60 percent of the state's *tortibonos* had 'disappeared' (*Excelsior*, 27 August 1989). Secofi condemned a network of PRI Diconsa storeowners and *colonia* leaders in southern Veracruz.

To digress for a moment, why did the administration turn on its allies in Veracruz? Discussing the 1980s, Fox (1994) describes how control of Conasupo's rural infrastructure often oscillated among mostly pro-government *campesino* groups. Perhaps this type of intra-group PRI rivalry prompted a crackdown in Veracruz. Community pressure and fear that local conditions on the ground may spiral out of control may have motivated Secofi. For example, in November 1990 Ignacio Ovalle announced another case of widespread abuse in which Secofi seized three local distributors with 26,000 unauthorised coupons. Supposedly, local complaints about the trafficking of illegal coupons 'got out of hand' (*Excelsior*, 9 November 1990). Allies became more of a burden, generating more public outrage than political support.

Perhaps a crackdown on *colonia* leaders in Veracruz amounted to a battle in a larger war, for the highly publicised Veracruz raid occurred in late August 1989, and thus coincided with the 'policy formation period' discussed in Chapter Two. There were two additional well-publicised raids in this period: the first involved a Mexico City Diconsa manager and former director of candidate selection for the PRI; the second, a network of Diconsa agents falsifying import licenses along the northern border. These examples of abuse touch only pervasive *tortibono*/PRI corruption, what Mexicans sarcastically dubbed *votobonos*. Since Conasupo documents from the 1980s and public comments by Ignacio Ovalle attest that the agency understood the political obstacles that would obstruct any attempt to reorient the *tortibono* scheme, then arbitrary crackdowns on violators may have been a strategy to put social pressure on corporatist intermediaries to endorse the CMP and, more generally, a decision to tighten Conasupo's loose distributional constraints in the light of growing abuse.

The government announced in July 1990 that *tortibonos* would be discontinued in November 1990. Salinas justified this policy change as part of the CMP's promise to target resources. In Mexico City, protesters blocked streets and access to Secofi offices from 16 to 23 July 1990, demanding among other things the restoration of *tortibonos*. At one point, 40 *colonia* organisations descended upon Secofi. In a prompt turnaround, Ignacio Ovalle unveiled a new targeted scheme on 5 August 1990, which guaranteed access to *free* tortillas to all 840,000 households from the *tortibono* scheme.

In October 1990, under the CMP, individual state Conasupo offices assumed control of a renamed tortilla scheme known as the *Programa de Subsidio al Consumo de Tortilla* (PSCT). The PSCT unfolded in two stages. First, Conasupo swapped *tortibonos* for another coupon (dubbed *tortivales*) that furnished the same quantity of tortillas, free of charge, thus elevating the subsidy from 50 to 100 percent.[4] According to Conasupo (November 1994b),

> This was the application of a selective and targeted subsidy scheme that guaranteed transparent and rational use of resources, replacing universal subsidies [i.e., *tortibonos*].

Ignacio Ovalle anticipated that 'if the federal government doesn't allow political parties to manipulate the new programme, it will be able to avoid intermediaries and deal directly with households' (*Excelsior*, 9 November 1990). Curiously, Conasupo classified *tortibonos* as a 'universal' subsidy while at the same time utilising the old beneficiary list to dispense *tortivales*, permitting the old households to consume free tortillas.

What measures 'guaranteed transparency' this time since the beneficiary list stayed the same? In Mexico City, executive-appointed Mayor Manuel Camacho Solís would now distribute *tortivales* instead of Diconsa's 'politicised' representatives.[5] Under the PSCT Conasupo distributed coupons outside Mexico City through the national mail service. In March 1991, citing 'substantial abuse' in the delivery of *tortivales* by post (Conasupo, 1992), Conasupo sanctioned another arrangement outside the D.F., in which, until 1992, directors of state Conasupo offices distributed coupons.[6] Conasupo concedes serious problems arose in PSCT's initial phase:

Although there was a planning system, this was incipient and did not translate into a basis of rigorous analysis ... and was overly complex in its elaboration and management.

The selection of beneficiaries who received *tortivales* was done by a very general criteria ... thus, during the period of *tortivales* the subsidy was applied with a list from the *tortibono* programme of Diconsa that basically consisted of *pertinent persons from unions, colonia associations and popular organisations...* (Conasupo, November 1994b ... emphasis added)

Undoubtedly, *tortibonos* and *tortivales* presented examples of policy recreations that led to incremental innovation and the perpetuation of the old model of state-society relations. In fact, the PSCT filtered subsidies through the CNOP, CT and CTM until 1993, and it delivered 281,000,000 *tortivales* or free kilos of tortillas to 1.8 million urban households each day from November 1990 to March 1991, when the PRI was campaigning against the PRD for the upcoming mid-term election.

The second or 'automated' phase of the PSCT began in May 1991. Here Conasupo distributed bar-coded cards to households on the PSCT list and shoebox-sized, magnetic machines to record card data at affiliated *tortillerías.*[7] Although announced in May, Conasupo commenced distributing cards in the election month of July. By December 1991, 273,000 bar-coded cards went out to households in 202 cities, up from 71 cities in May. New locations fell into one of two categories: (i) a population surpassing 25,000 residents or (ii) communities within designated metropolitan zones who signed a *concertación* agreement with President Salinas – here cards and machines recreated the familiar 'executive-local bridge'. Conasupo, however, continued to distribute *tortivales* at a steady rate, explaining why official households ballooned from 840,000 in 1990 to 2,100,000 in 1991.

In October 1991, after the PRI success in the mid-term Congressional elections, the 172nd session of the Administrative Council of Conasupo established a new parastatal, *Fideicomiso para la Liquidación al Subsidio de la Tortilla* (Fidelist) to operate the PSCT. Fidelist's arrival signalled a recognition that the old Conasupo bureaucracy (notably Diconsa) could not deliver tortilla subsidies according to a neoliberal ethos. In effect, Fidelist marked a parallel bureaucracy inside Conasupo because a

Technical Committee composed of Conasupo's director of social programmes (Technical Committee president) and representatives of the ministries of Commerce, Finance, Budget and Planning, and Treasury, supervised Fidelist development.[8]

There were sharp differences in the top-level management of the Tortilla Programme under the Technical Committee as opposed to Diconsa administrators. The Technical Committee requested, for example, that the director of Fidelist produce monthly reports on budgetary targets, subsidy distribution, and general progress in bureaucratic efficiency.[9] After an initial organisational period Fidelist assumed control of the PSCT in May 1992. The combination of *tortivales* and automated delivery of tortilla subsidies outlined above continued through mid-1992. According to the *1992 Annual Conasupo Report* (Conasupo, 1992),

> The objective of Fidelist is to realise the payment of subsidies to the corn flour industries and affiliated *tortillerías*, under a system of absolute transparency and guaranteeing strong co-ordination with Conasupo's central and state offices.

Graph 4.1 Total Beneficiary Households in the Tortilla Programme (1986-1996)

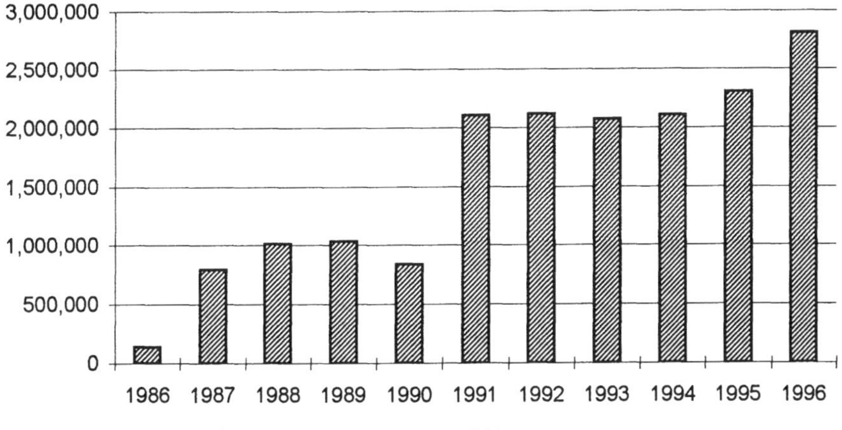

Source: Informe de Gobierno (1996), Conasupo (1991)

Nevertheless, problems with the Tortilla Programme resurfaced under Fidelist management. Fidelist discovered cardholders routinely visited several *tortillerías* per day in the D.F., Monterrey, and Guadalajara. Complicating matters, the new automated-card system encountered some significant problems. For instance, if a card was stolen or damaged, the official procedure removed it from the PSCT list by registering the card's bar code on a black list. What soon became a problem is that the black list could not exceed 6,000 entries. In the DFMA alone, site of 6,000 officially registered households, Fidelist calculated an astonishing 600,000 cards in circulation during 1992 (Conasupo, 1992). This chaos inflated payments to *tortillerías* by 39 percent in 1992.

Incremental Steps Toward Needs-based Distribution (1993-1994)

In December 1992, in the municipality of Chimalhuacán, State of México, Fidelist piloted a modified card-based system that programmed cards for specified *tortillerías* and restricted daily quantity. The new card redressed earlier shortcomings and soon the PSCT witnessed a sizeable drop in payments to *tortillerías* in the DFMA. In 1993 Fidelist distributed 1.8 million modified cards across Mexico and the reaction was prompt: expenditure in the DFMA declined from ($US) 8 million per month at the end of 1992 to less than ($US) 1.3 million at the end of 1993. In late 1992, to monitor the new technology, Fidelist matched all *tortillería* payments to authorised cardholders on a weekly basis to isolate abusers. By December 1992 Fidelist expelled 55 *tortillerías* and fined another 95 in the DFMA. Further, Fidelist confiscated resources in some cases where payment exceeded a *colonia*'s registered cardholders.

- Second semester of 1992, recovered ($US) 250,000; 57 percent in DFMA

- First semester of 1993, recovered ($US) 220,000; 94 percent in DFMA

- Second semester of 1993, recovered ($US) 50,000; 61 percent in DFMA

- First semester of 1994, recovered ($US) 27,000; 14 percent in DFMA

The modest sums recovered (less than 2 percent of the 1993 total in the DFMA) and action against the small total of 150 *tortillerias* (a total representing less than 3 percent of the total in the DFMA) should be kept in mind so that these steps toward reform or tightening of Conasupo's loose distributional and budgetary constraints are seen in the proper perspective – e.g., incremental rather than radical innovation.

However, under Fidelist management the momentum for reform shifted in 1993 and 1994. Community complaints largely disappeared from Mexican newspapers; a general depiction that diverges with the *tortibono/tortivales* era. Perhaps subsidy cuts in other areas of traditional social policy and the success of the Solidarity Programme (the Solidarity logo was affixed to Fidelist subsidy cards) accounted for this unusual level of silence. Alternatively, new technology played its role by squeezing former types of abuse.[10] At the conclusion of the Salinas years, it was impossible for 70 percent of subsidies to disappear unknowingly as had been observed in Veracruz, or that 600,000 undocumented cards could be circulated in the DFMA. Starting in 1994, Fidelist published weekly consumer and inventory reports. It also monitored consumption patterns of individual households and, if warranted, distribution was discontinued by the removal of codes from the computer. In fact, streamlining the PSCT according to new technology and constant dissemination of information to the public modified perceptions at Fidelist over who controlled the programme.

> The Ministry of Treasury controls our budget and determines the rhythm of expansion and contraction in the distribution of new cards... within days we can deliver additional cards if Hacienda expands our budget... likewise, we simply discontinue cards when our budget is cut... this is no longer a complicated programme (Interview, Mexico City, Office of Fidelist, 4 April 1997).[11]

Yet, because the demand for the Tortilla Programme surpassed the available supply there was an unavoidable element of discretion. Given past experience with Conasupo tortilla subsidies, there is reason to look closely at how policymakers selected *tortillerias*, participant households and *colonias*.

Selection of Tortillerias (1992-1994)

A seemingly endless chain of *tortillerias* operated across Mexico and literally thousands appear in Mexico City, Monterrey, and Guadalajara. Fidelist averaged 46,493 monthly payments to *tortillerias* and in the DFMA affiliates surpassed 5,000. What guided Fidelist selection? This is an important question since selection affected survival in the marketplace for *tortilleria* owners.[12] Securing a machine would guarantee Conasupo customers on top of their regular consumers and grant them access to subsidised Conasupo corn.

Fidelist targeted *tortillerias* in communities that fit a particular socioeconomic profile. Once selected, *tortillerias* signed a contract with Fidelist before receiving a machine. In the agreement the prospective affiliate pledged to uphold the guaranteed price and to supply free tortillas to cardholders. Failure to do so, according to the official guidelines, automatically terminated the contract and discontinued the flow of Conasupo corn to the *tortilleria*.

Committing affiliates to the official tortilla price granted a certain degree of leverage first to Diconsa (when it ran the Tortilla Programme), and later to Fidelist. If merchants embarrassed the government either by inflating prices or marketing subsidised Conasupo corn/tortillas to restaurants instead of cardholders, the deal was off and Diconsa/Fidelist turned to other local *tortillerias*. However, widespread price inflation suggested that Diconsa/Fidelist anticipated and accepted a measure of distortion on the ground. By 1992 this grey area spawned the Manual of Norms and Procedures for Attending to *Tortillerias*. Here Fidelist delineated concise guidelines for participation and created separate offices in Mexico City, Guadalajara, Puebla, and Monterrey, in which *tortillerias* could file complaints against local Fidelist agents (Conasupo, 1992). New institutional responses, however, have proven insignificant against the scale of the problem, a point articulated by Fidelist employees. However, the fact that *tortillerias* refrained from adjusting prices in line with inflationary market conditions after 1986 indicates at least the tacit observance of a price ceiling. Contractual leverage, together with Conasupo's influence on local supply (i.e., cheap Conasupo corn) and demand (local Conasupo consumers) contributed to this outcome. Taking this point one step further, it is possible to formulate a tentative timetable in which the government yielded to a shadow price regime at *tortillerías*.

Observers note a general level of compliance with regulated food prices after 1982, in part because enforcement featured in the government's emergency welfare policy (Ochoa, 1994, Ch.10). As noted above, in 1986 the Tortilla Programme separated itself from Diconsa stores and began utilising *tortillerías*. Government-financed Diconsa stores lent themselves to easier monitoring of tortilla prices (though they were prone to other forms of abuse); however, *tortillerías* represented private enterprises and were subject to the pressure of market forces. After the switch to *tortillerías*, Mexico soon entered a high inflationary period (1987-1988), a time when severe price distortions hit controlled basic commodities. The government recognised that *tortillerías* faced bankruptcy at the official rate set in the 1987 and subsequent anti-inflationary pacts, marking an instance where a shadow price regime covertly became official policy. In the 1988 presidential campaign Carlos Salinas remained silent on tortilla subsidies that favoured DFMA consumers in general, and the Tortilla Programme that favoured DFMA official unions in particular. In 1988, the government again elected to maintain a low tortilla price and accept a degree of distortion at *tortillerías*.

The pattern of this formative period (1987-1988) carried over into subsequent tortilla policy. In 1990 Salinas liberalised general food prices except for tortillas, beans and milk. Fidelist acknowledges that cardholders and regular consumers confronted widespread price inflation under Salinas. Public exchanges in the media between *tortillería* unions and the government shed light on the grey area (i.e., the gap between real and official prices). Unions repeatedly requested an increase from 2 to 3 or 4 to 5 pesos to stave off bankruptcy. However, a Fidelist respondent explains that 'the official price (at the time) was only 1.2 pesos'! (... who pockets the difference?) 'the *tortillerías*, of course' (Interview, Mexico City, Office of Fidelist, 22 April 1997). Hence, in these unpredictable, locally-driven markets across urban Mexico, cardholders in the CMP's targeted scheme paid the balance between shadow and official prices, while non-card holding consumers paid the prevailing shadow price.

Contractual guidelines also shielded Fidelist from private competition. Private tortilla maker Maseca hinted at developing a network of *tortillerías* to tap the Mexican preference for fresh tortillas. The Fidelist representative to Maseca comments:

> Maseca asks for our machines in their *tortillerías*... fine by me... as long as they sign the contract... but they [Maseca] cannot do it because only our affiliates receive the government subsidy... Maseca cannot survive at the official price... (Interview, Mexico City, Office of Fidelist, 22 April 1997).

Whereas Fidelist affiliates received free Conasupo corn, Maseca purchased corn domestically (which was subsidised but not free) and sometimes internationally. It was in no position to compete for Fidelist's pool of two million urban households consuming (nearly) free tortillas.

Another repercussion of the official contract with *tortillerías* is that it encouraged *tortillería* owners to internalise part of the monitoring costs at the community level. Local competition for machines has acted as an incentive to *tortillerías* to furnish information on price violators. Fidelist also approaches *tortillerías* concerning consumer abuse, seeking information on multiple card users or those known to earn in excess of two times the minimum wage. The question was posed to the Fidelist official responsible for *tortillerías*: 'it would seem that this gives merchants influence over who gains access to the programme within the community? Wasn't this a problem in the past?' He replied, 'yes it does, but the computer must approve of all new cards' (Interview, Mexico City, Office of Fidelist, 22 April 1997). His disclaimer referred to socioeconomic means testing and the fact that cards, in theory, only went to people in low-income communities. The formal procedures set up by Fidelist mask a more fundamental and common reality. To some extent, the selection of communities has already taken place very early on by local power brokers, and the jockeying for position of *tortillerías* at the local level is often the last stage in the sequence of more subterranean processes of elimination. Demand for Conasupo tortillas outpaced the supply throughout the Salinas term, and amid this environment there was still room for local intermediaries to select winners and losers.

Targeting Colonias

Given that low-income *colonias* exceeded Fidelist resources, who made final distribution decisions?[13] The official answer is: 'Ultimately, people at the state-level decide', that is, the 202 directors in cities covered by the PSCT, who typically collaborated with state governors (Interview, Mexico City, Office of Fidelist, 4 April 1997). However, while it is correct to say that state-level actors may influence information arriving in Mexico City (e.g., the selection of *colonias*), clearly the latter maintained tight budgetary control. For instance, Morelos Conasupo Director Emilio González Anguiano explained why 325 Conasupo stores and other Conasupo infrastructure in his state lacked financing to purchase goods: 'Politics surround the distribution of resources to states...you have to have a base in the federal government or your state loses out ... [Conasupo's budgetary allocations arc] a racket system' (*Excelsior*, 7 January 1989).

More recently, antagonism between opposition governors and Fidelist has also surfaced: 'We now have opposition governors in Mexico and they want to take the programme from us, the government' (Interview, Mexico City, Office of Fidelist, 7 May 1997). This partisan comment – are governors outside the government? – was directed at a budgetary battle in February 1997 sparked by then PAN Governor of Guanajuato Vicente Fox's petition to decentralise the Tortilla Programme. For Fox the Tortilla Programme signified a relic of centralised, one-party rule. Chapter Six returns to this issue but the point that needs to be stressed is that the centre-local relationship surrounding the Tortilla Programme retained a clear political dimension. With the Tortilla Programme, some administrative power was dispersed to local agents without relinquishment of centralised control or decentralisation of budgetary power. If political conditions deteriorated, few obstacles prevented the executive from authorising additional resources (i.e., cards) into a local setting. A tendency toward centralisation or streamlining with the Tortilla Programme is also found in the next two case studies.

Household Selection

In the Tortilla Programme's 202 cities, a February 1992 socioeconomic survey estimated eligible households at 3,773,500, of which Fidelist delivered benefits to 2,080,900 households or 55 percent (Conasupo, November 1994a). Whether tortilla subsidies reached low-income households had never been a main priority in the Diconsa years; however, after 1992 achieving this objective preoccupied Fidelist. Before discussing measures undertaken to secure this outcome, it is instructive to step back and elaborate on how Fidelist formed the original PSCT list in 1991.

First, it transferred 1.8 million households to the PSCT list, including the 840,000 households that comprised the *tortibono* list. Thus, in his press conference on 30 November 1991, President Salinas left out a key point when he replied to critics of the PSCT that 'free tortillas only go to households after an analysis is done of their socioeconomic situation' (*Crónica del Gobierno de Carlos Salinas de Gortari 1988-1994*, 1994: 407). In truth, no process appraised old households, inviting the same pertinent union and *colonia* leaders to resurface in the PSCT. Second, Conasupo added 273,400 households in October-November 1991 as the PSCT incorporated 131 new cities. In these locations socioeconomic surveys tested *colonia*s and follow-up interviews confirmed the accuracy of information. Third, Conasupo verified and added 335,000 households with no prior experience from the original 71 cities from April–June 1991. Fourth, Fidelist incorporated 110,000 households in new locations without appraising household income status. In 1992, when Fidelist officially took over PSCT, it tested all new households (441,263), and in the following year a further 406,517 in the interior, and 226,414 in the DFMA. In 1993 and 1994 Fidelist processed 604,031 socioeconomic profile questionnaires, granting special priority to the states of Michoacán, Baja California, Hidalgo, Nuevo León, Sinaloa, and Veracruz.

After formulating the PSCT list and distributing around 2 million cards, Fidelist conducted a comprehensive, family-by-family, evaluation of the beneficiary list in the first semester of 1992. By September 1994 this verification process prompted Fidelist to visit 79 percent of the PSCT's 2.1 million households. Likewise, it was able to situate each household on a socioeconomic scale: high/medium high, medium, medium low, and low. Similarly, between November 1992 and March 1993, Fidelist profiled each *colonia* in the PSCT's 202 cities. Households in the bottom two categories of the socioeconomic scale qualified, yet to the government's dismay surveys discovered that 55 percent of households were in the top two categories. In Mexico City, a more alarming 70 percent of households appeared in the top two categories. Of course, the Council's initial decision to incorporate the *tortibono* list into the PSCT list helps to explain these findings.

Graph 4.2 Total of Beneficiary Households 1991-1994 (x1000)*

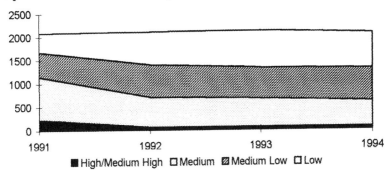

*Through September 1994
Source: Conasupo (November 1994b)

**Graph 4.3   Total of Beneficiary Households from Interior of
Country 1991-1994 (x1000)***

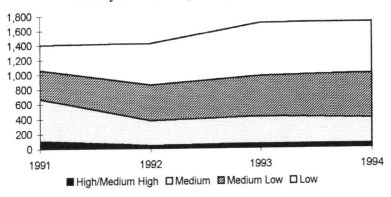

*Through September 1994
Source: Conasupo (November 1994b)

This 1992 survey data prompted the Permanent Programme to Purify the Beneficiary List (PPPBL). This campaign authorised 547,000 household visits outside the DFMA between March-May 1992, which in turn led to the discovery and expulsion of 231,000 ineligible households. Attention turned to the DFMA between June-November 1992, and here, two million visits managed to locate 280,000 of the 686,000 listed households; that is, surveyors could not account for over half of DFMA beneficiaries. In the next year, Fidelist recorded high rates of expulsion: 230,023 households outside DFMA and 470,217 households from the DFMA (Conasupo, 1993). New households offset expulsions, thus Fidelist maintained an official list of 2.1 million from 1991-1994 (graph 4.2).

Graph 4.4   Total of Beneficiary Households from D.F. Metro Area 1991-1994 (x1000)*

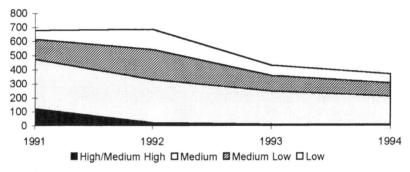

*Through September 1994
Source: Conasupo (November 1994b)

While a process of reshuffling comes into view in graphs 4.2-4.5, it is important to remember that total households jumped from 840,000 in 1990 to 1,961,000 in 1991 and stabilised thereafter at 2,100,000. This is pertinent because it becomes apparent that under the PSCT the Tortilla Programme progressively delivered resources effectively to poor households located in the interior of the country; notice that the bottom two socioeconomic categories accounted for 71 percent of households at the national level by 1994. Though the DFMA share dropped sizeably – 37 percent in 1993 alone – the bottom two socioeconomic categories still accounted for a mere 43 percent in 1994. Arguably this suggests an unwillingness to break the traditional pattern in the DFMA, a fact that was partially masked by the overall expansion of the Tortilla Programme between 1990-1991. Nonetheless, it was a significant departure from the past that, by 1994, expenditures in the DFMA fell to 10 percent of the nation-wide total. After 1992 Fidelist offices conducted statistically significant random household visits triennially and initial discoveries turned up positive. Fidelist reported 100 percent of households in 25 states (a list that did not include the D.F.) satisfied eligibility requirements in December 1993. Evidently, successful targeting occurred in new cities, while old patterns of distribution lingered in the DFMA.

Graph 4.5 D.F. Metro Area Percentage of Conasupo Tortilla Subsidy

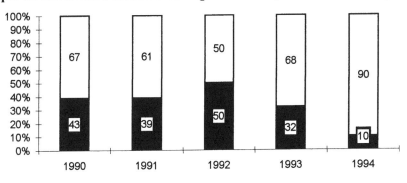

■ D.F. Metro Area □ Interior of Country

Source: Conasupo (1995)

To summarise, this section on the Tortilla Programme between 1984 and 1994 revealed a pattern of policy 'recreation' that produced meaningful, though incremental, reform and continuity in certain state-society relationships (notably in the DFMA). As far as the Salinas years, targeted subsidies grew from 1989 to 1992; however, initial steps to monitor or restructure the delivery of subsidies only began in 1992. This populist rather than neoliberal choice 'to distribute first' and 'to reform later' suggests that the PRI's restored electoral legitimacy after the 1991 mid-term election provided a more propitious environment for needs-based distribution. In this respect it is important to emphasise Conasupo's 'bureaucratic capacity' during the Salinas years. Conasupo incorporated 137 cities in 1991 and verified 79 percent of participant households from 1992 to 1993, this implied a considerable reservoir of bureaucratic resources, organisation, and infrastructure that was ready to respond to executive priorities.

The Government Milk Programme

Antecedents. In 1972 President Echeverría gave *Leche Industrializada Conasupo*, or Liconsa, the mandate to intervene in the production, distribution, and marketing of dairy products; and granted Conasupo an import monopoly over milk powder (NDM) and dehydrated butyric fat (required to reformulate milk powder). During Mexico's petroleum boom in the 1970s, President López Portillo pumped significant resources into Liconsa expansion and, despite the overall constraints on public spending after 1982, de la Madrid increased Liconsa intervention, including the processing of dairy products.

Nicholson, an economist who specialises in North American dairy markets, conceives of Liconsa's gradual import dependence as a byproduct of a subsidy-based, anti-inflation policy to curb supply-side pressure, itself a policy driven by Mexico's rapid urbanisation and population growth rates.

> Seventy percent of Mexican citizens, some 61.5 million people, lived in urban areas in 1992, and urbanization continues to increase... Already, one in four Mexicans lives in or around Mexico City, and an estimated 65 percent of dairy products are consumed in the Valle de México (Nicholson, 1995: 2).

His analysis relies heavily on demographic shifts through the 1970s. He contends that a demographic transition precipitated a modern, urban-based, consumption pattern for milk in which demand out-paced domestic production by the 1980s.[14] In this environment, milk powder imports served to moderate urban price inflation, most notably in the DFMA.

No blueprint co-ordinated Liconsa development across *sexenios*; instead, its infrastructure and organisational development evolved with specific priorities delineated by different executives. Echeverría stressed purchases from Mexican dairy farmers, and Liconsa constructed reception and cooling centres where dairy farmers from the Altos de Jalisco, Tlaxcala, Veracruz, Nayarit, and Zacatecas could market output at a fixed price. Echeverría and López Portillo encouraged milk production with high prices; however, producer subsidies eroded after 1982 and production dropped off under high costs and insufficient marketing infrastructure. Domestic milk production climbed 4.1 percent annually from 1970 to 1980, yet it fell to 0.8 percent from 1980 to 1988 (Muñoz Rodríguez, 1990: 887). López Portillo and de la Madrid initiated the processing of dairy commodities, identified as an area overlooked by domestic entrepreneurs.[15] Finally, de la Madrid, Salinas, and Zedillo have prioritised cheap milk distribution in urban zones. Urban distribution has mostly relied on Liconsa's small retail outlets or *lecherías* that have marketed subsidised, reformulated milk powder and fresh milk.[16] Even today, women standing before a *lechería* service window, usually in the dark hours before sunrise, remain a fixture in the Mexico City landscape.

Conasupo, not Liconsa, auctioned unused milk powder to private processors. According to Nicholson (1995: 28),

> The roughly 30 percent of NDM (milk powder) not used by Liconsa's social programs currently are auctioned to private industry monthly or quarterly, depending on need. In the 1980s, Conasupo apparently provided NDM to domestic processors at subsidized prices..., but now appears to be extracting quota rents by selling to domestic processors at prices above world market prices.

Similarly, *El Financiero* (9 May 1990) reported that Conasupo auctioned milk powder to Liconsa and private milk producers at an equivalent price, but sold to producers of dairy derivatives at double the Liconsa price. Apparently, post-1982 budgetary pressures caused policymakers to squeeze private industry to help enlarge Liconsa milk distribution. To a degree this survival strategy laid the ground work for manoeuvres authorised under the CMP, such as auctioning processing factories to expand Liconsa's network of *lecherías*. In either case, Liconsa appropriated resources from low-priority activities in order to enlarge its consumption related infrastructure (i.e., *lecherías*).

According to official guidelines, a household should obtain a Liconsa subsidy card if it (i) earns below two minimum salaries and (ii) possesses children below the age of twelve. Eligible households obtained four litres per child each week at a fraction of the official price. At *lecherías*, cardholders purchased at a subsidised price directly, and at Diconsa stores they received a 70 percent discount on 'Boreal' brand milk, a firm that the government has shared a special arrangement.

Graph 4.6   Beneficiaries of Tortilla* and Milk** Programmes (1986-1995)

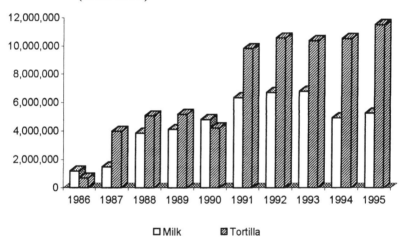

□ Milk   ▨ Tortilla

* Tortilla calculation multiplies number of households by five
** Milk calculation only refers to the number of children beneficiaries; hence the total figure is higher.
Source: Informe de Gobierno (1996)

Mexico began liberalising dairy markets in 1986, after it entered the GATT, a move that automatically lowered import tariffs by around 20 percent (Outlaw and Nicholson, 1994). De la Madrid's policy mirrored the World Bank's 1986 recommendations for Mexican food markets, in particular its advocacy of targeted consumption subsidies as opposed to universal subsidies. In the 1990s, Salinas unilaterally scrapped price controls in the domestic dairy market (cheese, cream, yoghurt), aside from milk. Moguel (1993: 55) notes however that Salinas took lactose products off the NAFTA agenda.

Graph 4.6 charts total tortilla and milk beneficiaries from the mid-point of the de la Madrid *sexenio* through the initial year of the Zedillo term. A formative period, 1986-1988, marked a developmental stage in targeted milk subsidies that was comparable to the inaugural Diconsa (tortilla) Programme. In this period, however, Liconsa sometimes catered to households earning more than two minimum salaries in the DFMA, a continuation of pre-1986 operations, which often left the Milk Programme in the hands of corporatist intermediaries (Ochoa, 1994; Lustig and Martín del Campo, 1985). This was not a controversial policy, given that the government kept the retail price for all non-Liconsa milk far below the true market price; tortillas in the *tortibono* era operated according to the same logic. There was no compelling reason or zero-sum context – i.e., a sense that access to Liconsa milk subsidies for some entailed an evident 'loss' for other groups – thus pressure from below did not manifest around targeted milk benefits. Of course, the erosion of general subsidies due to high inflation, and officially adopting 'targeting' at Liconsa, in the second half of the de la Madrid term gradually altered the environment in which Liconsa policy unfolded.

In 1989, Salinas immediately pumped resources into Liconsa milk distribution. Around the DFMA, Liconsa constructed, according to Ignacio Ovalle, 500 *lecherías* to benefit 2 million households in the administration's first 100 days alone (*La Jornada*, 11 March 1989). Salinas continued to enlarge the circle of Liconsa beneficiaries, punctuated by exceptional growth in 1991. Liconsa beneficiaries swelled from 3.8 million in 1988 to 6.9 million in 1994 (see graphs 4.6 and 4.7).

Distribution of Liconsa milk and Conasupo tortillas experienced extraordinary geographic expansion between 1988 and 1994, while progressively accomplishing a more equitable balance inside and outside the DFMA. However, once again we find that, rather than relocating operations outside the DFMA, privatisation and additional budgetary outlays to Liconsa fuelled new territorial expansion. According to INEGI/CONAL (1992) statistics, Liconsa situated 50 percent of *lecherías* in the DFMA as late as 1991. Note that the Milk Programme reached 631 municipalities and the Tortilla Programme 36 cities in 1990, both figures climbed to 1,370 municipalities and 202 cities in 1991. Graph 4.8 charts growth in the number of *lecherías*: 2,230 in 1990 and 5,683 in 1991.

Graph 4.7   Geographic Development of Milk and Tortilla Programmes (1988-1994)

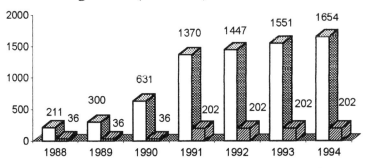

□ Municipalities (Milk) ☑ Cities (Tortillas)

Source: Conasupo (1994)

Graph 4.8 Growth in Liconsa *Lecherías* (1988-1995)

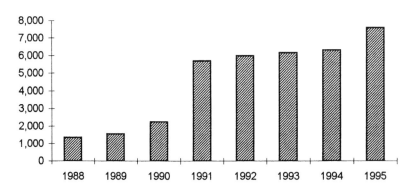

Source: Informe de Gobierno (1996)

In the short span of one year, these (geographically) limited programmes were transformed from being significant in major urban centres, yet highly centralised, to being large-scale, nation-wide operations. Again, if we simplify the milk and tortilla policies to a trade-off between integrating new households via old methods (clientelism) versus assuring handouts arrived at poor households (neoliberalism), the balance overwhelmingly sided with the first option through 1992.

Purifying the Liconsa List

According to Nicholson (1995: 27), 'In 1992, Liconsa specified a goal of providing subsidised milk to all eligible households (some 12 million people) by the year 1994'. In subsequent years, he correctly notes, Liconsa production fell considerably short of its objective. Nicholson's economic analysis asserts that the sharp devaluation of Mexico's exchange rate at the end of 1994 was a structural obstacle which impeded Liconsa production – e.g., imported milk powder became too expensive. We can infer that, for Nicholson, the official goal may have been realised, had external variables not interceded. By contrast, sociologist Gurza Lavalle (1994) contends that the logical fulfilment of an unholy alliance between Mexican technocrats and international capitalists is the force behind policy in Conasupo's traditional markets. Closer inspection of the 1992-1994 period, however, reveals the need for an alternative to either the economic interpretation or this particular sociological account.

Conasupo representatives, political parties, academics, and beneficiaries all suspected that Liconsa wasted public resources and largely catered to partisan interests. Before 1992 the government did no monitoring of the Liconsa list, which, similar to tortilla schemes, granted special access to unions in the DFMA. Under de la Madrid the CT and CNOP distributed Liconsa subsidy cards (Conasupo, 1983d, 1987). In the 1980s, failure to target benefits and monitor the supply of Liconsa milk, alongside cuts in Liconsa employee salaries, cultivated an environment ripe for abuse. If the government displayed no urgency in monitoring milk subsidies, why should Liconsa employees? Salinas agreed to explore the issue in 1993, after public pressure surfaced from various sources and as black markets for Liconsa milk continued to crop up across Mexico City, Monterrey and Guadalajara.

In 1993 Liconsa contracted *Instituto Tecnológico y Estudios Superiores de Monterrey* (ITESM) to conduct exploratory socioeconomic surveys in the state of Colima (Conasupo, 1993). In May 1993 it surveyed 10,545 households at 19 *lecherías* and discovered a 40 percent ineligibility rate. It blamed unions and corrupt Liconsa officials. If 4 in 10 households turned up ineligible in a small state operation such as Colima, what might surveys uncover in the DFMA? One Conasupo (September 1994) document surmised,

> The accelerated growth in the Milk Programme (65 percent between 1988 and 1991) and its operating guidelines provided the basis for multiple control problems with the beneficiaries list.[17]

Observers describe political manipulation of the Milk Programme under Salinas as extensive.[18]

To put DFMA operations into some general context, before the Chamber of Deputies Commission on Supply and Distribution of Basics, housewives that participated in the Milk Programme alluded to a multiplicity of corrupt acts at *lecherías*. For example, in addition to irregular supply, *lechería* operator number 339 from zone North 75 in *colonia* Jardín Azpeitía pocketed the women's change, threatening to cut them off if they protested. Interviewed housewives 'refused to give their names to the Deputies for fear of future reprisal' and sceptically retorted that 'nothing would change' under the proposals recommended by Salinas (*Excelsior*, 9 January 1990). Deputies from the Commission visited a number of *lecherías* around the DFMA and reported black markets at each stop.

In June 1993 Liconsa summarised the Colima survey before session #248 of the Administrative Council of Liconsa. A Conasupo report explains that the Council reflected on the mis-allocation discovered in Colima and requested a national verification study under the stewardship of the office of social programmes at Conasupo (Conasupo, 1993).

Any path leading to a needs-based Milk Programme (discontinuity/neoliberalism) unavoidably ran through the DFMA (continuity/clientelism). In the second semester of 1993, the office of social programmes hired ITESM to survey 20 DFMA *lecherías* that officially supplied 18,342 households. Until 1993 the quantity of milk delivered per *lechería* corresponded to its household list. ITESM managed to locate 12,630 households, it left comply warnings at 2,857 households after follow up visits, it failed to physically locate 1,728 households, and it failed to begin investigating 1,127 households due to insufficient information. Hence, before this neoliberal scheme to 'target the poor' could determine whether survey participants satisfied eligibility requirements, ITESM discovered a 30 percent leakage rate, e.g., the difference between quantity delivered and households accounted for. Of course, household relocation and tenant informality, common features in low-income *colonias*, played a part in this outcome. Likewise, another salient factor was a thriving black market in the DFMA that enticed Liconsa employees to expand or maintain participant lists.

Director for Conasupo Distribution in the DFMA Ignacio Barrón Carmona commented that the black market in 1990, usually visible on the street corner opposite a community's *lechería*, furnished prices around 200 percent above the official Liconsa price (*Excelsior*, 9 January 1990). Liconsa Director Enrique Sada Fernández agreed and noted that, in the DFMA, Liconsa sold at 112.5 pesos per litre (in 1990) while the black market price was 350 pesos. Clear parallels between the Tortilla and Milk Programmes surface regarding official prices and their articulation at the local level.

Conasupo never disclosed ITESM's DFMA pilot survey but there was reason to suspect that a negative outcome unfolded, for the Council deliberately excluded the DFMA, State of México, and Hidalgo from future surveys.

> Where it was decided to postpone surveys until there existed appropriate conditions to proceed... It will remain pending for the next administration to move the verification process to the D.F., the State of México and Hidalgo... (Conasupo, 1994b).

No explanation elaborated what these 'appropriate conditions' entailed. But given the unpredictable climate surrounding the eligible population as well as the intermediaries involved in DFMA operations, it is not hard to see why coherent needs-based targeting, the government's official policy since 1983, was finally abandoned in 1993.[19]

Of course the best-intentioned, well-place technocrat faced major, perhaps insurmountable, obstacles in the DFMA if his/her mandate was to reform without discontinuing Liconsa milk distribution. Likewise, rapid expansion of subsidies certainly did nothing to advance the cause of better monitoring in the first half of the Salinas term. First, past consumers of Liconsa milk that fit the profile of lower-income households (households that earned above two minimum salaries were still likely to be characterised as 'lower-income' and unable to purchase at the market price), but who did not qualify for milk subsidies, expected Liconsa resources and simple elimination invited a political backlash.[20] Second, assuming that there was indeed strong executive support for a reform package of private-sector audits, community participation, or new technology, who at Liconsa might manage and defend the process in the DFMA? Liconsa employees totalled in the thousands, and many encouraged black markets. Community participation, the Salinas formula elsewhere, offered no solution to the widespread abuse prior to final distribution. Community complaints suggested that, in addition to corrupt *lechería* operators, very often milk never arrived. Again, under what scenario can one foresee a successful needs-based targeting scheme developing out of the traditional Liconsa operations in the DFMA?

Outside the DFMA, State of México, and Hidalgo, Liconsa policy advanced in three stages. First, interviewers hired by the office of social programmes questioned 179,961 households from a total of 418,987 in 23 states between August and December 1993. Second, it questioned 623,921 households in 28 states from January to June 1994. At the end of 1994, Liconsa had surveyed nearly all households outside the D.F., State of México and Hidalgo, or roughly half the programme. Third, Liconsa mailed notices to those households not visited, outlining that a failure to participate in the survey by July 1994 would result in automatic expulsion.[21] In sum, Liconsa verified 839 *lechería* lists, 13 percent of the nationwide total in 1993 and a further 1,409 *lechería* lists, 22 percent of nationwide total in 1994. The net result uncovered a 47 percent ineligibility rate. Liconsa promptly expelled ineligible households, causing a 28 percent cut in total beneficiaries in 1994, or 40 percent of households outside the DFMA.

To summarise, the Salinas administration rejected petitions to test lists until late 1993 and subsequent surveys, in Colima and elsewhere, discovered high ineligibility rates. Even after deciding to reform operations,

Liconsa pressed forward in the interior of the country yet bypassed the DFMA. Neither Nicholson's economic interpretation nor Gurza Lavalle's framework accurately accounts for Liconsa's dual policy. Analogous to the Tortilla Programme, during the Salinas years there was an unwillingness to disengage from past distribution patterns tied to traditional allies in the DFMA.

Targeting Other Basic Commodities, Diconsa

Antecedents. The parastatal *Sistema de Distribuidoras Conasupo, S.A.* (Diconsa) appeared in 1961 to co-ordinate Conasupo's retail stores and distribution apparatus (boats, trucks and railroad cars). Since the 1960s, Mexican presidents officially employed Diconsa's retail network to combat *intermediarismo* or speculation in urban food markets, to fill a void in domestic marketing infrastructure, and to redistribute national income. In the early 1980s, a study by Solís (1984) found that while Mexico possessed sufficient distribution infrastructure in terms of total stores – for example, stores per person compared favourably to the US – there was a problem of over-concentration in final sales. In 1976, 2 percent of Mexico's food stores accounted for 50 percent of national sales, leading Solís to suggest that over-concentration encouraged inefficiency. Officially, the government used Diconsa to overcome this imperfection in the marketplace. By 1987 Diconsa retail operations reached 95 percent of Mexican municipalities or a potential pool of 58.8 million consumers (Salinas, 1988). Given Diconsa's national orientation, it became a major public sector employer with a workforce surpassing 22,000 in 1987.

The National Development Plan 1983-1988 stressed that targeting subsidies would be crucial if Mexico was to cope with its economic crisis. In the de la Madrid years, targeting Diconsa subsidies and cost-cutting implied fewer commodities on store shelves. For instance, official policy instructed rural co-operatives to focus on basic commodities such as corn, beans, rice, and sugar. However, at large urban stores, Diconsa stockpiled between 5,000-10,000 commodities, including clothing, televisions and luxury goods. It fact, basics in the Mexican diet constituted a minor proportion of total Diconsa sales under de la Madrid: corn, beans, rice, and sugar, accounted for 12.1 percent in 1982, 15.6 percent in 1983, 17 percent in 1984, 15.9 percent in 1985, and 19.2 percent in 1986.

Diconsa's official guidelines limited its subsidies strictly to poor households, but this blueprint bore little resemblance to what occurred in practice. Diconsa policy reflected familiar political calculations, which manifested themselves clearly in the five Diconsa programmes deployed by de la Madrid to regulate consumption of basic foodstuffs: (i) the Rural Supply Programme, co-administered with the CNC, (ii) the Popular Urban Supply Programme that involved the CNOP, (iii) the Union Store Programme that involved the CT, (iv) the Institutional Programme that involved public sector unions, and (v) the General Public Programme, where affiliation was less precise (Conasupo, 1987a). Four of the five programmes channelled food subsidies to the PRI's corporatist branches, and therefore the programmes, bureaucracy, infrastructure and workplace norms that Salinas inherited were all steeped in partisan politics. Solís (1984: 493) observed in the early 1980s that Diconsa's operations 'barely touch the lowest-income groups'.

The situation was actually even more blatant. In 1983, to cope with union pressure, Diconsa expeditiously distributed 3 million 'baskets' – each was a monthly ration of corn, corn flour, wheat flour, milk, eggs, cooking oil, sugar, beans, rice, pasta for soup, salt, potatoes, tomatoes, dried meat, cookies, sardines, coffee, chilies and onions – and 3 million Diconsa coupons/vouchers (good at Diconsa stores) to labour unions; re-capitalised 120 union stores and 115 institutional stores (public sector unions); created the *Programa de Apertura de Tiendas Congreso del Trabajo* (new union stores), *CODEF-conasupo* (programme for the DFMA), and *Centro Comercial SEP-SNTE-conasupo* (stores for public education workers); and signed inter-institutional agreements for Diconsa resources with, among others, the government of Mexico City (DDF), CNOP, PRI, BANRURAL, SRA-FIFONAFE (Secretary of Agrarian Reform), INI, SARH, FERTIMEX (the National Fertiliser Company), and CNC (Conasupo, 1983d). In addition to infrastructure modifications, between 1983 and 1986 de la Madrid delegated significant control of daily operations at Conasupers to official unions through so-called Administrative Agreements of Co-responsibility with Diconsa, another mode of official *concertación* (Conasupo, 1987a). After 1982 Diconsa policy followed the Tortilla Programme by formulating a coupon scheme targeting eligible Diconsa consumers (the Consumption Credit Programme). Businesses, public institutions, and unions dispensed coupons, exchangeable for free Diconsa merchandise. Overall, such handouts benefited official labour unions (table 4.0); however, subsidised Diconsa goods remained available to the public at large. In 1986 when the government sought an anti-inflationary pact reliant on further wage and price controls Diconsa subsidies formed part of a compensatory package offered to a debilitated and disillusioned corporate labour sector. 'In response to demands from the CT', Diconsa distributed 3.6 million coupons to unions for merchandise valued in excess of ($US) 3 million between March and December 1986 (Conasupo, 1987a). In 1986, Diconsa delivered another 800,000 baskets valued at ($US) 2.5 million to the CT. Furthermore, Diconsa assuaged official union tension in 1986 by inking 250 *concertación* agreements with individual unions for new stores; a move incorporating a potential 2.5 million new consumers. A special budget for Presidential Programmes financed these stores. Presidential Programmes, which also included natural disaster relief, ballooned under Salinas until 1993 when the Administrative Council acknowledged 'considerable abuse' and curbed funding (graph 4.9) (Conasupo, 1994b). Monitoring whether food subsidies reached poor households was not dismissed outright. Policymakers originally authorised a Diconsa beneficiary list in 1983 but no steps to implement such a policy ensued.

Both de la Madrid and Salinas adopted a *concertación* formula to select new store locations. *Colonia* leadership or labour unions typically filed a petition for a Diconsa store, pledging to share the resource burden by donating community labour time and perhaps construction materials – Diconsa policy offered a blueprint for the well-known 'Solidarity formula' of state-society partnership, later embraced to great advantage by Carlos Salinas. In turn, a petition to Diconsa instigated a dialogue with community and labour groups. Yet neither President de la Madrid nor President Salinas predicated policy on socioeconomic criteria; determining who used Diconsa remained a mystery until the end of the Salinas term. Around 300 Conasupers accounted for 70 percent of total sales by 1988. It is important to stress that these large-sized Conasupers were tied to official labour unions because later, in the debate surrounding their closure, some observers contended that these stores were located in poverty stricken areas; this was simply not the case. The government erected Conasupers to cater to public workers and official labour unions, not the urban poor.

Momentum toward needs-based distribution in the cases of tortillas and milk subsidies occurred in 1992 and 1993; at Diconsa, an initial turning point arrived in 1993. The *1994 Annual Conasupo Report* (Conasupo, 1994b) reads,

> In 1988 self-owned stores, concession stores [i.e., Conasupers and union stores], and community stores composed the Diconsa system. With this structure, Diconsa subsidised consumption in a general manner...without prioritising zones with the highest instances of poverty.

To distribute according to economic need, Diconsa first required information on its consumers and store locations. Oddly enough, López Portillo, de la Madrid and Salinas (until 1993) utilised Diconsa to redistribute national income, yet no record documented the final destination of food subsidies. Likewise, when Salinas later discontinued Conasupers and constructed thousands of Community Stores he did so without such data – i.e., Diconsa policy was not 'neoliberal' before or under Salinas.

Graph 4.9   Budget of Conasupo's Presidential Programmes ($US 1000)*

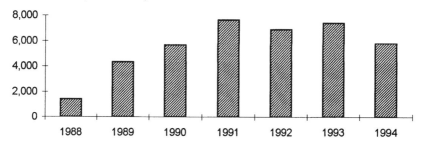

* Estimated budget for 1994
Source: Conasupo (September 1994)

However, while Conasuper closures proceeded apace Diconsa constructed thousands of new retail stores via *concertación* agreements. Soon the new stores became more expensive to operate than the Conasupers due to high transportation costs, the largest component in the Diconsa budget. Until 1989, Diconsa 'made money in the cities' and 'lost money in the mountains and the jungles' (Interview, Mexico City, Office of Fidelist, 22 April 1997). The CMP modified the old equation; as of 1990, Diconsa simply lost money because of high transport cost and the privatisation of 589 Conasupers.

Table 4.0   Participants in Consumption Credit Programme (1983-1987)

Group	Amount ($US)
• National Sugar Worker Union (57 plants)	1,200,000
• Banrural Workers	3,300,000
• Ejido Credit Union of the Yaqui and Mayo (5,000 households)	560,000
• Coffee Workers of Nayarit	180,000
• Other Ejido Organisations (23 ejidos)	83,000
• GRUSOL Rice Works in Culiacán	250,000
• Port and Fish Industry Workers in Mazatlán	226,000

Source: Excelsior (1 November 1988)

Given the backdrop of the de la Madrid years, what measures assured that *concertación* agreements under the CMP reached low-income *colonia*s as oppose to being bartered via the 'executive-local bridge' as before? No reference to the Diconsa Community Supply Programme or the CMP's Community Store model surfaced in annual Conasupo reports in 1990, 1991, or 1992. In fact, the only evidence to document the programme's existence before 1993 came from CNC and CTM representatives who confirmed that their members had gained control of stores.[22] The *1993 Annual Conasupo Report* discusses the 'inauguration' of the Diconsa Community Supply Programme. In late 1993, Diconsa produced a procedural manual to outline rules and regulations in the selection of *colonias* for the programme. Thus, here is another case where dispersing resources came first (1989-1992) and the development of an organisational structure came second (1993-1994).

Graph 4.10 Total Diconsa Beneficiaries (1991-1994)

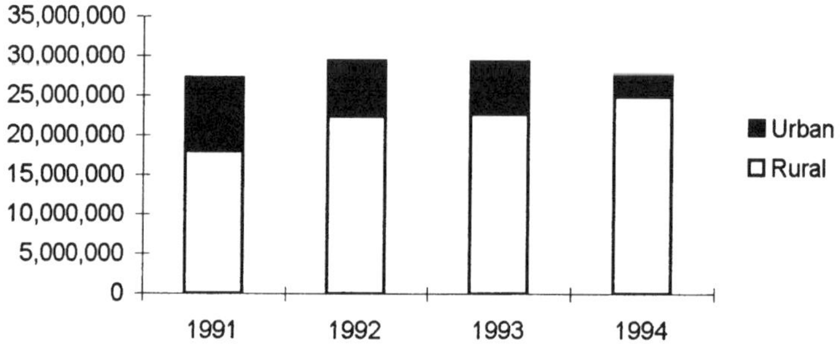

Source: Informe de Gobierno (1996)

But the shift in Diconsa policy went beyond manuals or official guidelines. In 1993 Salinas hired ITESM to conduct a survey to (i) determine the socioeconomic profile of Diconsa users and (ii) to determine the structure of household spending of Diconsa consumers. Officials announced that the ITESM survey would guide the government's final determination of which stores to close, relocate, and maintain. A Conasupo (September 1994) report cites the ITESM study's conclusions:

> ... the users of Diconsa stores do not live in locations characterised by low or very low instances of poverty... they do not have socioeconomic characteristics and a household spending structure characterised as low-income....

The 1993 ITESM survey marked the first attempt at a socioeconomic profile of Diconsa and the outcome led Salinas to decree a gradual closure of all urban stores in March 1994. Graph 4.10 reveals that a rural shift predated March 1994 concerning Diconsa sales and total beneficiaries. In 1991, information on Diconsa beneficiaries first appeared when Diconsa consumers numbered 18 million rural and 9.2 million urban. By 1994, the figures stood at 24.9 million rural and 2.6 million urban, indicating that a mere 10 percent of Diconsa consumers came from urban areas. Thus the decision in March 1994 formalised a process that commenced when Salinas started privatising Conasupers. Graph 4.11 shows a transfer of infrastructure to rural areas. From 1988 to 1994 urban stores fell from 7,222 to 1,074 and rural stores jumped from 15,447 to 19,564.

Graph 4.11   Diconsa Infrastructure of Rural and Urban Stores (1961-1995)

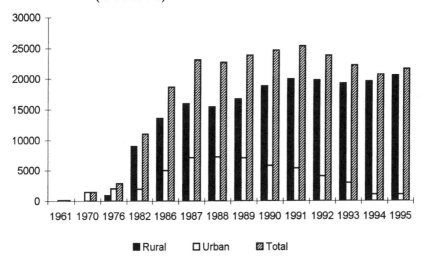

Source: Informe de Gobierno (1996) and Conasupo (1987)

What we have shown is that without taking steps to monitor the distribution of Diconsa subsidies, Salinas encouraged a major reshuffling of infrastructure. Conasupo (1994b) note that Diconsa closed 21,451 stores by

1994 or 73 percent of the 1988 infrastructure. However, in graph 4.11 total stores never fluctuate above 5,000 stores, implying Salinas opened around 15,000 stores (or 3,000 per year) after October 1989. Since Diconsa opened a mere 300 stores in 1989, the average from 1990 through 1994 must have been even higher.

Summary: The CMP and the Recreation of Consumption Subsidies

To summarise, it is instructive to flag three key points: (1) the CMP generated timely and significant political capital for President Salinas, especially in the first half of his term; (2) the CMP prompted a process that 'reshuffled' Conasupo's traditional consumption services; and (3) political considerations rather than budget constraints guided Conasupo policy in the area of consumption subsidies. This chapter investigated consumption subsidies before and under the CMP. Subsidies were perhaps the most significant aspect of Conasupo operations vis-à-vis wider patterns of state-society relations because of the potential impact on millions of Mexican households. The CMP prioritised a policy of 'targeting'; however, the Salinas years witnessed unprecedented numbers of households gaining access to Conasupo, usually through a process of executive-local negotiation. In this way, the CMP precipitated a successful 'recreation' of the old model under a new guise.

As regards the sequencing of policy innovations, figure 4.0 distinguishes phases in a matrix ranging from *more of the same* (the old state-society model) to *initial reform* (co-existence of old and needs-based distribution) to a *radical break* (needs-based distribution). Although 1992 initiated movement from left to right on the matrix (with the notable exception of tortillas and milk in the DFMA), the overall picture is one of incremental, geographically-oriented innovation, or a blending of old and new (e.g., a 'recreation'). Admittedly, movement from left to right on this matrix over-emphasises technical steps taken to tackle traditional problems with unions and groups earning more than two minimum salaries in the DFMA. An implicit assumption here is that a radical reorientation of Conasupo and a coherent neoliberal alternative had to overcome these problems. By implication, and certainly a shortcoming of the matrix, it fails to capture potential 'new problems'; for example, operations at new

Diconsa stores, the conducting of new *concertación* processes and the repercussions of increasingly centralised, executive management.

More of the Same	Initial Reform	Radical Break
Tortibonos (1986-1990) *Tortivales* (1990-1992)	PSCT I (1991-1992) PSCT II, DFMA (1993-1994)	PSCT II, Interior of the Country (1993-1994)
Milk Programme (1988-1992) Milk Programme, DFMA (1992-1994)	Milk Programme, Interior of the Country (1992-1994)	
Diconsa Target Programme (1988-1992)	Diconsa Target Programme (1993-1994)	

Figure 4.0 Recreating Consumption Subsidies (1988-1994)

What factors contributed to a pattern that crosscuts the bureaucracies of Liconsa, Diconsa, and Fidelist? Nicholson pointed to public sector budget constraints. Yet, Mexico's severest budgetary crunch under Salinas transpired from December 1988 until the successful rescheduling of Mexican foreign debt in early 1991. In this interval, the unprecedented and reckless expansion of consumption services was a throwback to the clientelistic *populismo* of 'pre-neoliberal' executives. Interestingly, the three case studies above revealed that de la Madrid responded in very much the same way during economic difficulties in 1983 and 1986. Conversely, Salinas' maiden steps toward needs-based distribution (the government's post-1983 policy) materialised in a comparably favourable fiscal context after 1992. Furthermore, that President Salinas increased the budgets of his two signature social welfare initiatives, Solidarity and the Programme of Direct Producer Subsidies (PROCAMPO) in 1993 and 1994 does not support Nicholson's argument regarding Conasupo policy at the end of the Salinas term. So it is not evident that 'budget constraints' lend the best guide to Conasupo policy, at least not in the manner presented by Nicholson.

In another interpretation of the Salinas years, Ochoa (1994: 286) concludes:

> While for years many observers argued that to dismantle the State Food Agency (Conasupo) would wreak havoc for the official party, such political problems have not occurred because the State Food Agency was gradually dismantled and because Salinas has substituted a new catch-all social welfare agency, PRONASOL [Solidarity].

Ochoa is correct that the government circumvented political havoc, yet perhaps his reference to gradual dismantling and Solidarity misread the lessons of this chapter. Iconsa privatisation and Diconsa closures under the CMP underlie his contention that Conasupo was being dismantled, but this overlooks a concurrent process of re-intervention or expansion of subsidy services. He also fails to appreciate the significant technical, bureaucratic, personnel and financial/budgetary walls that separated Conasupo and Solidarity. Despite the confusion caused by the new labelling of Conasupo services under the CMP (see Chapter Three), this chapter has shown that Solidarity never 'replaced' traditional Conasupo services, nor did it supplant the administrative/bureaucratic apparatus that historically provided them. Perhaps the best illustration of continuity at Conasupo is the fact that Raúl Salinas was the key figure behind *concertación* with community groups during the de la Madrid years and from 1988 to 1992.

From graphs 4.12, 4.13 and 4.14, it seems more accurate to conclude that Salinas staved off a political backlash by slicing the Conasupo 'consumption subsidy pie' into new and usually smaller units. Increasing the number of households and extending services into new communities and regions, while at the same time decreasing the quantity of distributed basic goods, characterise how the CMP 'recreated' consumption subsidies. The following question by Cornelius (1995: 139) has important implications for the issue of continuity and discontinuity:

> Can new compensatory policies be devised that are both consistent with the fiscal constraints of the new macroeconomic model and able to cushion the social costs of economic restructuring and prevent mass explosions of discontent?

Although he is sceptical in general, consumption subsidy policy under the CMP seems to fit this prescription.

Graph 4.12   Output and Beneficiaries of the Tortilla Programme (1988-1994)

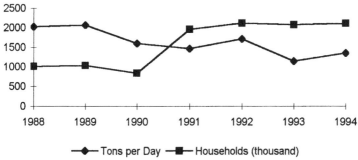

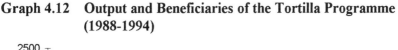

Source: Informe de Gobierno (1996)

Chapter One argued that political capital flowed from two sources: the final distribution of goods and a process of negotiation (or *concertación*). Conasupo policy, notably from 1988 to the end of 1991, generated unparalleled political capital. The Salinas administration under the CMP negotiated and delivered Conasupo consumption services to thousands of lower-income communities across Mexico, both in a hurry and without a major budgetary increase. Likewise, it is now apparent that 'delivering the goods' via clientele or informal norms was encouraged. Empirical investigation of the way in which the government delivered Conasupo resources via unstructured, local-executive negotiation puts aggregate statistics in a useful framework; indeed, Conasupo tortilla subsidies (to the same list of beneficiaries) jumped from 50 to 100 percent in 1990, while the traditional beneficiaries of the Milk Programme maintained access to the same quantity of subsidised milk per week. Cornelius (1995: 142) notes that Conasupo and not Solidarity helps explain why 'extremely poor urban dwellers' dropped from 6.5 million in 1989 to 4.8 million in 1992. That Conasupo generated political capital is clear enough with the Tortilla and Milk Programmes, the situation is less precise with Diconsa due to its concurrent processes of privatisation ('lost political capital') and the construction of thousands of smaller rural, urban and union stores ('generation of political capital').

Graph 4.13   Quantity, Infrastructure and Beneficiaries of the Milk Programme (1988-1994)

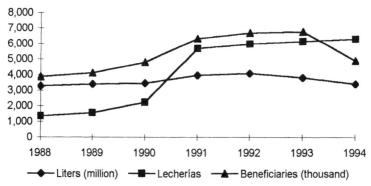

Source: Conasupo (1994)

This generation of political capital in the first half of the Salinas term undoubtedly contributed to a successful campaign that neutralised left-centre (Cárdenas/PRD) opposition support in the DFMA (29 percent in 1988 to 13 percent in 1991), among women (20 percent in 1988 to 5 percent in 1991), among unionised voters (22 percent in 1988 to 7 percent in 1991) and among working class voters (24 percent 1988 to 10 percent in 1991). This interval witnessed *concertación* dialogues in 3,453 lower-income urban communities for *lecherías* (500 in the DFMA in Salinas' first 100 days) and approximately 3,000 lower-income urban/rural communities for Diconsa stores. Furthermore, 1.1 million new, lower-income urban households gained access to the Tortilla Programme for the first time. Rodríguez and Ward (1991: 25) explain that the urban PRI machine pressed President Salinas for more resources to 'win back votes' after 1988. Our discussion indicates one way in which this request was granted. Likewise, Varley (1996: 209) suggests that the PRI felt that to maintain power it had to become the 'party of the urban poor'; expansion of the Tortilla and Milk Programmes seems to fit this theory. It is also important to underscore that PAN support among these electoral categories (DFMA, females, unionised and working class) fluctuated much less than the PRD (see table 1.0), which suggests that the PRI's gain in 1991 was mostly at the expense of the PRD.

Graph 4.14   Total Diconsa Subsidies and Infrastructure (1988-1994)

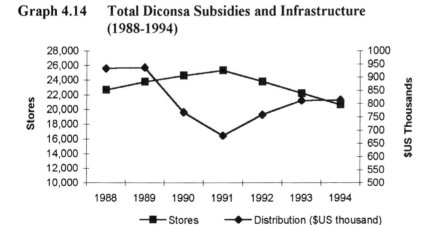

Source: Conasupo (1994)

In another respect, the 'recreation' process under the CMP squeezed antiquated corporatist channels (privatisation of union-run Conasupers), yet without abandoning them (new Infonavit stores, 250 *concertación* agreements safeguarding union benefits, etc.). In fact, vacated space in the marketplace under the CMP was not necessarily filled with the Solidarity programme, coherent needs-based distribution, or the private sector. Frequently, if not predominantly, it was *more of the same* through 1991, a process of exit and re-intervention.

However, once the post-1988 crisis of electoral legitimacy had been overcome with the PRI's mid-term electoral triumph in July 1991 – and the PRD's dismal showing at the same time – the environment at Conasupo changed and what ensued was a period of tentative reform and a period of consolidation. In October 1989 Ignacio Ovalle (*Proceso*, 6 November 1989) answered his critics within the PRI:

> Those who attack the plan [CMP] now will stand in line and they will look to organise in order to win concessions for *lecherias* and community stores.

In part, Conasupo policy shifted after 1991 because Ovalle's prophecy came to pass; traditionally loyal allies of the government did organise and did win concessions and the status quo was re-established.

Finally, other interpretations of Conasupo policy that have been raised simply cannot explain the dual pattern discovered inside (continuity) and outside (discontinuity) of the DFMA. Rubio and Newell (1984: 267) write: 'The very closed nature of the Inner Family prevents a detailed analysis of the individual agreements or alliances at different times; the allocation of resources does give a clue as to what sectors, in general, have benefited in each sexenio'. The Tortilla and Milk Programmes attest to the primacy of the public sector unions and lower-income groups in the DFMA that the government appeals to for legitimation. These groups are mostly lower-income, but above the two-minimum wage threshold ('the poor'), and cannot easily make the switch to the private market. The expansion coupled with the unwillingness to reform these programmes in the DFMA formed part of a historic bargain with allies of the government, and to remove such benefits threatened to strain it dramatically and perhaps disrupt it; a gamble the Salinas administration was not ready to take, especially with the PRD threatening on the left.

Chapter Five turns to administrative reform and the organisation of the Conasupo apparatus under the CMP. Again, the six-year policies of other executives tried to impose administrative reforms at Conasupo without much success. So why should it be different under the CMP? Looking 'inside Conasupo' not only helps to answer this general question but it also provides a useful empirical perspective on the relationship between continuity and discontinuity inside the public sector, a feature of the Mexican system that is intimately connected to patterns of state-society relations.

Notes

[1] President Salinas announced his intention to liberalise the tortilla price on various occasions including October 1989 (*La Jornada* 23 October 1989) and at a press conference 4 July 1990 (*Crónica del Gobierno de Carlos Salinas de Gortari 1988-1994*, 1994). Salinas never discontinued general consumption controls for corn, tortilla or beans, but he liberalised other products, including milk after 1991.

[2] Interestingly, Ochoa discovered that, at that time, Mexico City's business class endorsed a proactive, interventionist policy.

[3] 'Even independent unions would profit', interjected Fidel Velázquez after Conasupo and the CT modified their *concertación* agreement in February 1986 (*El Cotidiano*, 1986: 37). Further, Conasupo documents reveal that official unions in the DFMA captured the lion's share of *tortibonos* under de la Madrid (Conasupo, 1987a).

[4] The reader should be aware that the minimum salary purchased 59.5 kilos of tortilla in December 1987, but the figure declined to a mere 15.8 kilos in May 1991 (Lozano *et al.*, 1991). ECLA (1995: 77) reports that the 'Real Urban Minimum Wage in Mexico' (Average annual indexes, 1990=100) behaved accordingly:

1980: 252.9	1985: 181.2	1988: 136.4	1989: 111.4	1990: 100
1991: 95.8	1992: 90.9	1993: 89.4	1994: 89.6	

With purchasing power falling, 'free tortillas' signified a meaningful handout to lower-income urban households that gained access to this programme.

[5] Before becoming an elected position in 1997, the D.F. mayoral post was a coveted patronage assignment in the PRI's spoils system. According to one account, 'Camacho treated the public unions well with handouts, his rallies were always well attended, especially by the trash collection and public transportation unions' (personal

correspondence with Francisco Zapata, El Colegio de México, 26 September 1996). Camacho's handouts included *tortivales*.

[6] That the CMP's designers thought successful targeting could be achieved via the D.F. mayor and 'delivery by post' reveals the types of problems that confront targeted schemes predicated on a 'predictable' world. It is not too difficult to image why the Mexican postal service was not the most efficient intermediary between Conasupo's Mexico City planners and the urban poor outside the D.F., a population that is highly mobile, often illiterate and often located in informal living arrangements.

[7] Reimbursing *tortillería* owners was straightforward. Each week a Conasupo representative extracted a balance from a machine via a laptop computer and wrote a check to the owner; 'the whole process usually takes five minutes' (Interview, Mexico City, Office of Fidelist, 4 April 1997).

[8] 'We are a special programme within the Diconsa budget', explains a Fidelist administrator (Interview, Mexico City, Office of Fidelist, 4 April 1997). 'The Technical Committee, as the governmental organ of Fidelist, adopted the functions of receiving, analysing and approving, in each case, the activity reports presented by the director of Fidelist on the current spending budget, financial statistics, and rules of operation' (Conasupo, November 1994a).

[9] However, it should be pointed out that the private bank Banamex paid *tortillerías* before 1992, but Conasupo severed ties after citing 'operational irregularities'. Fidelist assumed operations at Banamex's 91 state and 8 regional payment offices. In April 1992, it hired the publicly-owned *Banco Nacional de Comercio Interior* (BANPECO). The official explanation was that it preferred to separate finances from other activities to 'resolve the mentioned problems with Banamex and to improve efficiency and transparency in the process of subsidy transfer' (Conasupo, 1993). However, switching payments from a private bank, where, in theory, activities are accountable to shareholders and market incentives, to a public institution that would be exposed to the political pressures (and 'soft budget constraints') discussed in this book, does not fit a 'neoliberal' logic.

[10] Likewise, Fidelist discontinued the practice of allowing the CT and CNOP to distribute cards in 1993, although communities still had to sign *concertación* agreements with the executive.

[11] Fidelist explains (Interview, Mexico City, Office of Fidelist, 4 April 1997) that processing household applications used to take six months, but by 1993 it dropped to less than a month.

[12] The supervisor of *tortillería* selection notes that 'yes, there is considerable competition among *tortillería* owners for machines... and yes, becoming affiliated can make or break an operation' (Interview, Mexico City, Office of Fidelist, 7 May 1997).

[13] Selection proceeded in three steps: first, local Fidelist agents suggest eligible *colonias* to Mexico City supervisors; second, after selection Fidelist dispenses fliers in the *colonia* and advertises door-to-door; and third, after disseminating information households must register for the programme, and take a socioeconomic means test (Interview, Mexico City, Office of Fidelist, 4 April 1997).

[14] Institutional factors also encouraged a production deficit: price and subsidy policies hurt producers; the Mexican Constitution restricts farm size, subjecting large land-holdings to possible seizure; before 1990, Mexican law prohibited the use of grain (corn, wheat, and sorghum) not produced on-farm as feed grain to protect Mexican grain producers; and dairy farmers could not import grain before 1990 (Nicholson, 1995: 12). Muñoz Rodríguez (1990: 886) blames Mexico's dairy sector problems on its traditional productive system and its failure to develop the potential of tropical zones.

[15] In the mid-1980s Liconsa operated 18 processing plants and de la Madrid boosted fluid milk production by 62 percent (*Excelsior*, 13 June 88).

[16] In the DFMA Salinas supplemented *lecherías* with a home delivery programme where a fleet of Liconsa trucks transported milk to households. Liconsa also utilised community Diconsa stores to deliver milk. Liconsa has and continues to participate in government nutrition programmes through inter-institutional arrangements with public schools and public agencies (INI, DIF and IMSS). Finally, Liconsa traditionally delivered milk across the public sector, to hospitals, nurseries, cafeterias for public workers, Diconsa's Popular Kitchens, and the military.

[17] Ochoa's (1994: 318) case study on Liconsa concluded that 'in 1989 and 1990, the recombination and sale of milk continues to be a mainstay of the State Food Agency, albeit directly targeting the poor'. Here the problems with accepting the government's official packaging, come into focus.

[18] One academic researcher comments, 'Liconsa distribution routes in Mexico City were produced daily, shifting with the electoral landscape' (Interview, Oxford, UK, 12 November 1995). Liconsa's ex-technical secretary to the director of the Milk Programme comments, 'During the Salinas period it was a disaster' (appendix 6.0, respondent No. 4).

[19] It is worth noting that Conasupo was evidently prepared to restructure DFMA operations before Salinas balked at the prospect. A 1993 Conasupo report declares that after ranking *colonias* in the DFMA by socioeconomic criteria, the office of social programmes drafted two new programmes: (i) Criteria for Determining the Maintenance or Elimination of *Lecherías* and (ii) Selecting Establishments (*lecherías* and Diconsa stores) for New Technology (Conasupo, 1993).

[20] The author's view on this subject comes from personal experience. He found himself caught up in a UNAM student riot along *Avenida Insurgentes* in December 1997; a reaction to price increases for milk and metro tickets.

[21] Again, repeating earlier comments on a similar policy concerning the Tortilla Programme, life among the lowest-income urban population is not apt to be 'predictable' enough to make this policy a success. Questions of literacy and the appropriateness of 'targeting the poor via the post' aside, this is not the way households gained access to their milk subsidy card (usually obtained via the CNOP or PRI under de la Madrid), which would present clear obstacles to 'targeting via post' at the local level.

[22] In November 1989 Ignacio Ovalle announced the construction of 62 large Diconsa stores and 2,000 smaller stores for the first half of 1990, where the large stores would be run jointly by 'a representative of the CT' and Liconsa and Diconsa officials (*Excelsior*, 5 November 1989). Economic Assessor of the CTM Porfirio Camarena Castro confirmed,

not surprisingly, official union support for Diconsa policy under Salinas. The 'achievement of Solidarity [Community Stores]', according to Salinas in November 1989, was to maintain the consumption of workers and unions. Ignacio Ovalle and Porfirio Camarena Castro corroborated that President Salinas promised labour unions preferred access to new stores (*Excelsior*, 5 November 1989). In May 1990, Director of Infonavit Emilio Gamboa announced that 250 Infonavit stores had already been constructed, benefiting 610,000 union households (*Novedades*, 28 May 1990). Growth in Infonavit stores, however, levelled off in 1992, and by 1993 Conasupo began closing some stores because they 'served the middle-classes' (Conasupo, 1994b).

5 Administrative Reform under the CMP (1990-1994)

Introduction

This chapter offers an empirical analysis of administrative reforms under the Conasupo *Modernización* Plan (CMP), to examine whether they followed the continuity-discontinuity logic and timetable discovered in Chapters Three and Four. It is conceivable that economic or political events outside Conasupo – for example, the PRI electoral victory in July 1991 – could explain a general policy shift in the management of Conasupo subsidies, without meaningful administrative reform. Were this the case, then it would be expected that a future transformation of the political landscape would invite another politicised recreation of Conasupo.

In discussing administrative reform of the Conasupo bureaucracy, our broader interest in continuity-clientelism and discontinuity-neoliberalism can be viewed somewhat differently. Previously, general 'informality' or a lack of transparency in Conasupo operations helped sustain the old model of clientelism and encourage six-year recreation cycles and a pattern of incremental change toward (but never reaching) 'formality' and transparency. To break this cycle, greater formality, transparency and accountability had to be imposed across the Conasupo bureaucracy. There is evidence that such a process neither occurred as President Salinas entered office nor surfaced under the original CMP. Upon closer analysis, and in a way parallel to earlier discussions, it becomes evident that the Salinas years witnessed a constant tension and interplay between the pressures for informality and formality.

Level One: Administrative Council of Conasupo

- Council President: Secretary of Commerce (Secofi)
- Council Members: Secretaries of Treasury, Budget and Planning, Agriculture, Finance, Executive Chief of Staff and Sedesol (after 1991).

Level Two: Mexico City or Central Office

- General Director of Conasupo
- Technical Office (after 1992)
- Offices of Finance, Planning, Agricultural Marketing, and Legal Council
- Office of Social Programmes (supervised Fidelist until 1992)
- Central Branch Offices or Decentralised Branch Offices (Diconsa, Liconsa, Impecsa, Miconsa, Boruconsa and Fidelist)

Level Three: State or Regional Offices

- State Conasupo Offices
- State/Regional Branch Offices (Diconsa, Liconsa, Impecsa, Miconsa, Boruconsa and Fidelist)

Figure 5.0 The Conasupo System

This analysis of administrative arrangements covers different levels of operations (see figure 5.0). In this respect, two core themes surface in the presentation of empirical data. First, there was regular tension between the Council (level one) and Conasupo policymakers in Mexico City (level two), though it never approached overt conflict. The former exerted pressure for more formality (new monitoring mechanisms, meticulous normative guidelines, formalising recruitment criteria, etc.) while the latter promoted more traditional arrangements. The scope and pace of policy initiatives fluctuated, and it was uncertain whether Conasupo should primarily aid the government's anti-inflation strategy (level one) or fight poverty and redistribute national wealth (level two). At different moments, administrative reforms oscillated between decentralisation and centralisation, and between patronage commitments and neoliberal objectives. Likewise, features characteristic of technocratic/neoliberal administration or principles of private management (competitive awards, labour flexibility, Total Quality Control Management) competed with more customary 'informal' practices. Arguably, this policy incoherence flowed from the fact that Carlos Salinas propounded a reform agenda at odds with itself by sanctioning two antagonistic administrative projects. On the one hand, the executive instructed the Council to modernise the Conasupo bureaucracy in anticipation of structural reforms of the national economy. On the other hand, at Conasupo, Carlos Salinas installed the Ignacio Ovalle-Raúl Salinas team, shrewd *politicos* who were not renowned technocrats (see Chapter Two).

A second recurrent theme in this chapter covers a similar type of tension, between the Council or Mexico City policymakers (levels one and two) and state offices (level three). State offices – what Grindle (1977a) labelled 'personal fiefdoms' – represented a strategic arena for the struggle between informality and formality inside Conasupo. This was an issue that also had clear implications for state-society relations given that the millions of Conasupo beneficiaries and intermediaries typically dealt with local officials. Specific policy proposals precipitate these two tensions, and they are analysed in section one.

Analysis of the informality-formality dynamic also appears in general theorising on the Mexican public bureaucracy, in particular in discussions of recruitment, educational training and technocratic influence over public policy (Centeno, 1994; Smith, 1979; Camp, 1985; Bailey, 1988, 1994). Centeno's well-known 'technocratic revolution from above' synthesises what others imply: neoliberal bureaucratic elites, exemplified by the Harvard-trained Carlos Salinas, manufactured a restrictive bureaucratic environment by coding public policy in technocratic language that in turn circumscribed 'who could participate' and 'who could enter' policy-making circles.[1] Centeno's conception of technocracy belongs amid modern elite theories of political power. Some refer to 'neo-elitist theories' as those that add agenda-setting power and non-decision-making power to empirical-dependent, pluralist-inspired studies devoted to who consummates policy decisions (Bachrach and Baratz, 1962; Cox, Furlong and Page, 1985). Centeno justifies his model by charting who acquired prominent positions in the Salinas administration and stressing their commonalties (education, recruitment, past work experience, etc.). 'The revolution from above', for Centeno, was not a strategy to reorient unilaterally the preferences/interests of those who participate in the political arena; instead it centred on installing the right people in the right jobs, but without rendering traditional politicians obsolete.[2] The success of the Salinas reform agenda often depended on this particular division of labour because unimpeded or 'too much technocratic revolution from above' promised to incite a backlash within traditional bureaucracies as well as the PRI, and, if employed recklessly, could potentially culminate in 'no revolution from above' and a shift in power within the PRI elite to rival, less technocratic groups.

From a different viewpoint, of the multiple relationships forged by politicians, parties and constituencies, access to the bureaucracy is part of a wider practice of clientele reciprocity – as opposed to an ideological or perhaps regional/ethnic bond. In one conception of Centeno's technocracy, Salinas appears as a shrewd politician who created a formula to monopolise access to the bureaucracy, and with it (*vis-à-vis* his rivals within the PRI) the division of the spoils; that is, monopolisitic clientship. Was Salinas exceptional compared to other political leaders outside Mexico who endeavoured to consolidate and secure power? Centeno argues that he was not different, and conveys this message by suggesting that 'the technocratic revolution' was fundamentally a weapon in a civil war raging between antagonistic poles within the PRI. Salinas, by linking recruitment and influence over public policy to technical skills, in some cases subjugated but more typically marginalised individuals within the PRI whose power and career paths were tied to the party – or, members of what Gibson (1997) labels the 'provincial coalition' as opposed to the public bureaucracy.

Section two shows how the Conasupo experience not only lends supportive evidence to Centeno's basic premise on political power, it also adds depth and value to the conception of 'the technocratic revolution' by providing an empirical view below the elite level, probing deeper into the contested terrain of the public bureaucracy. It reveals the *micro* components of a more robust picture of institutionalising 'who could participate', thus clarifying the unknown space between entry-level secretarial posts and Jaime Serra Puche (the main 'revolutionary' in this instance). Specific personnel decisions, as well as restructuring recruitment norms and guidelines, also illuminate a discernible rhythm wherein 'informality' came under renewed pressure from a technocratic/neoliberal agenda.

However, this case study's wider interest in continuity and discontinuity, and this chapter's attention to informality and formality also add a few more reservations to those made by Centeno concerning the probable conclusion and success of 'the technocratic revolution' in Mexico. Centeno's influential work was written around 1992, a period when much discussion centred on President Salinas, 'the actor' who had a coherent blueprint to reorganise radically the Mexican government, and on how members of society would relate to it in the future, that is, state-society relations. When the Salinas project collapsed in December 1994 (discussed in Chapter Six), the constraints that had always influenced Mexican presidents in their management of state-society relations reasserted themselves. Demands for legitimacy, clientele reciprocity, the tacit rules of the six-year cycle, and the costs to insure a measure of 'continuity' during the transition from one PRI administration to the next, combined in a way that called for a more balanced structure-agency framework for general theorising on state-society relations.

Finally, section three explores an ambitious education/retraining strategy of the Council that aimed at institutionalising a new 'bureaucratic culture' among Conasupo employees – arguably an illustration of Centeno's 'revolution' and the Salinas 'blueprint' in a concise but observable context. For the chapter's discussion of bureaucratic culture, it is construed as Conasupo reformers embrace the term: 'general workplace expectations of public employees in addition to the standard expertise or practical training attached to administrative functions' (Conasupo, November 1994b). This definition layers culture with institutional (regularised patterns of expectations) and descriptive (technical skills) qualities, a departure with customary longitudinal references to long-term time horizons and incremental adaptation 'to the body of rules and values that particular societies [or bureaucracies] produce' (Mény, 1993: 149).

Institutional Arrangements and the Tension Between Formality and Informality

This section focuses on four operational procedures that partially overlap and three strategies to improve administrative transparency and accountability. The logic is that the degree of 'informality' in these areas affected the capacity of policymakers to 'recreate' Conasupo, both in October 1989 and thereafter. In figure 5.1, *auditing, planning* and *budgeting* encompass these procedures at central and state offices. *Co-ordination between central and state offices* examines state office reform and steps to reverse PRI clientele networks that thrived under de la Madrid's decentralisation policy. *Tax collection* focuses on the Value Added Tax that the milling industry and private dairy, candy and cattle firms paid to Conasupo. *Inventory* refers to managing reserves of grain, milk powder and other basics. As far as strategies are concerned, *rule/norm making and enforcement* encompass innovations to formalise Conasupo's status in domestic food markets and restrict its operations to a normative or rule creation, surveillance and enforcement capacity. The *participation model* implies the inclusion of beneficiaries in administrative duties, a strategy to open new space for channelling community demands and coercing local agents to improve services (see Chapter Three). Finally, *privatisation* can also be viewed as a strategy to address the general problems of administrative informality.

Figure 5.1 summarises policy innovations that appear in operational manuals, agency memos and annual reports. Cosmetic reforms in the past justify separating *first efforts* and *coherent policy change*. Note that privatisation stands out as the exceptional case due to the prompt auction of Iconsa plants and Conasupers in 1989. At a general level, the lesson from figure 5.1 is that, between 1989-1991, the Salinas administration had not prepared Conasupo for fundamental administrative reform.

Cosmetic Changes at Conasupo: 1989-1991

In October 1990 Jaime Serra Puche acted on behalf of the Council and drafted 80 Conasupo reform targets under the Programme of *Modernización* of Public Enterprises (PMPE). The Council revised the PMPE annually. Because some Council members leaned toward discontinuing Conasupo outright in 1989, examining the PMPE helps ascertain the Council's priorities and general sense of the boundaries or constraints surrounding reform once President Salinas rejected the idea of dismantling Conasupo at the start of his term.

	1988-1989	1990	1991	1992	1993-1994
Auditing, Planning and Budgeting*	NA	NA	FE	FE	FE
Auditing, Planning and Budgeting**	NA	NA	NA	FE	FE
Co-ordinating state and central offices	NA	NA	NA	FE	FE
Tax Collection	NA	NA	NA	**CPC**	**CPC**
Inventory	NA	NA	NA	FE	FE
Rule/Norm Making and Enforcement	NA	NA	NA	FE	**CPC**
Participation Model	NA	NA	NA	FE	**CPC**
Privatisation	**CPC**	**CPC**	**CPC**	**CPC**	**CPC**

*   Central Conasupo Office
** Branch and State Offices

NA	=	*No Action*, or no policy change (traditional 'informality')
FE	=	*First Efforts* at policy change (less 'informality')
CPC	=	*Coherent Policy Change* (more 'formality')

Figure 5.1   Formal Administrative Reforms (1988-1994)

Whereas the 1990 PMPE authorised expeditious privatisation of Iconsa and Conasupers, it produced only minor administrative reforms of traditional Conasupo operations. By the end of 1991 Conasupo had acted on 33 targets, each depicted as 'temporary' or 'subject to reconsideration', apart from the privatisations. In October 1991 the *Annual Conasupo Report*

(Conasupo, 1991) depicted the following as 'significant changes' introduced under the PMPE:

- At the central office, initial measures toward integrating external and internal regulations for human resources, finances, and materials (i.e., *first efforts* to reform the central office).
- The Integral Programme of Orientation and Information for Citizens (i.e., increased basic information on Conasupo programmes).
- Conasupo began to mechanise the registration and control of the central office administrative budget (i.e., *first efforts* to reform the central office).
- 'Exchanged points-of-view' with Boruconsa to formulate and execute the gradual decrease in grain subsidies (concentrated traditional services on corn/beans but no attempt to restructure Boruconsa *per se*).
- Initial discussion concerning guidelines for 'social control' of Conasupo services (i.e., the first official discussion of the participation model).

At the end of 1991 Conasupo also verified that 47 targets – depicted as 'permanent tasks' or 'structural reforms' – required attention from the original 1990 PMPE. Aside from the PMPE, Conasupo policymakers, not the Council, formulated the Programme of Administrative Simplification (PAS) in October 1991. Here the agency prioritised (i) deconcentrating the human resources department, (ii) simplifying standard purchases and sales documents, and (iii) harmonising weight and quality regulations at Boruconsa and Andsa. Generalising on the depth and relevance of these initiatives, performance through 1991 largely amounted to cosmetic revisions. In this respect, policymakers at the Council and at Conasupo put more energy into increasing consumption programmes and generating revenue via privatisations than into administrative reform.

From the outset, the Salinas Conasupo team faced several well-understood obstacles, including some that had to be confronted immediately in order to improve financial coherence. Ignacio Ovalle, for instance, criticised outgoing officials for failing to follow standard operating procedures at state offices and branches (see Chapter Three). Particular displeasure centred on the absence of accurate records of private account balances from the previous presidential term (Conasupo, September 1994;

Excelsior, 5 December 1988) – a clear instance of the traditional 'informality' involved in managing Conasupo.

What postponed administrative reforms until 1992? The reader should be aware that Secofi rather than Conasupo supervised privatisations and also spearheaded modifications in general subsidy and price policies, perhaps the two principal administrative reforms under the CMP. It is therefore difficult to argue that Conasupo policymakers confronted a situation of bureaucratic overload in the area of administrative reform. Further, in the case of the participation model, rough guidelines were given in an introductory handbook for central office circulation in October 1991. Where Conasupo delayed precise guidelines until its new wave of infrastructure expansion had been largely completed (see Chapter Four), the opposite has been observed with Solidarity initiatives. Perea and Moscoso Rodríguez (1995: 35-49) note that in the city of León, Solidarity initiatives like *Escuela Digna* and *Niños en Solidaridad* stipulated meticulous guidelines as early as 1989. They contend that the influence of municipal presidents was marginalised, in 1989-1990, by a detailed, rule-generation process that transpired in Mexico City. García Falconi (1996: 57) found the same to be true with *Mujeres en Solidaridad* in Querétaro. With the Conasupo participation model, Raúl Salinas piloted its advancement into rural areas between 1983-1988 and was responsible for the campaign in urban areas after 1988 (involving Diconsa stores and *lecherías*). Thus, 'practical operational knowledge' was already present. Despite this expertise, Conasupo delayed an official operational plan for state offices and branches concerning the participation model until October 1992 (after Raúl Salinas had left his position at Conasupo), while a monitoring apparatus first appeared in late 1993. Administrative reform or steps toward 'formality' therefore followed, rather than preceded, the wave of new Community Stores and Community *Lecherías* constructed between 1989 and 1991.[3]

Technocratic Reform at Conasupo: 1992-1994

In October 1992 the Council added new targets to the PMPE, and as early as November and December 1992, Conasupo policymakers formulated policy to satisfy 55 targets (37 permanent and 18 temporary). In 1993 the latter proceeded to act on another 36 targets (14 permanent and 22 temporary), and in 1994 an additional 38 targets (8 permanent and 30 temporary). The pace, scope and priority areas that followed as of 1992 all seemed to indicate that policymakers inside and outside Conasupo began reassessing a host of complex administrative issues. The *1992 Annual Report* (Conasupo, 1992) outlined that reforms promulgated between November-December 1992 aimed to accomplish the following:

- Fortify communication between central office and state offices;
- Apply the Programme of Social Control ('participation model') at state offices and branches;
- Compose administrative manuals outlining standard operating procedures at the central office;
- Perform analysis on the appropriate future organisational structure of Conasupo;
- At 32 state offices, create a new system to develop guidelines for obtaining accurate information at warehouses, Diconsa stores, and other state-level operations (Programme to Modernise and Bolster State Offices).

This list of reforms emphasised vertical integration or mechanisms for co-ordinating, monitoring, and normalising interaction between state (level three) and central (level two) offices. As a first step, in 1992 the central office analysed procedures and employment guidelines at state offices in Jalisco, Zacatecas, Tlaxcala, Tamaulipas, and in the DFMA. Where Chapter Four noted reluctance to reform subsidy programmes in the major metropolitan areas, here Conasupo prioritised the DFMA and Jalisco for administrative reform. Conasupo (September 1994) summarises its 1992 events accordingly:

> Conasupo has adopted new norms and procedures through the Programme to Modernise and Bolster State Offices, whose purpose is to design a new organisational model and fortify the capacity of state offices to contribute to institutional objectives and a more efficient use of resources throughout the Conasupo system.

However, it was not until August 1993 that Conasupo produced a manual of norms and procedures at state offices. Furthermore, the overall tone of the

August 1993 report depicts reforming or 'reining-in state offices' as a work in progress.

In 1992 policymakers at Conasupo also amended the PAS. This prompted 16 initiatives between 1992-1994 (4 in 1992, 11 in 1993, and 1 in 1994). In 1993 additional pressure for vertical transparency and standardisation surfaced with the Integral System of Information (discussed below), which largely harmonised disconnected and dysfunctional planning, finance, and budgeting operations across the Conasupo apparatus. In 1994 the PAS led to first-ever operational guidelines for Conasupo's various schemes that fell under the label of Presidential Programmes and Social Assistance, two traditional categories of Conasupo activities that delivered basic goods by arbitrary executive decree.

In April 1992 the Council unveiled the Integral System of Information (SII). SII was an ambitious project designed by private accounting firms hired by the Council to integrate registration procedures for new programme participants, inventory management, standard budgeting procedures, financial planning and regular generation and dissemination of accurate, up-to-date information on all aspects of Conasupo. Figure 5.1 classifies SII as a *first effort* in 1992 for the category *auditing, planning* and *budgeting* because implementation in many areas occurred after October 1992. SII translated into Conasupo's maiden attempt to formulate a comprehensive administrative system, that is, both 'vertical' (the central and state offices) and 'horizontal' (Conasupo and Diconsa, Liconsa, Fidelist, and Boruconsa) integration. By October 1993, SII established new standard operating procedures and integrated approximately 80 percent of the parastatal's operational system. Hence, in the short interval of twelve months, the Council, via SII, rewrote and imposed greater 'formality' concerning how Conasupo functioned, delineated tasks, assessed performance, and monitored or supervised operations and personnel.

The roots of SII sprang from a Council decision to hire the private accounting firm *Arturo Elizundia Charles, S.C.* to audit Conasupo accounts in 1991. External audits had been performed before and critics at the time had legitimate grounds for questioning the autonomy of auditors. Foremost, auditing Conasupo accounts meant probing the affairs of a sitting president's brother, hardly propitious conditions. After consulting with the general director, the firm submitted a summary to the Council prior to a meeting held October 1991. Perhaps significant or indicative of the report's contents, the Council took several unilateral, unanticipated steps in this meeting. For example, it eliminated The Office of Planning and relocated Raúl Salinas to Sedesol, as the co-ordinator of *concertación* for Solidarity. The Council also eliminated The Agricultural Marketing Office and relocated its Director Juan Manuel Pasalagua (Raúl Salinas' brother-in-law) to Sedesol as well. Finally, the Council relocated Director of Miconsa Salvador Giordano to a different post, Sub-secretary of the *Contraloría*, in charge of combating public sector corruption. The Council constructed a new Technical Office (inside the Conasupo general director's office) to manage the tasks traditionally handled by these discontinued offices. Discontinuations, therefore, did not occur because their functions had become redundant but rather as a measure to relocate former directors and centralise operations. The impulse for this bureaucratic reshuffle would seem to have been the report submitted in October 1991.[4]

Table 5.0 Uncollected Value Added Taxes (1988-1991)

Total	($US) 126 million
Wheat millers	($US) 4 million
Conasupo branches*	($US) 35 million
Accumulation of the Value Added Tax from 1988, 1989 and 1990	($US) 45 million
VAT for 1991	($US) 42 million

*Diconsa, Liconsa, Boruconsa and Fidelist
Source: Conasupo (1993)

In practice, to what degree did SII impose formality on Conasupo operations? In pragmatic terms, 1992 marked the first time that one could secure regular and accurate information about Conasupo operations. More than anyone else, the new system aided Conasupo, Sedesol, and SARH policymakers in Mexico City, facilitating tighter control from the centre over decentralised offices. Weekly reports on tortilla beneficiaries, processors, inventory and suppliers, for example, enabled Fidelist to monitor the Tortilla Programme from Mexico City carefully. Conversely, such information was not available under either the *tortibono* (1986-1990) or *tortivale* (1990-1991) schemes. It is also possible to examine how SII precipitated more formal and accountable arrangements with specific groups of traditional Conasupo intermediaries.

For instance, SII applied pressure for transparency in two notable problem areas: *tax collection* and *inventory*. Table 5.0 shows the sources of uncollected Value Added Tax (VAT) revenue; the total of ($US) 126 million equalled 64 percent of Conasupo's outstanding debt total in 1991. Uncollected taxes reveal the traditional informality surrounding Conasupo's business arrangements and amounted to arbitrary subsidies that seemed to favour certain businesses over others (see Chapter Two). In general, as the research by Elizondo (1996, 1993) attests, a culture of lax tax collection has been a political device of the government in the twentieth century. Between April and October 1992 improved tax collection slashed Conasupo's total outstanding account burden by approximately 85 percent (Conasupo, 1993), a figure significant not only for its pecuniary value, but also for the efficacy with which auditors detected and recovered revenue. What explains the aversion of the Salinas Conasupo team (including the Council) to pursuing this action upon arrival in 1988 or later when it crafted the CMP in October 1989? Why utilise privatisation as a strategy to procure money for expanding Conasupo's infrastructure (Diconsa stores, *lecherias*, etc.) when simple fiscal measures would have achieved the same end? The answer was that uncollected taxes involved long-standing political arrangements, and it was not clear until after 1991 that Salinas was willing to improve accountability and transparency to this area.

SII also tightened Conasupo's accounting system under the System of Compensation of Debts, in which individual accounts were updated bimonthly, starting in 1993. Though this marked a step toward coherence in Conasupo's accounts with private firms, nonetheless the system was selective rather than comprehensive. At the end of 1994, it incorporated the newspaper *El Nación*, miscellaneous transport companies, and Liconsa, but excluded Diconsa suppliers as well as other manufacturers such as Maseca and Minsa. Hence, a large degree of informality remained in Conasupo accounting procedures at the end of the Salinas term.

In addition to the partial monitoring of Conasupo's private accounts, beginning in 1992, auditors began examining earlier transactions in order to recoup, where possible, lost revenue. In 1994 investigators scrutinised subsidy payments to wheat millers between 1989 and 1992. The point of contention was whether marketing records of approximately 200 private millers corresponded to the figures they submitted to Conasupo, for the government reimbursed millers on the basis of the quantity distributed at the official price. The process recovered approximately ($US) 3.3 million by August 1994 and the Council estimated that an additional ($US) 45 million remained tied up in the court system as of December 1994 (Conasupo, September 1994).

A comprehensive inventory system for grains and other products, part of SII, commenced in May 1992. Although official government records documented Mexican grain purchases and quantity in storage,[5] Conasupo explained that at Diconsa and other branches no one knew what was purchased, when, and from whom through 1988 (Conasupo, September 1994). SII improved this environment. Further, with subsidy programmes, hereafter policymakers at branches (Diconsa and Liconsa) and the central office (The Office of Social Programmes and Fidelist) accessed weekly information on conditions at individual Diconsa stores, *lecherias*, and *tortillerias*. Likewise, in October 1993 the Council authorised a new physical inventory system in 32 states, which documented Conasupo assets such as equipment for transport, shortage, processing, and distribution. Representatives from the central office as well as external auditors supervised the physical inventory system as a precaution against distorted information reaching Mexico City. Given that this was the first comprehensive account, perhaps it was not surprising that the process encountered a few problems. Hundreds of cars and other vehicles could not be accounted for in the DFMA, for instance.

The Council upgraded Conasupo's internal audit system in 1992. Private firms engineered a modified system (The Annual Control and Audit Programme) that concentrated on inventory/storage, revenue generation, human resources, and tortilla subsidies. It authorised 532 random audits in 1992, which identified irregularities in 244 cases (46 percent). In the same year Conasupo resolved 128 cases (52 percent). By comparison, between

1988-1991 Conasupo's old audit system uncovered 443 cases of irregularities and Conasupo took action on 74 cases (17 percent). Within a one-year span the new system, reliant on private consultants, improved action on reported complaints from a low rate of 17 percent (1988-1991) to 52 percent (1992). This signalled greater formality, yet the fact remained that 48 percent of reported irregularities received no attention. In 1993 Conasupo produced 31 revisions to the audit programme and acted on 246 outstanding cases; interestingly, 225 cases involved accusations against state offices while a mere 21 cases focused on the central office. Here it seems that 1993 saw the exertion of pressure to formalise activities at state offices; nonetheless, the high total of reported irregularities at the end of the Salinas term indicates how far the 'formalisation process' still had to go.

Table 5.1   Official Complaints Regarding Conasupo Activities (1988-1993)

	1988-1991	1992	1993	Total
Received	292	174	222	688
Resolved	181	24	177	382
Not Resolved	111	150	45	306
Percentage of Cases Resolved	62%	14%	80%	

Source: Conasupo (1993); own calculations

In theory the *participation model* would either revamp or construct institutional channels in order to process community petitions and criticism. Normally, the government preferred to channel this dialogue through corporatist intermediaries, which were originally constructed to perform this interlocutory task. However, the CMP gradually channelled dialogue through the new participation model (and sometimes outside corporatist intermediaries). For instance, in 1992, Conasupo received 177 demands and complaints, of which it reported action on 139. In 1993 the Council's efforts became more sophisticated, specialised and transparent after adopting two new programmes: the Programme of Social Vigilance (demand petitions) and the Programme of Complaints and Denouncement of Responsibility (complaints). During 1993 demand petitions experienced a sizeable upsurge (423) over the previous year.[6] Conasupo approved 300 petitions and left 123 pending at the end of 1993, while it received 218 demand petitions and acted on 183 in 1994. In 1993 Conasupo processed 222 complaint petitions from communities.[7] Table 5.1 shows an escalating number of complaints and, in 1993, a high percentage of resolved cases.

Table 5.2 Actions Under Programme of Institutional Supervision

	1992	1993	1994
Tortilla Programme	23,915	23,010	30,130
Purchases	13,131	15,194	13,790
Sectoral Support	17,178	14,425	13,425
Verifying Merchandise	8,477	11,074	14,336
Transporting Merchandise	6,747	8,771	20,089
Sales	2,529	15,916	26,587
PACE (rural marketing programme)	4,789	5,539	9,860
Rural Diconsa Stores	8,788	2,667	688
Milk Programme	4,438	1,344	1,037
Wholesale Distribution (Impecsa)	5,631	1,039	39
Total	95,623	98,979	129,981

Source: Conasupo (1992,1993,1994)

In 1992 the Council also authorised a new institutional scheme, the Programme of Institutional Supervision (PIS), to monitor staff performance across the Conasupo bureaucracy. Table 5.2 charts the development of the PIS between 1992-1994. 'Actions' signified instances where central

Conasupo policymakers and private firms carried out on-site inspections of programmes and evaluated employee performance, but these were not formal audits. Particular attention was given to corn sales to small business and *tortillerías* in Baja California, Baja California Sur, Chihuahua, Sonora, Sinaloa, DFMA, and Yucatán, as well as international points of entry, in particular cross-border trade in wheat and milk in northern states. The PIS marked a conspicuous, post-1991 attempt by the Council to reduce administrative informality at Conasupo; in fact, no comparable effort to monitor operations can be identified before this programme.

The Push for a Transparent Bureaucratic Structure

The Council's general approach to administrative reform at Conasupo centred on the consequences of 'informality' and revealed a view that imprecise, sometimes inappropriate, and largely unenforceable norms and guidelines encouraged sub-optimal outcomes. In the past, faulty 'standard operating procedures' cultivated subversive norms and practices, and inevitably distorted technocratic objectives and workplace expectations. The path forward – according to this actor-centred framework that de-emphasised well-known institutional constraints at Conasupo – called for the meticulous scripting of bureaucratic life to alter the traditional incentive structure. A few examples show the Council's logic vis-à-vis administrative reform.

First, the Council flagged the absence of guidelines as the cause of institutional patronage, excessive bureaucracy/personnel and non-meritocratic recruitment at state offices. For example, no procedures restricted entry into state offices to qualified personnel – in fact, there was no official definition of qualified personnel. In 1993 the Council answered by ordering a position-by-position verification of each post and associated responsibilities, as well as a wave of standard operating manuals.

Second, at the port of Veracruz and at state Conasupo offices in Morelos and Tamaulipas, a series of incidents witnessed Conasupo distributing corn, beans and milk previously designated as 'contaminated' by health inspectors. The Council sought no resignations, but rather demanded that Conasupo formulate a manual to clarify the procedure for disposing contaminated food. Considering the volume customarily handled by Conasupo it was striking that no guidelines existed before 1992.[8]

Third, internal analysis of the *tortibono* programme adopted the framework described above, despite the fact that coupons were distributed through Diconsa stores and corporatist intermediaries. The Council (Conasupo, September 1994) explained:

> The distribution methodology... [with *tortibonos*] did not contemplate clear criteria for the participation of beneficiaries in the programme, leading to errors in the inclusion of families that did not require the subsidy and ... the lack of an active beneficiary list did not permit accurate evaluation of the impact and effect concerning welfare benefits to attended families, nor the calculation of the real cost of the programme.

Problems with the *tortibono* programme are depicted as the failure of policymakers to contemplate, or perhaps render precise, an appropriate selection and monitoring criteria. In the end, imprecise 'rules of the selection game' caused confusion with actors on both sides of the public/private divide, culminating in a sub-optimal use of resources. The Council's framework did not include corporatist intermediaries and party politics, or explain why technocrats failed to verify the beneficiary list. The Office of Social Programmes (Conasupo, November 1994b) offers a parallel assessment:

> Due to the programme's [i.e., *tortibonos*] distribution and sales procedures, it did not permit the establishment of strict controls that would have permitted the agency to know exactly who were the beneficiaries of the programme, and in short measure, whether the benefited population deserved to receive the subsidy.

These passages suggest that reversing the situation called for greater transparency and normative detail. Subsequent analysis of issues such as rural programmes, Diconsa and Liconsa services, the selection of construction contracts by state offices, operations at Boruconsa and Andsa warehouses, payment of account balances and collecting taxes followed the same logic that conceived of *cause* (erroneous guidelines) and *effect* (flawed operations) in isolation of other considerations (party politics, corporatism, etc.).

Year/Manual Description

1993:

- New guidelines at Andsa and Boruconsa warehouses for regularising inventory data – key change, reports produced every 21 days rather than 75 days.
- First manual for outlining procedures of the Tortilla Programme.
- First manual for outlining procedures for the (i) acquisition, (ii) reformulation, (iii) distribution and (iv) marketing of milk powder.
- Manual: General Administrative Norms
- Manual: Norms for Personnel Administration and Institutional Development
- Manual: Norms and Procedures for the Administration of Material Resources and General Services
- Manual: Organisational Manual for State Offices and Defining the General Administrative Language used in the Federal Government.

1994:

- First guidelines for both presidential programmes and social assistance programmes
- Manual: Policies and Guidelines for Acquiring, Renting and Lending of Services Related to Institutional Resources
- Manual: Policies and Guidelines of Public Work
- Manual: Norms for the Implementation, Cancellation and Final Delivery of Institutional Resources
- Manual: Procedural Manual for National Purchases, Sales and Transportation
- First official guidelines for Special Operations, Self-Transport, Railroad Transport and Maritime Transport

Source: Conasupo (1993, 1994)

Figure 5.2 Normative *Modernización* Programme (1993-1994)

One final issue shows the Council's desire to add formality to Conasupo operations at the end of the Salinas term. In November 1993 the Council announced The Normative *Modernización* Programme, an initiative that produced a series of technical manuals. Figure 5.2 outlines this drive to delineate clear boundaries for Conasupo in the marketplace, and to formalise bureaucratic life across the system. One manual – Defining the General Administrative Language used in the Federal Government – went so far as to stipulate the appropriate language that Conasupo policymakers had to adopt when communicating with the federal government (i.e., the Council).

A Strategy of Import Substitution

This section shows how informality and formality featured in recruitment and promotion guidelines at Conasupo's central and state offices. The Council promised deep cuts in Conasupo personnel back in December 1988; however, table 5.3 shows that rationalising the bureaucracy at central and state offices was delayed until 1993. Note that table 5.3 excludes Conasupo's decentralised branches where privatisation likely resulted in greater job losses; however, there is an absence of data to confirm this outcome.

Apart from reclassifying a small number of posts in 1990, it took a May 1991 mandate from the Council to initiate any rationalisation, and within a month Conasupo squeezed 200 positions from the confidential and honorary groups. However, in 1991 the hiring of additional workers offset the impact of reductions and some intermediate/technical positions were simply re-classified as confidential posts. Conasupo recorded further declines in 1993 (11 percent) and 1994 (8 percent). However, the slow reduction in personnel between 1988 and 1992 offers more evidence that coherent administrative reform waited until at least 1992. Moreover, the extent of 'informality' in 1992 is revealed by the fact that Conasupo could not compute the total number of employees in the division of social programmes or within the Tortilla Programme (Conasupo, 1993).

Table 5.4 highlights a simultaneous process of deconcentration amid some movement to downsize the workforce. From 1991 to 1993, reductions at the central office (27 percent) surpassed those at state offices (5 percent). On the one hand, the central office lost roughly 100 high-level personnel between 1991-1993, while on the other hand, state offices gained additional supervisors. Apart from this distinction with supervisory personnel, at both central and state offices, less skilled, middle and lower-level employment decreased and higher skilled, intermediate/technical personnel increased. To some degree, Conasupo entered a period of transition from a patronage based parastatal with low skilled, official union workers to an information based, skill-oriented, and less unionised public agency.

A key feature of this transition was the arrival of intermediate/technical employees at central and state offices in 1990 and 1991. Agency records (Conasupo, 1991) stress the 'professional training' and 'professional work experience' of intermediate/technical employees. In addition to intermediate/technical employees, a supervisory reshuffle at the beginning of 1992 suggested a second, though limited, technocratic shift. María Teresa Ortega replaced Salvador Fano Galindo as general treasurer of Conasupo and Saúl Trejo Reyes replaced Roberto de Alba Herrán as director of finance. Ortega lectured in public finance at the Autonomous Technological Institute of México (ITAM) and was an esteemed IMF consultant. Likewise, although not a technocratic move *per se*, but reflective of a general policy shift in late 1991, Sub-secretary for Work and Social Provision Javier Bonilla García replaced Ignacio Ovalle (starting 1 January 1992) as general director of Conasupo – Ovalle won a seat in the Senate in the 1991 mid-term election.

At the behest of the Council, members of the original Salinas team (Raúl Salinas, Salvador Giordano, Carlos Alamán Bueno, and Manuel Pasalagua Branch) also vacated strategic posts at the beginning of 1992. Arguably, the Council's decision (at a meeting in October 1991) marked a wider policy shift from political capital *a priori* to the pursuit of tentative steps toward reforming the agency; a claim that is supported by at least two other considerations. First, it is apparent that the original Salinas Conasupo team successfully performed their duties between 1988 and 1991, for each was 'promoted' to prestigious public posts during 1992 and 1993. Second, as the emphasis of Conasupo policy switched, Salinas required fresh faces with different skills. Bonilla's political career, for example, was rooted in a corporatist background, whereas the strength of the Ovalle/Raúl Salinas team rested on their experience as executive negotiators in the *concertación* process *with* union leaders. It is important to stress that while Conasupo's personnel progressively adopted a more 'technocratic' or skill-based profile, the second general director was again a *politico* rather than a technocrat, thus maintaining the balance between continuity and discontinuity.

Table 5.3 Central and State Office Personnel (1988-1994)

	1988	1989	1990	1991	1992	1993
Supervisors	451	451	451	451	451	401
Intermediate/Technical	0	0	287	337	361	374
Confidential Workers	1,678	1,678	1,644	1,505	1,562	1,542
Base Workers	1,605	1,605	1,605	1,665	1,665	1,409
Honorary Workers	655	655	402	231	150	13
Total	4,389	4,389	4,389	4,189	4,189	3,739

Source: Conasupo (September 1994)

- *Supervisors* – office and department managers, policymakers (i.e., top-level)
- *Intermediate/Tech.* – statistical analysts and systems managers (i.e., upper-level)
- *Confidential Workers* – non-union, no contract security, better salary than base workers (i.e., mid-level)
- *Base Workers* – union employees, cannot be fired, low salary (i.e., lower-level)
- *Honorary Workers* – 'piece work' employees

Importing Technocratic Norms and Expectations

Although intermediate/technical personnel represented eight percent of Conasupo personnel in 1991, they performed a number of crucial tasks: internal audits and other quality control/monitoring functions, and co-ordinated new statistical planning, inventory and budgeting systems outlined above. Beginning in late 1990, in effect, the Council tried to import private sector experience, skills and workplace expectations via intermediate/technical personnel in order to operate and enforce a new institutional order at Conasupo. Yet this did not coincide with a down-sizing of the Conasupo bureaucracy, a development that shows how the CMP balanced formality and informality.

Table 5.4   Conasupo Employment at Central and State Offices (1991-1993)

	1991	1992	1993	% change
Central				
Supervisors	333	276	236	-29%
Intermediate/ Technical	100	113	173	
Confidential	1,099	927	782	-29%
Base	911	708	582	-36%
Total	2,443	2,024	1,773	-27%
State				
Supervisors	118	125	123	
Intermediate/ Technical	237	247	359	
Confidential	637	642	535	-16%
Base	754	701	633	-16%
Total	1,746	1,715	1,650	-5%
Total	4,189	3,739	3,423	

Source: Conasupo (1991, 1992, 1993)

Salaries for intermediate/technical workers compared favourably with private sector rates; this formed part of the Council's effort to adopt professional employee incentives at Conasupo.[9] An intermediate/technical employee from The Office of Social Programmes notes that 'salaries are good at Conasupo…especially after the second year' (Interview, Mexico City, Conasupo, 4 April 1997). A Fidelist technical analyst gave the same point of view (Interview, Mexico City, Office of Fidelist, 4 April 1997). Both employees possessed university degrees in economics, statistical training and were hired straight from university. A lower, assistant-level employee in The Office of Social Programmes ('confidential worker') commanded a considerably smaller salary but, interestingly, possessed the same economics degree from the same university as the two previous employees (Interview, Mexico City, Conasupo, 24 March 1997). She identified English language skills and perhaps a future masters degree in industrial organisation at the well-known *Colegio de México* to improve her job prospects in the private market, and as a potential path to advancement at Conasupo. Her case implied a significant degree of competition for higher paying, technical positions at Conasupo.

Conasupo personnel was eventually rationalised by means of three strategies. First, confidential, base, and honorary posts were no longer filled after 1991. This accounted for the 200 positions eliminated in May 1991, a further 100 places in August 1992, and 62 posts over the course of 1993 (Conasupo, September 1994). Second, the government furnished a financial package to Conasupo employees taking voluntary retirement. Basically, the government offered a small cash payment (weighted on work experience) and the health and social security benefits of long-term civil servants. Recourse to financial compensation reflected the contractual security of base workers who were guaranteed a job.

The absence of figures on monetary allotments at the central and state offices precludes further examination of the compensation scheme. However, there are data on Conasupo's decentralised branches, which can serve as a rough benchmark. In 1990 the voluntary retirement scheme first surfaced at Conasupo's decentralised branches, with the official justification that it would help prepare factories and Diconsa stores for privatisation.[10] In 1991, 12,219 Diconsa employees accepted voluntary retirement at a cost to the government of ($US) 2.9 million, corresponding to 27 percent of Diconsa's annual budget. At Impecsa 1,744 people accepted the plan, costing the government ($US) 2.8 million. The higher total of workers at branches, compared to Conasupo, is explained partly by the size of Diconsa operations and partly by the high percentage of unionised workers at Diconsa and Impecsa.

A third employment rationalisation process discontinued departments and offices, re-classified job-descriptions, and condensed salary levels. However, at the same time the newly formed Technical Office hired staff in 1991-1992. So alongside pressure for decentralisation – for example, the deployment of new supervisory and technical personnel outside Mexico City – there was a concurrent process to centralise decision-making in Mexico City in the new Technical Office. Article 21 of the first comprehensive organisational manual (Conasupo, 1994a) states:

> The General Director will be assisted by the Directors of Internal Control, the Technical Office in the General Director's Office, Co-ordinator of the Legal Council and other functionaries who all depend on him directly and will be authorised by the Council.

After 1991 the Technical Office gradually exercised control over Conasupo's statistical information as well as budgeting and planning systems. In a further articulation of Conasupo's emerging technocratic division of labour, Article 29.5 of the same document delegates to the Technical Office freedom to act in place of the general director when *concertación* and co-ordinating responsibilities monopolise his schedule. It is the Technical Office, moreover, that acts on Council priorities and, under Article 29.6, delineates mandates to state and branch offices. The Council thus constructed a new channel that, by-passing the general director would usher in reform. In fact, by empowering the hand-picked Technical Office, the Council formulated a structure in which technical reform (discontinuity) remained in the hands of technocrats and *concertación* (continuity) remained in the hands of *políticos*.

Transparency in the Employment Pyramid

Formalising bureaucratic life during 1993 and 1994 also led to a transition in the profile of Conasupo's occupational pyramid. In 1993 Conasupo harmonised the supervisory-level salary structure, for the first time rendering explicit suitable job experience and technical skill training for future employment and advancement consideration. In 1993 the Council exerted further pressure at the top through other administrative reforms, above all, mandating the complete documentation of expenses (for the first time) by all supervisory-level employees. In 1993, the Council also assured that 'professionals' would perform monitoring tasks and control new operating systems by decreeing that central and state Conasupo offices could only employ private firms from a pre-approved list provided by the Council.

Table 5.5 Evolution of Salary Levels and Job Categories (1988-1993)

Year	Confidential		Base		Inter./Technical	
	Levels	Categories	Levels	Categories	Levels	Categories
1988	19	45	15	58	0	0
1989	19	45	15	58	0	0
1990	16	40	15	67	5	11
1991	9	27	18	48	5	11
1992	9	27	18	48	5	11
1993	6	27	9	31	5	11

Source: Conasupo (September 1994)

Likewise, parallel with a trend in private sector labour markets, temporary contractual agreements rather than permanent union-affiliated contracts were more common after 1992. Restructuring job descriptions of confidential, base and intermediate/technical personnel began in 1991 (see table 5.5); however, 1993 marked a key juncture in this reclassification process, as different salary levels for confidential and base employees were harmonised (base salary levels declined from 18 to 9). Policymakers felt that reducing the categories of base workers realigned workplace expectations and responsibilities of this group with confidential employees. Institutionalising labour flexibility unfolded according to a specific discourse that accentuated professionalism as the path to upward mobility. The Council did not, however, challenge the legitimacy of the Conasupo bureaucracy or induce excessive job losses among the workforce that did not fit this profile. In part, this development shows how the 'technocratic revolution from above' unfolded in this particular context, where the Council ('the revolutionaries') had to maintain at least a partial balance between continuity and discontinuity given the policy goals and bureaucratic appointments of President Salinas.

This discussion in this chapter shows that an initial commitment to bureaucratic downsizing failed to materialise before 1992-1993, and was only partially implemented thereafter. When Salinas left office, the Conasupo workforce had decreased by 22 percent, with most cuts coming in 1993 and 1994. Institutional factors partially explained government reluctance to downsize. In 1988, base workers represented 37 percent of the workforce and contractual obligations complicated scaling back their numbers. Likewise, Conasupo had to hire supplementary, appropriately skilled employees. In 1990-1991, Conasupo hired 337 intermediate/operative workers, a total that surpassed the number of vacated and unfilled posts in the same period. Skipping ahead to 1992, 1993 and 1994, the scope of reform shifted as measures to rationalise the occupational pyramid marked a step toward constructing a meritocratic, norm-based, and transparent employment regime. In large part, the intention was to redefine the 'rules of the game' for future bureaucratic recruitment and advancement by balancing transparency where only ambiguity previously existed. By linking job responsibilities to sophisticated, statistical forms of analysis, the Council circumscribed the pool of potential entry and upwardly mobile candidates to individuals with technocratic or professional backgrounds.

Managing Transition Costs and Down-Sizing

Conasupo's experience offers another lesson: to avert a political backlash over job losses at long-running, public bureaucracies, reformers may profit from at least token financial compensation to threatened groups. Nineteen Conasupo unions from across the Republic mobilised and converged on Mexico City on 23 November 1989. Protests lasted several days and angry employees blocked streets as well as the entrance to the Chamber of Deputies. Events and employee perceptions of the CMP incited union frustration. Whereas a degree of ambiguity has always been customary in back-room corporatist deal making, in this case Conasupo union leaders obviously felt deceived. From their perspective, Ignacio Ovalle had assured the relocation of all union members a month earlier in a *concertación* agreement with Diconsa union leaders. This deal facilitated a propitious environment for the scaling back of traditional Conasupo functions without precipitating a worker backlash, according to the unions.

Implementation of reform posed a different reality, however. In late October and early November 1989 the government closed 14 urban Diconsa stores, resulting in 220 job terminations and the relocation of a mere four employees. Furthermore, the government scheduled another 126 store closures for December 1989, jeopardising 1,400 union jobs. Antonio Herrera, Diconsa union president in Michoacán, declared that 25,000 CTM-affiliated jobs were in jeopardy if the government continued to close urban stores as scheduled in 1990. He also predicted labour unrest over the issue.

Various union presidents – Crisóforo García (D.F.), Antonio Herrera (Michoacán), Alfredo Zúñiga (Veracruz), Hipólito Vicente Anselmo (Oaxaca), and Refugio Ocampo (Puebla) – also outlined a strategy to stop the threat to 19 Conasupo unions in 1990. First, the group solicited the assistance of Jesús Lozano, president of the FSTSE (a major public employee union). Second, the Diconsa unions tabled an alternative plan to unilateral privatisation and store closures based on renewed dialogue with unions and construction of new stores in marginal areas.

Co-ordinated union mobilisation dissipated after the protests of November 1989, although spontaneous protests by beneficiary groups continued. Perhaps instrumental to this was the fact that, whereas the potential for a sizeable labour response existed, given a reservoir of union workers across the Conasupo system, no degree of unified action materialised in late 1989. The absence of layoffs at central and state offices provides a partial explanation for this. Moreover, Liconsa operations and personnel increased to keep pace with the investment in the Milk Programme while Boruconsa and Impesca employment remained stable between 1988-1992. Together these factors isolated Diconsa from the rest of the Conasupo system.

Diconsa possessed the largest contingent of threatened workers and was the obvious loser in the initial phase of the CMP. Here demobilisation after November 1989 requires another explanation. One element that influenced Diconsa unions was the first wave of store construction in marginal and rural areas in 1990, which added a degree of legitimacy to a promise to relocate and not discontinue Diconsa. But equally important was managing the issue of financial compensation. The gradual dismissal of 25,000 CTM-affiliated Diconsa workers over the course of 1990 posed a potential political obstacle. Opposition members in the Chamber of Deputies welcomed a surge in worker mobilisation in November, albeit for contrasting reasons. The PRD never endorsed Conasupo privatisations. The PAN, an advocate of privatisation in general, nonetheless opposed a PRI-led auction of public assets.[11]

Beyond party politics, Diconsa workers had the potential to galvanise public opinion: given the concentration of its infrastructure in the DFMA, Diconsa could symbolise a social welfare agency that enjoyed popular support among low-income Mexicans (notably in the DFMA). Accounts of the CTM-led mobilisations in November 1989 note the presence of vocal *amas de casa* (housewives) drawn from around Mexico City, who were concerned about their traditional food subsidies. Against this backdrop, the financial compensation package emerged, which was not mentioned in the original CMP. For the Diconsa workers, the payoff amounted to a palliative rather than a financial boon; nevertheless, an added incentive was in place to accept what was understood as inevitable reforms.[12]

Constructing a New Bureaucratic Culture, Workplace Expectations

The previous section examined how innovations would influence future recruitment and mobility at Conasupo; however, it was also recognised that the existing labour force was not scaled back in great numbers. In a sense, this represented the need to balance continuity and discontinuity. This raises an interesting administrative dilemma, however: what to do with a Conasupo labour force that was steeped in the norms (clientelism, informality, etc.) of the 'old model'? The Council's reaction merits careful examination. It authorised an ambitious education/training campaign that was intended to culminate in a homogeneous base of knowledge ('the technocratic revolution'), the bedrock of a new bureaucratic culture at Conasupo. In this final section, the goal is to clarify how policymakers understood the relationship between administrative formality and informality, yet without drawing a final conclusion on its eventual impact. This discussion lends a more qualitative level of analysis of the specific steps to reorient the workplace expectations and the informal institutions that structure bureaucratic life.[13] Could the Council reorient the existing Conasupo labour force to obey a new set of workplace institutions? Were this the case, it would offer an alternative to privatisation and add depth and scope to the notion of a 'technocratic revolution from above'.[14]

Conasupo summarised the underlying objectives for its education/retraining campaign accordingly:

> To instil the appropriate organisational elements that introduce schemes to elevate employee knowledge/skill, service quality, and workplace excellence; *to facilitate a change in the administrative culture* and to improve the office environment (Conasupo, September 1994... emphasis added).

In this context, a skill deficiency was viewed as paramount. Reformers conceptualised the Conasupo bureaucracy as a market of individuals requiring investment in human capital, and, in the process, they neglected or assumed away other considerations associated with party politics, past recruitment patterns and the expectations of Conasupo's intermediaries and final beneficiaries.

Before 1991 job training had been rare at Conasupo. However, a multitude of courses, seminars, and workshops on Total Quality Control Management (TQCM) appeared in The Preparation Programme (1991) and its ambitious successor The Preparation, Productivity and Motivation Programme (1992-1994). In the past many employees entered into Conasupo posts at the beginning of a *sexenio*, sometimes with no employment history at the agency or any coherent job orientation.[15] Executive-appointed supervisory personnel posed a particular dilemma.

The *1991 Annual Conasupo Report* (Conasupo, 1991) remarks,

> The quality of the services that Conasupo offers depends on the qualifications and attitudes of employees. For this, The Preparation Programme in 1991 represents a supportive, complementary instrument in the *modernización* process initiated at Conasupo. Internal and external instructors offer courses oriented toward improving employee knowledge and dexterity, which will contribute to the efficient development of worker skills needed to achieve entrusted tasks.

Table 5.6 aggregates the number of events (courses, seminars and workshops), hours of instruction, and participants; unfortunately, the absence of data precludes an analysis of 1991. Education/retraining events potentially introduced TQCM concepts to the entire workforce in 1993-1994. Of course, crude averages hide the distribution across the labour force. For instance, some reports indicate that events concentrated on central office supervisors in 1991. On the other hand, in the next two years the pattern switched to personnel at state offices. In a three-year period 11,350 Conasupo employees attended 906 TQCM-related events, or 21,580 hours of instruction. By any standard in the public or private sector, what transpired at Conasupo between 1992-1994 amounted to a significant infusion of technical training.

Table 5.6   **The Preparation, Productivity and Motivation Programme (1992-1994)**

Year	1992	1993	1994	1992-1994
Number of Events	242	369	295	906
Hours of Instruction	7,358	8,294	5,928	21,580
Total Participants	2,348	4,891	4,111	11,350
Hours per Employee	1.76	2.22	1.73	5.71
% of Workforce	56%	131%*	120%*	

* In other words, some employees participated in multiple forums.
Source: Conasupo (1992, 1993, and 1994); personal calculations

The intellectual quality or rigour of these events deserves separate comment. The Council employed respected sources to design, deliver, and monitor the transference of information to Conasupo staff. Events often corresponded to a university-level business or statistical course, where university professors gave weekly courses over a period of months. Alternatively, others simulated an intensive, short-term schedule that is common in the private sector. A strong collaborative presence of the

Instituto Tecnológico y Estudios Superiores de Monterrey (ITESM) illustrated the first type of arrangement while private business and consultants – for example, the South African technology firm *Informática Mexicana, Consultoría y Diseño*, customer service consultant *El Premio Nacional de Calidad*, and private accounting firm *Arturo Elizundia Charles, S.C.* – illustrate the second category. The calibre of instruction thus compared favourably with private sector or top-flight university training.

Table 5.7 provides a description of the education/retraining campaign. Titles of courses reveal much about the nature or inspiration behind this project. In 1991, still undeveloped and tentative (for example, ITESM had not been hired), the campaign centred on a handful of Mexico City supervisors. However, note the following passage, on The Preparation, Productivity and Motivation Programme, from the *1992 Annual Conasupo Report* (Conasupo, 1992).

> The programme gradually incorporates diverse total quality control courses with the objective to implant in the medium term an integrative programme on the material... the programme first emphasises technical courses for supervisory employees and later introduces the same knowledge, management concepts, techniques and tools of total quality control across the organisation ... in parallel form, there are in place other courses focused on operative-level employees [i.e., base and confidential employees] with the objective of establishing a basis for a change in attitude that would permit the organisation to achieve a higher level of service quality.

In 1992 the Council solicited the services of ITESM, the intellectual spring for technical instruction in Mexico. It developed, taught, and monitored (e.g., follow-up testing) courses for Conasupo employees such as New Key Aspects of a Quality Work Environment and Contemporary Ideas on Total Quality Control. In 1992, besides ITESM, the Council enlisted the services of other academics at regional universities for collaborative projects, all of which was new to standard policy at Conasupo.

Improvements in the general skill-level of Conasupo employees were a point of emphasis. For instance, a course in Basic Culture introduced all employees to rudimentary concepts of information technology in a context that underscored its relevance for future office performance. ITESM customised courses for staff to anticipate new monitoring, budgeting and planning systems, themselves the foundation of the TQCM framework under construction. Before the 1992 launch of The System of Supervision and Programme Evaluation, the Council enrolled 162 central and state Conasupo office supervisors and 74 Boruconsa supervisors in an intensive ITESM preparatory course. Instruction was customised to suit the collection, processing and analysis of statistical data fundamental to this new programme. In general, information-related material formulated an integral part of the education/training campaign. In 1992, 149 of the 242 events covered information-related material: introductory computer knowledge and internet access, basic statistical analysis, and inter- and intra-governmental information networks.

The collaborative role of ITESM in the campaign intensified in 1993 and 1994. The aim continued to be the dissemination of TQCM doctrine and 'thus to continue extending the information culture to support the automation of the agency's processes' (Conasupo, 1993). ITESM spearheaded two sub-programmes in 1993. First, The Special Technical Preparation Subprogramme (STPS) organised a series of courses and workshops to educate personnel on special areas of Conasupo operations. STPS encouraged employees to participate in university seminars, conferences and research projects pertaining to public administration in addition to specific areas such as the transport and storage of agricultural goods. Overall, the STPS organised 115 events or 3,372 instruction hours, with 1,301 employee participants (844 central office, 457 state offices), of which there were 274 supervisors, 258 intermediate/technical, 363 special operatives (i.e., specialised tasks, for example, health inspectors), 178 secretarial, and 228 administrative support staff. Despite the fact that events favoured Mexico City staff, 31 percent of participants corresponded to secretarial and administrative support, that is, the lowest-level bureaucratic posts. To some degree, therefore, the TQCM philosophy had the potential to trickle down beyond the strata of rule makers and enforcers to those who 'followed the rules' and performed basic tasks, delivered goods, and received and dispensed information to the public.

Second, The Subprogramme of Total Quality Control (STQC) arranged 82 events or 1,268 instruction hours, with 2,096 employee participants (339 central office, 1,757 state offices), with 284 supervisors, 491 intermediate/technical, 710 special operatives, 295 secretarial, and 316 administrative support staff. State offices accounted for 84 percent of participants, hence the transmission of the TQCM philosophy stretched beyond Mexico City. Again, by incorporating lower-level employees this programme achieved a level of comprehensiveness. The STQC required that state office directors and their department managers attend an ITESM course in Contemporary Ideas on Total Quality Control; the same course was furnished to Mexico City supervisors in 1991-1992. For middle management and lower-level personnel, ITESM developed a modified course – For a Quality Environment at Conasupo. The *1993 Annual Conasupo Report* provides additional details of the STQC.

> Part of these two courses calls upon the selection of two employees from each state office and managerial department to act as Total Quality Promoters, a position that requires an individual to attend a course entitled Formation of Total Quality Promoters at Conasupo (Conasupo, 1993).

Total Quality Promoters performed an interlocutory function and constituted an information channel running from state offices to ITESM co-ordinators. This enabled ITESM to supervise its ongoing experiment in administrative reform. Furthermore, to assure that Conasupo employees grasped TQCM material, in what ITESM labelled a 'medium term education/training process' rather than a one-off exercise, it collaborated with Conasupo supervisors and department managers from 8 state offices on a motivational course – A Better Future (Conasupo, 1993). Instead of technical training, it presented a broad framework for why employees ought to embrace the model being introduced. In effect, it formulated a functional argument conceptualising public sector management in general and Conasupo in particular, as integral for future economic, political, and social development in Mexico.

Table 5.7   The Preparation Programme (1991) and the Preparation, Productivity and Motivation Programme (1992-1994)

1991

- Courses in fiscal management, inventory and warehouse control, secretary management, civil protection and hygiene and security in the workplace: *intermediate/technical and confidential workers*
- Courses in information generation, workplace accountability, statistics, administration and technical marketing: *supervisory workers*

1992

- 19 courses, including (i) New Key Aspects of a Quality Work Environment and (ii) Contemporary Ideas on Total Quality Control: *supervisory, intermediate/technical and confidential workers*
- Additional courses included (i) Advanced Public Administration, (ii) A Contemporary Programme of Public Administration, (iii) Material Resource Management and (iv) Quality in Public Service: *intermediate/technical and supervisory workers*
- Events in basic secretarial skills, accounting, supervision, quality control, logistics and transport, and planning: *all employees*
- Training course to introduce The System of Supervision and Programme Evaluation: *Conasupo supervisors* (162) and *Boruconsa employees* (74)
- Four modules to disseminate new information material: (i) Contemporary Methods, (ii) Network Administration, (iii) Basic Culture, and (iv) Development: *all employees*

1993

- Special Technical Preparation Subprogramme (STPS): *all employees*
- Total Quality Control Subprogramme (STQC): *all employees*
- Information Culture: *all employees*

1994

- Four subprogrammes: Procedural Updating, Special Technical Preparation, Basic Skills, and Preparation for Attending to the Public: *all employees*
- Course in the information preparation programme for Conasupo personnel: *all employees* ('Basic Culture') and *intermediate/technical* (other subprogrammes)

Source: Conasupo (1991, 1992, 1993, 1994)

By 1994 the campaign centred around four subprogrammes: Procedural Updating, Special Technical Preparation, Basic Skills, and Preparation for Attending to the Public. Procedural Updating scripted norms and procedures of primary functions at Conasupo and aimed to establish precise job descriptions for supervisors to evaluate and monitor future employee, office, and department performance. Special Technical Preparation organised a series of courses:

- Storage and Conservation of Grains and Seeds
- The New Law of External Marketing and its Regulations
- Custom Laws 1994
- Forms of Payment and International Marketing
- Control of Quality Statistics in Production
- Aspects of Corporate Finance
- Payroll Management
- Quality Cash Flow Auditing

Basic Skills increased state-level education/training by diffusing the ITESM course in Contemporary Ideas on Total Quality Control to additional employees. Preparation for Attending to the Public professed to 'sensitise employees to the needs of clients' (Conasupo, 1994b). It introduced perspectives on customer service and a private sector, consumer-oriented ethos. The private firm *El Premio Nacional de Calidad*, to cite one example, ran a customer service course in 1994. Although government subsidies were not consumer-driven *per se*, Conasupo nonetheless adopted private-sector marketing techniques. It collected socioeconomic, consumption and regional data on client communities, utilised private advertisement consultants to broadcast product information via radio and TV, and regularly surveyed consumer preferences and complaints (Interview, Mexico City, Office of Fidelist, 4 April 1997).

In sum, after Conasupo policy shifted at the end of 1991 and the Ovalle-Salinas team had exited, reformers launched a far-reaching campaign to alter workplace expectations in conjunction with the formal measures outlined in the previous section. At one level, education, training and clarification of tasks and skills became part of a larger enterprise to link Conasupo employees to larger issues of political, economic and social development in Mexico. At another level, an apparent normative assumption about a linkage between workplace expectations and employee skills seems to lay beneath the entire education/training policy.

Summary: Administrative Reform and Constructing a New Bureaucratic Culture at Conasupo

In conclusion, discussing administrative reforms under the CMP points to a few central issues related to the timing of initiatives and the general balance struck between informality and formality (and between continuity and discontinuity). This chapter completes the analysis of the CMP, and the findings above need to be seen in conjunction with earlier observations on consumer and producer subsidies.

Consistent with Chapters Three and Four, the start of a coherent commitment to neoliberal/technocratic administrative reform did not follow the Salinas Conasupo team into office in December 1988 or feature under the original CMP in October 1989. In fact, the evidence suggests that Conasupo policy management under Salinas should be depicted in two phases, roughly before and after the 1991 mid-term election. In the former, the promise of neoliberal/technocratic administrative reform never gained momentum, as Conasupo rapidly increased its subsidy coverage. In the latter, the Council not only endeavoured to impose a strong degree of formality through manuals, guidelines, private audits, etc., but it also sought to construct a new neoliberal/technocratic bureaucratic culture through an ambitious education/retraining scheme. This suggests that the CMP unfolded according to a populist/clientelistic rather than neoliberal timetable.

A common thread runs through Chapter Five: the interplay of informality and formality, a tension that relates directly to earlier discussions of 'recreations' at Conasupo. The profile of administrative reforms reconfirms a familiar trend, that the CMP caused incremental change rather than the radical innovation promised at the beginning of the six-year cycle. Familiar budgetary and distributional constraints on policymakers (and on 'the technocratic revolution') produced a balance between continuity and discontinuity. In this sense, the CMP prompted an ambitious retraining scheme yet avoided firing the existing Conasupo labour force; it adopted sophisticated monitoring schemes yet maintained traditional, *politico*-managed *concertación*; and it empowered technocrats via the new Technical Office yet maintained the interlocutory role for *politicos* (Ovalle and later Bonilla). In this last case, the CMP established that future Conasupo management would mix formality (the Technical Office would monitor Conasupo activities) and informality (the executive-appointed general director would monitor *concertación*). Whether this balance of continuity and discontinuity at the end of the Salinas years carried over into the Zedillo term is the subject of Chapter Six.

Notes

[1] Bailey (1994) and Torres (1996) offer comparable arguments on Sedesol and the Solidarity project. However, it is not being suggested that Centeno's framework for the study of elite control of both the state apparatus and policy arena is particular to Mexico. A long tradition of scholarship on bureaucracy notes that late nineteenth and early twentieth-century movement toward merit-based recruitment in Europe assured pre-existing recruitment from privileged backgrounds and certain universities (Smith, 1989: 226-234).

[2] The initial Salinas cabinet, for example, included '*burócratas políticos*' such as Fernando Gutiérrez Barrios (Gobernación), Jorge de la Vega Domínguez (Agriculture), Arsenio Farrell (Labour), Manuel Bartlett (Education) and Carlos Hank González (Tourism). In one expression of the 'the technocratic revolution', later in the term Hank González, the archetypal *politico*, could serve as Secretary of Agriculture, the spokesperson and intermediary for the executive, while an empowered and tight circle of technocrats like Luis Téllez and Jaime Serra Puche could orchestrate and reform agricultural policy (Grindle, 1995). Below we want to explore whether the Ovalle-Raúl Salinas team (*políticos*, continuity) and Jaime Serra Puche (technocrat, discontinuity) followed this pattern. On this division of labour inside the Salinas administration, see Centeno (1994: 141-142) and Centeno and Maxfield (1992).

[3] The timing and assertiveness regarding formal guidelines reveals one area where creating new social programmes and reforming old ones follow different paths. With Solidarity, the goal was to define operations in such a way that often excluded local actors (including locally elected politicians from the PRI, PRD and PAN). By contrast, with Conasupo the goal was to maintain a degree of informality so that local-level relationships could influence the direction of policy.

[4] The reader should be aware that on 11 October 1996 the PGR authorised the arrest of Raúl Salinas (already in prison at the time), Salvador Giordano and Juan Manuel Pasalagua for defrauding the government between 1988 and 1992. In part, the PGR's case was based on these earlier private audits.

[5] A 1996 Conasupo report on grain imports before 1993 notes that 'it was not possible to verify the records from earlier years completely' (Conasupo, October 1996). In other words, Conasupo performed only loose documentation of its imports before 1993.

[6] There were 164 petitions for future installation of *lecherías*; 161 for future installation of Diconsa stores; 75 corresponded to the central office in reference to future incorporation into the Tortilla Programme, donations of corn, and payment of harvests and emergency relief; 20 concerned Boruconsa services; 2 concerned Miconsa services; and 1 concerned Impecsa services.

[7] There were 81 petitions concerning Diconsa; 46 concerning Impesca; 45 concerning the central office and the Tortilla Programme; 33 concerning Liconsa; and 17 concerning Boruconsa.

[8] It is worth mentioning that the congressional investigation into the matter of contaminated grain concluded that it re-entered the Mexican market in large part because Conasupo employees sold it to cattle ranchers for profit. Another contributing factor was functional, a product of Conasupo's decentralised structure. State offices are, above all, instructed to resolve problems locally and avoid embarrassing policymakers in Mexico City. In one well-known case, contaminated beans landed on the local market when a state office feared shortages after a poor harvest. Interestingly, this state received the beans from a second state office that knew them to be contaminated, yet passed them on to avoid incurring the financial loss, thus transferring the problem to another state office.

[9] Varley (1996: 219) observes that Salinas raised salaries in the traditional land-titling bureaucracy as an 'anti-corruption' policy.

[10] In practice, it should be stressed that both Conasupo and decentralised branches requested funds from the Treasury Ministry, a member of the Council. Therefore, an outside source, not Conasupo, ultimately dictated the pace and scope of voluntary retirement.

[11] The centre-right opposition criticised actors who guided the process, in particular Jaime Serra Puche's penchant for secrecy in selecting private owners. In March 1990 a boiling point seemed to be reached when Serra Puche announced that the foreign multinational firm Anderson and Cleyton had purchased an Iconsa cooking oil plant responsible for 70 percent of Mexican consumption. A week earlier Serra Puche had addressed the Chamber and proclaimed the plant to be in the national interest and not open for private ownership.

[12] It should be pointed out that my interviews with high-level Diconsa employees indicate that these workers relocated quite easily into other public or private employment in 1990. For example, although Fidelist officially took over the Tortilla Programme in 1992, Conasupo started assembling personnel in 1990, with supervisory personnel often switching over from Diconsa (Interviews, Mexico City, Office of Fidelist, 22 April 1997).

[13] Appendix 6.0 provides a 1997 survey of the views of Conasupo employees.

[14] It must said that, by privatising, the government advances no closer to the normative state apparatus that the neoliberal model requires to monitor, disseminate data, and formulate neutral rules-of-the-game. Even the intransigent neoliberal acknowledges an obligation to build public sector capacity alongside measures that reduce its encroachment in the marketplace. Discussing New Right reforms in Venezuela, Mexico and Peru, Philip

(1992b: 465) comments, 'New Right approaches are surely far more dependent on appropriate public administrative structures than many of their advocates believe'.

[15] Conasupo's quality control staff (i.e., health inspectors) presents an interesting case. Their first formal job training occurred in 1991; similarly Conasupo initiated a first-time preparative training course for incoming quality control staff in 1992.

6 Conasupo and Social Welfare Policy (1994-1997)

Introduction

On 1 December 1994 another PRI president, Ernesto Zedillo, entered office and initiated the latest six-year cycle in Mexican state-society relations. Although President Zedillo possessed a legitimate electoral mandate, an unprecedented economic crisis soon confronted his administration. By the second week of December, a minor peso adjustment by new Finance Minister Jaime Serra Puche sparked a currency exodus. The social repercussions of the crisis have been astonishing. In December 1994 alone the government estimates that job losses topped 460,000 (Osorio Goicoechea, 1996). One study calculates that Mexican poverty jumped from 45.2 to 56.7 percent of the population between December 1994 and late 1995 – and, more dauntingly, that eight consecutive years of 7 percent GDP growth is required to return Mexico to 1994 poverty levels (Garduño Ríos and González Vega, 1998).

This chapter discusses whether and to what extent the old timetable, constraints and 'recreations' have featured in Conasupo policy in the first half of the Zedillo term. Because an initial crisis occurred in the six-year cycles of de la Madrid and Salinas, on the surface there is a measure of continuity linking 1983, 1989 and 1995. Admittedly, the chapter is often speculative and offers general caution in certain areas rather than firm conclusions. However, the initial context for policymaking invites reflection on broader issues of continuity and discontinuity in state-society relations. Has Conasupo generated political capital for Zedillo? More importantly, Chapters Three, Four and Five found that the Conasupo *Modernización* Plan (CMP) produced incremental rather than the promised neoliberal, technocratic alternative, and did not preclude the possibility of another recreation. Has this occurred under Zedillo?

The chapter is organised in two sections. The first offers a general discussion of Conasupo policy in the first half of the Zedillo term. Contrary to initial speculation, unlike Solidarity, the implosion of the Salinas project did not spell the end of Conasupo. This points to a degree of continuity between the Salinas and Zedillo terms and reconfirms the argument made at the beginning of this book that different constraints surround episodic executive programmes (Solidarity) and traditional programmes (Conasupo). However, there has been a number of important policy shifts, and in a way parallel to the CMP, these must be analysed carefully to separate the new from the old.

The second section analyses the formative process that led to the launch of the Programme of Health, Education and Nutrition (Progresa) in August 1997. Progresa is Zedillo's signature social welfare initiative and its development can be traced back to Conasupo policymakers. Progresa attempts to 'bundle' traditional social welfare resources for education, health and nutrition. The earlier conclusions on the CMP coupled with the general discussion of Zedillo's initial management of Conasupo, invite the question: if constraints prevented effective 'targeting' before and under the CMP why should we believe 'bundling' under Progresa is different? The evidence in this chapter suggests that there may be reasons to be cautious.

Ending an Irreconcilable Relationship

To preface this general discussion of Conasupo policy during the first half of the Zedillo term, a quantitative sketch clarifies a situation that some mistakenly depict as Conasupo 'withering on the vine' or 'completely privatised' (*La Jornada*, 13 May 1997). Table 6.0 shows two countervailing tendencies: (1) increases in consumption services and (2) decreases in intervention in grain markets. The number of households in the Tortilla Programme climbed 22 percent and the average quantity distributed increased 33 percent from 1995 to 1996 (Conasupo, 1997). To be sure, growth rates for Liconsa, Diconsa and Fidelist do not match the initial Salinas years; nonetheless, in Zedillo's first year in office Diconsa constructed approximately 1,000 new stores, and by 1996 it subsidised around 30 million consumers (roughly equivalent to 1988). Similarly, in 1995 Liconsa constructed 1,288 *lecherías*, and by 1996 it delivered milk to

5.1 million children and 200,000 adults in urban areas. As late as May 1997, Conasupo policymakers believed that the government had no immediate plan to curtail the expansion of consumption infrastructure; moreover, it was suggested that the trend under Zedillo was to locate Diconsa infrastructure nearer to urban markets (Interview, Mexico City, Office of Fidelist, 4 April 1997). Recently, *Proceso* (4 April 1999: 7) reported that, in 1998, Diconsa operations covered 24 million rural beneficiaries and 9.8 million urban beneficiaries (a significant rise in urban areas compared to 1994).

Table 6.0 Conasupo Activities between 1994-1996

	1994	1995	1996*
CONSUMPTION			
Daily Milk Distribution (1itres)	3,421,000	3,419,000	3,476,000
Lecherias	6,296	7,584	7,331
Children Participants (milk)**	4,906,000	5,244,000	5,192,000
Daily Tortilla Distribution (tonnes)	1,351	1,225	1,806
Households (tortilla)	2,103,000	2,301,000	2,804,000
Diconsa Rural Stores	19,564	20,553	21,032
Diconsa Urban Stores	1,074	1,061	961
Diconsa Rural Consumers	24,867,000	26,494,000	27,330,000
Diconsa Urban Consumers	2,645,000	3,114,000	2,274,000

continued...

PRODUCTION

Conasupo participation in the Domestic Grain Market

Corn	44.6%	30.9%	not available
Beans	24.8%	18.8%	"
PACE Beneficiaries (corn)	141,612	143,716	"
PACE Beneficiaries (beans)	30,415	27,682	"

* Estimated for December 1996
** Plus 200,000 adults
Source: Informe de Gobierno (1996)

Conasupo's schizophrenic existence amid producer and consumer interests increasingly produced 'zero-sum' conditions under the tight fiscal constraints of the 1980s (Salinas, 1984). The Conasupo policies of de la Madrid and Salinas recognised the problem, though their specific innovations failed to ameliorate it. However, on 28 December 1994 the Zedillo administration announced its intention to reorganise the Conasupo apparatus (*Diario Oficial de la Federación*, 28 December 1994). The nature of impending reform was unclear, but a memo (#101-280, 2 March 1995) written by Sedesol Director Carlos Rojas on 2 March 1995 announced to Zedillo's Conasupo General Director Humberto Mosconi and Conasupo workers a series of executive decrees. Foremost, he explained that the National Development Plan 1995-2000 had instructed the Administrative Council of Conasupo to split the traditional apparatus.

1965—1995

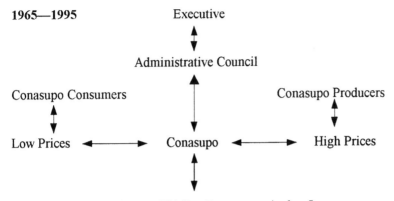

1995—1997

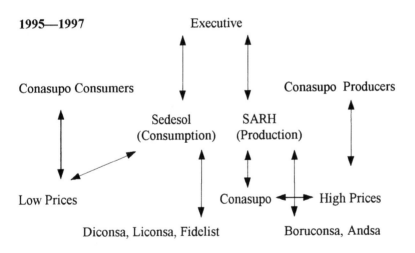

Privatised: Processing plants (Miconsa, Iconsa, Liconsa)
Privatised: Distribution infrastructure (Impesca)

Figure 6.0 Traditional Conasupo Formula

Figure 6.0 sketches how this decision reconfigured Conasupo. After May 1995, the Secretary of Agriculture (SARH) and Sedesol have partitioned traditional Conasupo services. SARH handles producer subsidies for corn and bean production, Boruconsa and Andsa operations, subsidies under the PACE scheme and other producer programmes – in addition, the central and state Conasupo offices are now accountable to SARH. Perhaps Zedillo's December 1994 selection as Conasupo Director General of Humberto Mosconi, a *politico* with a background in the CNC, indicates that the policy announced in March had been the new administration's policy from a much earlier date. Similarly, Sedesol, since May 1995, has managed Diconsa, Liconsa and Fidelist operations and employees. In the minutes of the Conasupo Council session #186 (9 May 1995) the Treasury Ministry instructed Sedesol to assume the functions previously performed by the Administrative Councils of Diconsa, Liconsa, and Fidelist (Conasupo, 25 October 1995).

What circumstances led Zedillo to split Conasupo? Studies of the Mexican presidential succession emphasise that an incoming executive usually attempts to distance himself from his predecessor, often through high profile, arbitrary manoeuvres, including abrupt policy changes in domestic food markets (Philip, 1992; Cothran, 1994; Camp; 1993). It is tempting to conceive post-1994 Conasupo policy as another incomplete policy cycle and executive manoeuvre during the sexenial transition. The logic of succession rituals accurately explain Zedillo's incarceration of Raúl Salinas on murder charges, his discarding of Solidarity, disbanding Solidarity Committees, and removal of Solidarity logos in 1995. These represented symbols (and relatives) of an unpopular ex-president. However, the intensity and scope of the Solidarity initiative basically removed Conasupo from the national discourse on social policy after 1991. Likewise, as far as succession rituals are concerned, Conasupo represented a parastatal with a social identity that predates Carlos Salinas. A policy shift in this area would not distance Zedillo from Salinas, but would rather distance him from an earlier populist era, not the best political strategy during a period of economic hardship that most blamed on the neoliberal management of the economy.

However, in the light of the Raúl Salinas jailing it is reasonable to speculate that Zedillo also anticipated the scandals likely to surface from the former's tenure at Conasupo, and therefore he pursued preventative action.

In Chapter Five, it was pointed out that the Council meeting of October 1991 saw the presentation of a private auditor report and the relocation of Raúl Salinas and other Conasupo functionaries. Given that these figures all stand accused of defrauding the agency between 1988-1991, there is reason to suspect that 'the Council knew' the scale of illicit acts that had occurred in the first half of the Salinas term. Were this the case, then Zedillo, as part of the Council, knew the scale of the problem.

In May 1995, reshuffling or 'recreating' Conasupo's bureaucratic arrangements – four months before any discussion of a congressional investigation of corruption at Conasupo – gave an alternative that also avoided discontinuing services at a time of high economic uncertainty. Splitting Conasupo fostered a perception, especially in the media, that it had been disbanded. David Márquez Ayala wrote in *La Jornada* (13 May 1997) that 'today, Conasupo is within view of being extinct, sacrificed for the neoliberal market'. The same edition finds León Bendesky suggesting that 'all statistics clearly signal the destiny of the organisation [Conasupo], that is, its disappearance very soon'. Yet these views that were focused on the two-year period between May 1995 and May 1997 accurately depict one side of the Conasupo story observed in table 6.0.

Aside from succession rituals and Zedillo's expedient 'damage control' measures, splitting the Conasupo system formalised a trend from the Salinas term: concentrating on expanding the coverage of consumption subsidies. In August 1991, Zedillo, acting as Secretary of Budget and Planning, Head of the Inter-sectoral Commission on Spending-Financing, and speaking for the Council, prematurely foreshadowed future developments when he stipulated that Conasupo services would thereafter fall under Solidarity (*El Financiero*, 7 August 1991). In response to this decision, Conasupo services adorned the Solidarity logo (Dresser, 1991). Yet, previous chapters have shown that a promise to transfer administrative control to Sedesol never complimented official propaganda. In turn, although Solidarity logos covered packages of Conasupo tortillas, bottles of Liconsa milk, Diconsa stores, and Boruconsa silos, the government maintained Conasupo's established bureaucratic arrangements. Most observers superimposed Solidarity, and later Sedesol, on top of Conasupo, even though the various components of the Conasupo apparatus exhibited very little substantive bureaucratic links, mutual planning and information sharing with Sedesol. Varley's (1996: 220) conclusions on Solidarity's land-titling activities and traditional land-titling programmes are instructive:

> In spite of the 'Solidarity' label attached to the regularisation programme and associated ceremonies, Pronasol as an agency appears to have had little to do with the process of regularisation in the Federal District; [the traditional land-titling bureaucracy] did the work and 'Solidarity' took the credit.

Back in 1989-1991, however, the casual observer had every right to be confused. In a routine repeated throughout the Salinas years, at a venue during the 'Third Annual National Solidarity Week' President Salinas announced new Diconsa stores – 188 rural stores, 82 urban stores, 23 Infonavit stores and 37 mobile units (*El Financiero*, 8 September 1992). Further, though the statistical annex of the executive's annual report to Congress (or *informe*) lists Diconsa and Liconsa as Solidarity schemes, again, this is misleading. While it was true that Municipal Solidarity Funds (funds available to Solidarity Committees) could be used to construct a *lechería* or Diconsa store, in the end Conasupo determined whether committees received services (Interview, Mexico City, Office of Fidelist, 4 April 1997). There is some evidence that a similar dynamic arose with health clinics. Solidarity Committees could choose to construct a clinic but IMSS had to approve the location. León Chaín (1996: 73-75), General Co-ordinator of the Popular Defence Committee (CDP) of Querétaro, argues that IMSS rejected such requests in CDP *colonias*. In addition to Solidarity guidelines, new stores and *lecherías* required a Conasupo *concertación* agreement. The point to stress is that the managers of Conasupo policy under Carlos Salinas did not include Solidarity and Sedesol architect Carlos Rojas.

The placement of consumer programmes under one ministerial head, Sedesol, may also be linked to the disharmony in the Council that Zedillo encountered during the Salinas years. Council proceedings over subsidy payments to Maseca are one illustration (see Chapter Two). Zedillo dissociated himself from any wrong-doing with the defence that Jaime Serra Puche, as president of the Administrative Council, overruled him and other council members concerning the legality of payments to Maseca. Control of Conasupo, irrespective of the multiple versions of the Maseca story (Aguilar

Zínser, Serra Puche, Zedillo, DePalma, etc.), was evidently porous, informal and exposed to personal agendas.

Undoubtedly, the Conasupo bureaucracy no longer resembles its former stature following the May 1995 split. However, it is an open question whether this policy has 'reformed' or merely shifted traditional Conasupo programmes to other executive-oriented bureaucracies. Was this another round of reshuffling/recreation and dressed up incremental change akin to past schemes at the parastatal? The question is salient because table 6.0 shows that traditional Conasupo consumption services have grown.

Who was running this apparatus after May 1995? At Conasupo, neither radical staff reductions nor a fresh round of administrative reforms ensued as a result of the May 1995 policy shift. Policymakers inside and outside Conasupo generally recognise that administrative reforms under the CMP (see Chapter Five) were appropriate and now require time to bear fruit. New meritocratic guidelines that structure recruitment and internal promotion, for example, have upgraded workplace skills at a steady pace.[1] Distinct from the past, however, traditional components of the Conasupo apparatus now comply with an agenda drawn up by SARH or Sedesol, and not the Administrative Council or Secofi.

Let us concentrate on consumption subsidies and Sedesol. If the perceptions of Fidelist managers approximate the situation at Diconsa and Liconsa,[2] there remains a conviction among long-serving administrators that they still run their own programmes. Yet, there is also a broad recognition that traditional Conasupo services are now one spoke in the Sedesol wheel and should no longer be identified with Conasupo or perceived as the same decentralised, independent operations (Conasupo, 8 August 1995). In essence, inasmuch as Secofi managed Conasupo policy in concert with President Salinas, Sedesol manages traditional Conasupo consumption services in close liaison with President Zedillo. For some, the partition symbolised the end of the old Conasupo. The comments of a twenty-two year Conasupo veteran (Interview, Mexico City, Office of Fidelist, 22 April 1997) were laced with sarcasm, animosity and nostalgia: 'Once an umbrella of decentralised agencies performing separate functions, two ministries now control everything'. In interviews with Fidelist employees, people referred to Carlos Rojas as their boss, a stark contrast to commentary on the Salinas years, which consistently referred to the Council and Jaime Serra Puche.

Fluctuations in Bureaucratic, Political and Ministerial Space

It is possible to add an empirical view of Conasupo-Sedesol integration. In early 1997, the outspoken PAN Governor of Guanajuato Vicente Fox filed a petition urging President Zedillo to devolve control of the Tortilla Programme to state governments. In March 1997, Fidelist drafted a report to the executive in which it justified preserving the status quo, arguing that economies of scale warranted centralisation at the federal level (Interview, Mexico City, Office of Fidelist, 7 May 1997). Later in March, both the governor and Sedesol accused each other of politicising resources to the detriment of poor Mexicans. But within weeks, Zedillo dismissed the petition as well as a request for a congressional debate on the matter. The Fox petition illustrated that President Zedillo's official decentralisation agenda of *federalismo nuevo* ('new federalism') in the social sector excluded traditional Conasupo consumption programmes.[3] The episode concluded in Guanajuato, at a meeting where Carlos Rojas and the director of Fidelist instructed Fox that if he wanted to design a PAN tortilla scheme in the future, by all means, he should lobby the Chamber of Deputies, which, like the United States House of Representatives, approves all federal spending.

Fox acknowledged some improvement in the Tortilla Programme under Fidelist management, hinting that the dispute boiled down to control. Further, this was not the first dispute of its kind. In 1992, the then PAN Governor of Guanajuato Carlos Medina Plascencia responded to the fact that Solidarity resources had bypassed PAN-held municipalities between 1989-1991, by spearheading a rival, participatory-oriented social scheme entitled *Barrios y Colonias*. The governor encountered major obstacles when implementing his initiative because PAN sympathisers, according to PAN officials, 'expected paternalism and were unwilling to participate' (Acedo Angulo *et al.*, 1995: 48). Beside the fact that the PRI-held Chamber was not likely to accept a PAN-sponsored proposal, perhaps this earlier experience encouraged the Fox strategy of capturing an existing programme rather than soliciting funds to operate a new or rival programme.

Carlos Rojas' leadership role in the dispute illustrates the modified hierarchy under Sedesol-Fidelist integration. Fidelist policymakers 'represented their interests' in drafting a forceful response and basically managed this dispute between 'us' (PRI/state) and 'them' (PAN) from beginning to end. Carlos Rojas was in view only during the official dialogue in Guanajuato. In the final Guanajuato meeting, for example, three Fidelist officials accompanied Rojas and handled the logistics and argued the government's position.

Turning to another example, the May 1995 decision also reoriented the responsibilities of Sedesol and Conasupo representatives below the level of Carlos Rojas in at least one respect. The Sedesol bureaucracy soon took over some of the social and political tasks customarily reserved for state-level Conasupo agents. Evidence to support this claim can be drawn from the research of Torres (1996) in Jalisco and Kaufman and Trejo (1997) in Puebla, Nayarit, Tamaulipas and Baja California, which analyse the politics of Sedesol operations under Zedillo. Both studies depict state-level Sedesol representatives regulating the distribution of public resources, including traditional Conasupo resources.

Torres' study is especially noteworthy. Sedesol actors are viewed by Torres as executive appendages. In discussing relief operations following an October 1995 earthquake on the coast of Jalisco, he documents the process whereby Sedesol agents systematically marginalised local *PANista* municipality presidents by controlling the flow of emergency resources. He gives a revealing glimpse of intra-PRI and inter-party (i.e., PAN, PRD, PT and PRI) contestation over social/political space and public resources in a specific context. One factor outside the Torres analysis is the origin of the resources that animate the clientelistic and partisan struggle under observation – food, tents, mattresses, or, in other words, traditional Conasupo resources. Conasupo organised relief operations across Mexico before May 1995 and its state representatives performed this intermediary, crisis broker, resource-oriented, function for the executive.

A Conasupo office (*Fideicomiso Comisión Promotora Conasupo para el Mejoramiento Social*) co-ordinated relief efforts between 1972-1987. President de la Madrid liquidated the office after discovering widespread corruption. President Salinas centralised relief duties under the general director of Conasupo. In December 1988, Salinas authorised various Conasupo Presidential Programmes under the stewardship of the general director to respond to natural disasters – floods, droughts, tornadoes, hurricanes and earthquakes. In 1992, as discussed in Chapter Four, private auditors hired by the Council uncovered rampant corruption in Presidential Programmes, and it scaled them back at the end of 1992.

Conasupo's natural disaster relief aided 716,500 families in 1988 but a comparatively lower figure of 181,500 families in 1994 (Conasupo, September 1994). The point to reiterate is that under Zedillo, it appears that Sedesol has replaced Conasupo in this particular area.

Moreover, there are tacit signs that Zedillo's Conasupo policy has prompted the fragmentation and intra-corporatist consolidation of former Conasupo functions. This is best illustrated in a three-year, joint CTM-CNC initiative. Beatriz Paredes Rangel (CNC), the late Fidel Velázquez (CTM) and PRI Governor of Zacatecas Arturo Romo Gutiérrez signed an agreement on 15 January 1997, 'that will allow the nation's workers to buy beans and other basic products directly from producers at half the normal retail price' (*The News*, 16 January 1997).

Starting in January 1997, the CTM and CNC began packaging beans in Zacatecas and distributing them to CTM offices in various cities. In effect, CTM trucks substituted for the Conasupo infrastructure, and soon, according to its architects, the agreement would include rice, lentils, oranges and meat. The governor of Zacatecas noted: 'The program is guaranteed to benefit both the bean producers and the workers. Producers will be getting a better price for their beans, and the workers will be paying less'; and the CNC leadership added: 'The farmers' organisation, the union and the ruling political party have a duty to focus efforts within the community, and add strength to the people's struggle' (*The News*, 16 January 1997). When questioned in a press conference on the quantities proposed, the CNC spokeswoman remarked, 'Whatever the workers can eat'. Later, PRI Senator and Assessor to the CTM National Committee Manuel Cadena Morales submitted a document to the Congress in March 1997 heralding the success of the Zacatecas pilot scheme (*Reforma*, 2 March 1997).

In a sense, this development witnessed the PRI taking matters into their own hands. But Diconsa, the programme that this new initiative mimicked, continues to expand under Zedillo. Therefore, control over the basic consumption of millions of households has started to fragment into an 'executive apparatus' catering to predominantly rural communities, and a 'party apparatus' catering to unionised urban consumers. It is too early to speculate on whether this is a prelude of larger things to come or an isolated instance; however, it does suggest a measure of continuity concerning the old norms of reciprocity and the expectations of traditional clients of the government and Conasupo.

Connections between the PRI and Conasupo resurface from time to time.[4] A *Proceso* (1 June 1997) interview with Roberto Campa Cifrián, the PRI's 1997 mid-term campaign organiser in the D.F., discloses that the PRI's official strategy for its candidates begins with an early morning visit to local *lecherías* to meet beneficiaries. Finally, in the coverage of the July 1997 mid-term election, several Mexican newspapers reported that the PRI had distributed 2,000 breakfast packages and 1,500 Conasupo lunches in the capital precinct of Alvaro Obregón, to encourage attendance at its mid-term campaign finale in the centre of Mexico City (*The News*, 1 July 1997).

A Historic Mid-Term Defeat, Campeche to Progresa, Another Recreation?

On 6 August 1997, President Zedillo announced the Progresa initiative that is apt to dominate the debate on social policy until the next executive succession, in the year 2000. Progresa's launch came on the heels of the PRI's defeat in the July 1997 mid-term election, and its pledge to 'bundle' the government's existing resources for education, health and nutrition represents either a radical policy departure or another recreation. Basically, Progresa attempts to enlarge a 1995 Conasupo pilot scheme from the southern state of Campeche (known as PASE). However, Progresa's link to the traditional Conasupo apparatus has yet to be analysed by scholars. Nor have observers taken notice or considered the significance of intra-governmental conflict and executive indecision over Progresa before August 1997. This section takes up both of these issues.

It is premature to comment on Progresa's performance, though it should be mentioned that, notwithstanding an enthusiastic article in *The Economist* (9-15 January 1999) and official government reports, no scholarly source foresees a decline in Mexican poverty resulting from this new initiative. One well-known social policy researcher sums up the prevailing attitude: 'The program (Progresa) as currently configured has no chance of getting to the deepest roots of poverty...The poor are poor because they exist within a context of labor exclusion and social inequality' (González de la Rocha, 1997: 4).

This section draws on interviews with Mexico City-based Fidelist administrators who designed and operated the PASE. The context and timing (March-May 1997) of the interviews is noteworthy not only for the approaching mid-term election in July, but also because it covers a critical period in which President Zedillo deliberated over different proposals to run a national PASE programme. To start with, PASE and Progresa share congruent and contrasting elements:

	PASE in Campeche (1995-1997)	**Progresa (6 August 1997)**
Target Area	Campeche's three largest cities: Campeche, Ciudad del Carmen and Champotón	Areas of extreme poverty in urban and rural regions: *phase one* (August-December 1997) states of Coahuila, Campeche, Chihuahua, Guanajuato, Hidalgo, Oaxaca, Puebla, Querétaro, San Luis Potosí and Veracruz; *phase two* (1998), add Chiapas (the highland and mountain regions) and Guerrero (mountain and coastal regions).
Target Population	24,924 families in 1996	400,000 families in 1997; 4 million families in 2000

continued...

	PASE in Campeche (1995-1997)	**Progresa (6 August 1997)**
Nutrition Components	- Monthly payments to families via electronic ('ATM-like') cards and machines located in 80 outlets marketing basic foodstuffs - Restricts eligibility and personalised cards to females - Substitutes for Conasupo's targeted milk and tortilla programs in urban areas - Monitors family purchases to ensure resources go for basic commodities - 70 pesos per month or ($US) 10.89 in 1995, ($US) 9.21 in 1996, ($US) 8.82 in 1997	- Distribute subsidies via ATM-like machines located at government-run stores - Restrict eligibility for personalised cards to females - 90 pesos per month, ($US) 11.34 in 1997; index future allotments to inflation rate
Education Components	(Unrealised under PASE as of May 1997) - Take over the DIF's (Defence of the Family) meal program in public schools - Student scholarships - Involve teachers and school administrators in the selection of participating students - Student attendance required to receive other PASE benefits	- Manage DIF meal program in targeted regions - Primary and secondary-level scholarships; priority to females - Student attendance required to receive other Progresa benefits

continued...

	PASE in Campeche (1995-1997)	**Progresa (6 August 1997)**
Health Components	- Participant families visit one of twenty affiliated health clinics - Participant families adhere to a regular examination schedule; special attention given to families with children below the age of 5 - Fidelist pays the salaries of doctors	- Participant families must visit affiliated health clinics - Participant families adhere to a regular examination schedule to maintain access to the program, special attention to families with children below the age of five.

Source: Conasupo (June 1995); Conasupo (May 1995), Conasupo (December 1996), Conasupo (1996), and *La Jornada* (7 August 1997)

In short, PASE's three components substituted private merchants for the traditional Tortilla and Milk Programmes and attempted to integrate or 'bundle' existing health and education support for the same target population. The cost associated with the three-city PASE scheme doubled Fidelist's budgetary outlay for the nation-wide Tortilla Programme (Interview, Mexico City, Office of Fidelist, 7 April 1997). Table 6.1 lays out the quantity of basic goods available to beneficiaries of the PASE (July 1995).

Progresa expanded much of the PASE. Phase one in the state of Hidalgo, for example, would include monthly allotments of 90 pesos to 37,000 families in 895 communities; scholarships for 43,000 children in 1,000 affiliated schools (70 percent primary and 30 percent secondary); and free medical coverage and nutritional supplements for 19,000 children under the age of two. Overall, costs in Hidalgo would surpass ($US) 1 million per month. Certain operational components crosscut either programme; in either case there is, for example, a reliance on direct resource transfers, integrated handouts, consolidation of traditional programmes (in the case of DIF), and attention to gender.[5]

Table 6.1   Products Purchased in PASE Scheme with 70 pesos (July 1995)

Product	Ave. cost in pesos	Store(s) visited
4 kilos beans	26.00	Super 10 (Centro)
4 kilos rice	18.00	Super 10 (Villa del Río)
2 litres cooking oil	17.00	Super Maz
1 kilo eggs	6.00	Maxitienda Resurgimiento
1 kilo sugar	3.00	Maxitienda Ave. P. Trueba
		Abarrotes 'El Labrador'
		Mercado Público
Total	70.00	

Source: Conasupo (December 1996)

Finally, both programmes centralise resources in Mexico City and preclude meaningful local input in the conception, design and execution of policy. Consequently, these are cases where 'agency' rests with executive branch bureaucratic actors alone. It is improbable that Progresa can reverse the situation. Substituting Fidelist and Liconsa intermediaries for private merchants formed a novel part of PASE, yet Progresa relies on Diconsa's rural infrastructure – a point returned to below.

Beneath these operational commonalties resides an analogous analytic dimension. PASE intended to 'bundle' resources in order to 'overcome the structural roots of Mexican poverty' (Conasupo, May 1995). Likewise, Progresa first appeared in a press conference held at a Boruconsa warehouse in the poverty-stricken community of La Florida, Hidalgo. Zedillo rationalised Progresa against a backdrop in which 50 percent of rural Mexican families resided in extreme poverty. Progresa's mission was to 'attack extreme poverty at its roots' and 'efficiently attack the vicious circle of ignorance, sickness, and malnutrition that has entrapped millions of Mexicans' (*La Crónica de Hoy*, 7 August 1997). 'With luck', explained the President, Progresa's reliance on direct resource transfers would produce greater efficiency and transparency (*La Jornada*, 7 August 1997).

Other issues separate PASE and Progresa, in part reflecting 'lessons learnt' from Campeche and in part reflecting familiar pressures for continuity and discontinuity in the management of social welfare resources. With monthly peso allotments under PASE, for example, Fidelist administrators clashed with the Treasury Ministry over fixing allotments at 70 pesos without inflationary adjustments from December 1994 to May 1997 (Interview, Mexico City, Office of Fidelist, 22 April 1997). The conflict touched a familiar tension: would 'bundling' be a tool to fight inflation or poverty? Resolving this dispute would have ramifications stretching beyond mere inter-bureaucratic rivalry; it would also affect public perceptions of Progresa and wider issues of continuity and discontinuity. Zedillo resolved the matter by setting monthly payments at 90 pesos and ordering inflationary adjustments every six months in line with the National Price Index of the Basic Basket of Goods.

Differences between PASE and Progresa also surface from the sheer scope of Progresa. Appropriate guidelines in a three-city scheme, in an under-populated, urban setting may not transfer smoothly to areas targeted under Progresa. In Campeche policymakers enjoyed adequate schools, medical clinics and market infrastructure to supply basic commodities and achieve the PASE's broader objectives. The absence of supply bottlenecks and ample market infrastructure furnished a propitious environment for a programme of direct cash transfers. Access to various supermarkets provided beneficiaries with the power to punish corrupt storeowners, something absent from traditional Conasupo services. Less favourable conditions await Progresa in the mountains of Chiapas, Guerrero and Oaxaca, and other rural areas.

It needs to be emphasised that the urban-oriented PASE aimed to substitute direct cash transfers for the traditional Tortilla and Milk Programmes. This process was only possible because all three programmes operated in urban areas and shared beneficiary lists as well as a similar card-based technology. Conversely, Progresa's rural orientation represents a complement to, rather than a substitute for, urban-based milk and tortilla schemes.

PASE and Progresa also recycled elements from Solidarity – examples include student scholarships and school lunches – and, most interestingly, Progresa reintroduces community participation and *concertación*. Progresa's original guidelines stipulate that municipal representatives, before posting participant lists at community buildings, will vote and approve all participant households. In this manner Progresa, like Solidarity and traditional Conasupo programmes, reduces community participation to a choice of whether to sanction decisions promulgated in Mexico City. Progresa's designers envision that municipal officials will, under certain conditions, add names to official lists – albeit this caveat is added without denoting how the government plans to monitor it. One suspects that this grey area and operational context may prove to be reminiscent of the Solidarity Committee experience or traditional *concertación*. As researchers increasingly discovered with Solidarity and Conasupo, will Progresa reproduce and reinforce existing power relations at the local level? Or, through technology and monitoring of intermediaries, can it demarcate a path toward more efficient, needs-based delivery of traditional social resources?

Undeniably, Progresa departs from the technocrat rigour embraced in Campeche. PASE relied on socioeconomic interviews and education courses before distributing subsidy cards to households or card-machines to merchants (Interview, Mexico City, Office of Fidelist, 4 April 1997). Progresa, it will be shown, failed to replicate these steps. However, before turning to the policy process that led to Progresa, it is worth taking a closer look at PASE since this was the supposed blueprint for subsequent policy.

Why Select Campeche?

There is some confusion as to why the government selected Campeche. Fidelist's official explanation centres on the reliability of Fidelist and Liconsa beneficiary lists in the state (Conasupo, May 1995). The logic was that problematic lists would jeopardise the initiative from the outset. Nevertheless, further exploration of the question 'why Campeche'? suggests the primacy of other considerations.

One high-ranking administrator recounts the advantages of Campeche's geography – 'Campeche has no mountains' – and port facilities as a context for policy experimentation (Interview, Mexico City, Office of Fidelist, 4 April 1997). As far as port facilities, he indicated that Campeche offered secure supply routes. These comments are suspect because PASE's architects (of which he was one) never framed it as a supply-side stimulant but rather the opposite – that is, as a demand stimulant. In fact, Fidelist submitted a report on PASE to the executive wherein policymakers allude to Campeche sites as self-sufficient in basics (Conasupo, May 1995). Upon further prodding, the respondent's interpretation changed direction; Campeche was depicted as a 'stable state' with minimal encroachment of opposition parties. In sum, Campeche's propitious location had to do with local politics that accorded policymakers space to experiment rather than geographic or supply considerations.

Another counterintuitive aspect associated with Campeche is that policymakers performed a trial of the bundling concept in an urban location, when Zedillo's stated objective, as early as 1994, was to reduce rural poverty. In Campeche, as in other poor and comparatively underdeveloped southern states, poverty pervades outside of urban centres. Against this backdrop, the selection of Campeche appears to be neither arbitrary nor realised strictly according to official discourse.

First, reforming entrenched resource programmes apparently called for a locality where PRI elites and traditional intermediaries had no reason to fear or obstruct innovation. Likewise, it would serve the government's interest to select a place where the opposition could not capture, interfere with or monitor PASE. Campeche presented a PRI stronghold; for example, in 1992 state-wide elections, the PRI won all 29 open majority-decided municipalities (Castillo, 1992). Second, the government wanted to assure the success of PASE so that when the appropriate time arrived to expand the programme to the national level it could point to a legitimate record. Locational preference therefore rested in part on formulating an 'image of success' and avoiding complications, rather than testing the scheme in a representative population. Finally, together the conception, final blueprint and execution of PASE amounted to a 'bureaucratic exercise' that neglected input from local officials or beneficiary groups. Thus, PASE digressed from the logic and rationale of decentralisation that was the core of Zedillo's *federalismo nuevo*; on the other hand, it also concurred with a more long-term policymaking style and inertia discovered in earlier chapters.

Was PASE an 'electoral exercise' as well? Campeche possesses 75 percent of Mexico's oil production but its small population renders it a minor piece in the national electoral map. Fifty percent of the state's voters reside in the three cities covered by PASE. However, any assessment of a direct electoral connection is complicated because the obvious yardstick, the 1997 mid-term election, was exceptional by historical standards.

Campeche politics boiled down to a handful of prominent families competing for control of the local PRI machinery (Romero, 1997; *Proceso*, 12 July 1997; *Proceso*, 28 June 1997; *Reforma*, Campeche election preview, 30 April 1997). The issue of oil cemented strong ties between Mexico City and the local PRI. But this political structure collapsed in the run up to the July 1997 gubernatorial race. PRI Governor Jorge Salomón Azar chose as his successor Antonio González Curi. Both individuals were not party activists and, despite securing elected office, local observers affixed the label of 'technocrats' to the pair. Their publicised ties to Zedillo served to bolster this classification. The González Curi nomination prompted PRI Senator Layda Sansores – a member of a local *PRIista* family whose father (Carlos Sansores) occupied the governorship as well as the head of the national PRI under López Portillo – to defect to the PRD. Observers associate the Sansores clan with the populist, redistributionist wing of the PRI which was out of favour with Zedillo in 1997. Moreover, in the Senate, Layda Sansores refused to endorse Zedillo's Value Added Tax (IVA) proposal in 1995, which personalised their conflict. Finally, PRI Senator Guillermo del Río Ortegón – ex-director of the state PRI party for a record six consecutive years – accepted the Workers' Party (PT) nomination. Campeche politics therefore assumed an unprecedented level of partisanship. Old foes adopted identical campaign rallying cries, for example, anti-corruption and negotiation of a better deal with PEMEX, and pursued similar campaign strategies of tapping clientele networks.

Disgruntled adversaries using alternative parties to compete for local power was not coherent multi-party competition. The PRD's foothold in Campeche was insignificant before Layda Sansores, and media accounts frame the contest as a battle pitting loyal and disloyal *PRIistas*. Candidate Sansores even suggested: 'Above all in Campeche the boundaries between political parties are diluted.... All come from one tree trunk' (*Reforma*, 30 April 1997).

The July 1997 election was tightly contested and opposition parties during and after decried systematic fraud. On 8 July 1997 a reported 12,000 PAN and PRD sympathisers marched in protest in the city of Campeche (*Proceso*, 12 July 1997). In the end, the PRD secured victory in only one municipality in Champotón (where the elder Sansores was born) and in two municipalities in Playa del Carmen. The PAN landed one municipality in the city of Campeche. For the governorship, the official totals from the State Election Institute (IEE) read as follows:

PRI	108,249	48.0%
PRD	92,898	41.2%

Regarding electoral clientelism, the prawn fishermen's union backed Sansores, a move linked to her father's loyalty base and past patronage. One local resident noted that 'the PRI give us medicines, donations [food packages], and offer us free drinks and T-shirts' (*Reuters News Service*, 23 June 1997). It was widely publicised that Zedillo's face appeared on cartons of Liconsa milk distributed by the local PRI weeks before the election (*Reuters News Service*, 3 June 1997). Finally, in May 1997, the newspaper *Reforma* exposed the fact that the PRI were distributing free medicine acquired at public clinics, an allegation to which candidate González Curi retorted 'we have always given medicines and we always will – people from outside Campeche don't know how we work' (*Reuters News Service*, 23 June 1997). Hence, in the eyes of the contestants and members of the electorate, voter loyalty in Campeche shared an intimate relationship with public resources.

PASE distributed benefits to approximately 25,000 families via a network of 80 local merchants in three cities that accounted for 50 percent of the state's population. In this electoral climate of multiple and competitive clientele networks, resources on this scale were significant. Likewise, the rigid bureaucratic formula and centralised orchestration of the pilot scheme – in contrast to decentralisation or 'community participation' – prevented locals from capturing these resources and favoured a particular group of policymakers in Campeche (i.e., González Curi), the same faction that Zedillo supported in this intra-PRI feud.

Initial Speculation on PASE in Campeche

Opinions about PASE range from 'mixed' to 'serious doubt' to 'indifference' regarding its potential to secure benefits in an efficient, transparent and timely manner. According to the Secretary of Administrative Development (Secodam), located in the executive branch, PASE fell short in meeting official targets. It found, for example, parents utilised cash transfers for non-basics, producing no marked improvement in household or children's nutrition levels (*Reforma*, 7 November 1996).

The mood or expectations inside Fidelist – at least between March and May 1997 – also varied. At the positive end, some conceived PASE as a rigorous, transparent and improved method to target the poor. Others voiced greater pessimism, viewing PASE as costly or basically another political ploy connected to the executive office. The inflated cost structure in Campeche – again, PASE expenditure surpassed the budget for the national Tortilla Programme – raised serious doubts for some about the programme's potential utility *vis-à-vis* traditional nutrition supplement programmes.

A government study (Sedesol, 1996) discovered that a smaller proportion of targeted households in Campeche utilised PASE compared to the proportion that had participated in the old Tortilla and Milk Programmes. This result is partly attributable to population movement in marginal communities. However, the study's opinion surveys in targeted areas also found that between 10 to 15 percent of respondents had never heard of PASE, suggesting uneven access to information in some segments of the targeted population.

Finally, on the prospects for a nation-wide PASE, some question the commitment to observing the preliminary steps that were instrumental in Campeche. By 1995 less than 3 percent of Campeche households participating in the PASE programme registered in the 'medium-high' or 'high' socioeconomic categories (Conasupo, May 1995). Meticulous groundwork before distributing resources was the key. In Campeche, Fidelist first scripted an official operation manual and surveyed the population, then oversaw training and selection of technology, and finally proceeded with the distribution phase. Therefore, the sequencing of PASE under Zedillo did not conform to the Conasupo reforms assessed in Chapter Four, where distribution of resources preceded coherent steps to secure that they found their intended beneficiaries.

Could the expanded PASE replicate this commitment given its 10-state, 400,000 family and four-month timetable (August-December 1997)? There is reason to be cautious. It becomes clear in the next section that both Fidelist and Sedesol delayed preparations for a national PASE as of late May 1997, due to President Zedillo's general indecision concerning this project's future bureaucratic arrangements.

The Build-up to Progresa, Inter-ministerial Rivalry and Executive Indecision

The sub-director of planning at Fidelist was asked, 'Who in society is pushing for a national PASE'? He responded sarcastically, 'the Ministries of Education, Health, Treasury and Sedesol' (Interview, Mexico City, Office of Fidelist, 4 April 1997). In a sense, his frank admission reveals that the pressures for continuity and discontinuity continue to feature in the management of traditional social welfare resources.

An initial disclosure of a national PASE occurred on 7 November 1996, when PRI deputies accompanied treasury officials in a press conference to announce a broad strategy to bundle welfare resources and adopt direct cash payments. According to Treasury Ministry Official Alejandro Valenzuela, 400,000 families from 11 regions in 10 states stood to benefit in 1997. PRI Deputy Antonio Herrera of the Chamber's Treasury Commission noted that the Treasury Ministry would dispense direct cash transfers until a card-based scheme became operational.[6] PRI Deputy Rosario Guerra Díaz summarised:

> The PRI deputies have a very clear idea that subsidies must comply with objectives and that a basic problem is that the general subsidies for bread and tortilla give the same benefit to people of high and low income. It is for this reason that we have been insisting that in place of a policy of general subsidies for basics, it would be better to have a selective subsidy for those who most need it, that is, to individualise subsidies rather than making them universal. We are insisting that the subsidies are not generalised but focused, and with luck, benefits can be increased to those who really need them (*Reforma*, 7 November 1996).

At this stage, two points should be emphasised. First, on 7 November 1996, the Treasury Ministry performed as spokesperson for a national PASE, and cash payments would be its responsibility. Second, observers inside and outside the media branded a national PASE (not 'Progresa' at this particular moment) an electoral manoeuvre. Observers, however, ignored several curious aspects of this episode. By what method would the Treasury Ministry allocate cash payments to 400,000 families in isolated regions of rural Mexico? Moreover, why was the Treasury Ministry spearheading the executive's most ambitious social project? Finally, how did an admittedly centralised scheme fit into *federalismo nuevo*?

On 30 November 1996, roughly a month later, Sedesol sub-secretary for regional development, Enrique Val del Blanco, conducted a press conference to re-launch the national PASE (*Reforma*, 1 December 1996). The targeted population was the same, but it was now one of Sedesol's decentralised Branch 26 programmes.[7] Branch 26, managed by the Sub-secretariat of Regional Development (part of SPP) under de la Madrid and switched to Sedesol under Salinas, supplanted the decentralised Solidarity programmes under Zedillo. Val del Blanco dismissed suggestions that electoral ambition motivated the policy, stressing that the opposition controlled two of the ten targeted states. The main point was that approximately one month after the Treasury Ministry announcement, Sedesol now appeared to sponsor a national PASE. No substantive steps to implement this policy ensued in November 1996 or in the months ahead, however.

On 17 March 1997, Zedillo outlined his 1997 social development agenda. The executive's presentation and press conference reiterated the national PASE parameters summarised back in November 1996 – though in subsequent years the executive intended to enlarge the national PASE to 91 regions and 1,376 municipalities in 14 states. The national PASE was thus 'expanded' by four states between November 1996 and March 1997. Yet while Zedillo discussed future expansion, at this stage ministerial leadership and a precise timetable remained unresolved. Zedillo commented that the national PASE 'is a policy for resolving in practice the problems of the people, and not a tactic to sell illusions' (*Reforma*, 18 February 1997). His intention of course was to distance the national PASE from the Solidarity legacy; however, it was an ironic assertion, given the national PASE's failure to 'appear' before August 1997.

Competing Proposals to Administer the PASE

There was no decision over ministerial control in late 1996 when the Treasury Ministry and Sedesol addressed the media. What explains this result? First, the evidence suggests that Campeche offered no coherent, transferable model for a ten-state, rural-based scheme. Fidelist paid doctors until February 1997 and ran the pilot PASE's clinics with marginal collaboration from health officials. As for the pilot PASE's education component, one respondent noted: 'We are still working on that' (Interview, Mexico City, Office of Fidelist, 7 May 1997). Finally, it was mentioned above that Fidelist and the Treasury Ministry quarrelled over finances in Campeche; therefore, in practice PASE produced very little ministerial harmony. To overcome this inflexibility, operations had to be centralised at Fidelist, a solution conceivable in the limited context of Campeche; but the scope of Progresa was another matter. Progresa prioritised rural areas, and Fidelist had no experience or infrastructure in rural areas.

Behind the scene, President Zedillo solicited proposals to run a national PASE in late 1996 and responses followed from the Ministries of Health, Education, Sedesol and Treasury, plus two state governors (Querétaro and Aguascalientes) – 'Everyone wants to run it', commented one participant (Interview, Mexico City, Office of Fidelist, 4 April 1997). PASE provoked an inter-ministerial conflict as well as paralysis in the policy process as participants perceived that the winner in the PASE contest would dictate social policy to the end of the Zedillo term.

The Health Ministry possessed at least two advantages. First, it offered nation-wide, rural and urban infrastructure. Zedillo's scheduled incorporation of 4 million families by the year 2000 placed a high priority on infrastructure. Second, other Latin American states, such as Chile and Venezuela, bundled welfare resources via the health care system; therefore, Mexico would not necessarily have to 'reinvent the wheel'. Also, the World Bank, a source of considerable revenue for social programmes under Carlos Salinas, embraced this model. The Education Ministry could also rely on comparable nation-wide infrastructure, though it lacked the necessary experience or expertise to be considered seriously.

Final deliberation narrowed on the Treasury and Sedesol proposals, a development that pitted the promoters of 'continuity' and 'discontinuity' in direct confrontation. Treasury officials suggested a nation-wide network of ATM-like machines across Mexico, where participants use service cards to collect weekly peso allotments. This plan would render the traditional web of Conasupo intermediaries obsolete. This proposal was not, however, unproblematic. It entailed significant infrastructure cost. Treasury officials also acknowledged that they required a full year to erect the ATM-network. Furthermore, the Treasury Ministry claimed no experience in the local complexities that accompany such a project. Who would deliver and service machines? Distribute cards? Teach peasants in conditions of extreme poverty how to use ATM machines? In all likelihood, it would hire the universities and private consultants typically employed by Conasupo.

At Fidelist, the idea of ATM machines along dirt paths in the mountains of Guerrero or Oaxaca struck a comical cord. 'Listen, in a rural town with 1,000 people you have, at most, three rich families or around fifteen people ... the rest are poor. Why spend millions and millions on machines, cards, and everything to ensure that 15 out of 1,000 people cannot access subsidies'? (Interview, Mexico City, Office of Fidelist, 7 May 1997). Another Fidelist administrator presented a series of photographs of impoverished *campesinos*, 'these are our customers' (Interview, Mexico City, Office of Fidelist, 4 April 1997). Fidelist officials questioned the commitment of treasury officials to such groups. The general sentiment was that if the executive insisted on a national, rural PASE, the government would be better served in terms of a cost-benefit analysis by raising subsidies at Diconsa stores. Though such criticism is sensible enough, treasury officials would certainly reply their concern lay not with the hypothesised three rich families but rather the entrenched, inefficient, deleterious government intermediaries and local political arrangements typically encountered in rural areas. Machines would put subsides on a more neutral, efficient and transparent foundation.

Fidelist performed an instrumental role in the Progresa story, for its top four administrators drafted Sedesol's proposal. The matter, for Fidelist, was straightforward: how to run a pilot PASE-like programme across rural Mexico? Fidelist suggested installing its piloted technology from Campeche in rural Diconsa stores and allowing Sedesol to handle student scholarships and health officials to co-ordinate healthcare services. However, the entire programme would fall under Sedesol's Branch 20 (traditional Conasupo programmes) and not Branch 26 (decentralised Solidarity programmes).

Infrastructure, experience, and cost favoured Sedesol. It could operate its strategy within days, due in large part to the location of Diconsa's infrastructure in the poorest regions of rural Mexico. Diconsa had expanded in 1995 and 1996, as the government constructed and re-capitalised 2,750 rural stores, 87 percent in Oaxaca (1,782), Chiapas (413) and Guerrero (193) (*Informe de Gobierno*, 1996). Sedesol personnel also had experience in out-reach and information-based programmes as well as the suggested technology, though admittedly such experience was limited to urban areas. In sum, one could argue that Sedesol's proposal was serviceable and expedient, although it dredged up more from the past (continuity) and offered much less in terms of new conceptions of social policy (discontinuity).

Two additional issues warrant separate consideration. First, familiarity and confidence in Diconsa can to some extent be attributed to personal, inter-bureaucratic links. Two of the four Fidelist administrators behind the Sedesol proposal previously occupied long-term positions at Diconsa. Second, the split of Conasupo in May 1995 moved Diconsa and Fidelist under the Sedesol umbrella, merging hitherto disconnected and competitive bureaucratic interests. In the absence of bureaucratic reshuffling, it would be difficult to foresee Sedesol endorsing a proposal largely dependent on Diconsa's infrastructure.

From PASE to Progresa: Continuity and Discontinuity

What circumstances permitted Zedillo to delay a national PASE until August 1997, despite the inevitable social and corporatist pressure associated with the economic crisis? If ever a Mexican President faced a hostile environment, it was Zedillo in 1995. One study calculated that 10.5 million Mexicans dropped from lower middle class into various categories of poverty in 1995 (Garduño Ríos and González Vega, 1998). It was significant that the economic crisis hit in 1995, the beginning of the six-year cycle. There were no imminent electoral tradeoffs, although a string of PRI losses in local elections in 1996, most importantly in the State of México, provoked protests from PRI activists in advance of the mid-term election. Another salient factor was that no one across the political spectrum contested Zedillo's electoral legitimacy; this issue undoubtedly distinguishes policymaking in 1995-1996 and 1989-1990.

After discussions with the pilot PASE's administrators the unavoidable impression one receives is that, rather than opposition parties, corporatist structures or a civil society roadblock, is was inter-ministerial rivalry and executive indecision paralysed the process. That the executive may decide 'tomorrow, next week, next month, next year or never' was a prevailing view, and that, above all, there was no sense of urgency (Interview, Mexico City, Office of Fidelist, 22 April 1997). Whereas Salinas scrambled in December 1988 to ameliorate the social upheaval unleashed by his controversial election and the challenge on the Left from the PRD, Zedillo displayed a degree of discretion in social policy and in the distribution of resources as late as May 1997.

However, in the July 1997 mid-term election the opposition seized control of the lower Chamber and the PRD's Cuauhtémoc Cárdenas won the mayorship of Mexico City. In turn, the pressures on Zedillo became political rather than economic, and the threat on the Left regained the momentum it lost after the 1988 election. Deliberations over the national PASE quickly stopped and within a few weeks the government implemented Progresa via the Sedesol proposal. Progresa's announcement and execution in the wake of the PRI's historic electoral loss, plus the decision to centralise control in Sedesol – while tying the hands of treasury officials by indexing future cash payments to the rate of inflation – indicate that political considerations drew the impasse to a close.

Sedesol edged out rival proposals because Zedillo sought an expeditious response. In August 1997 Zedillo announced that 'Progresa is possible because in our country we have institutions that have been constructed over many years and that we have continued and will continue to strengthen' (*La Jornada*, 7 August 1997). Hence thoughts of parallel structures *á la* Solidarity or bundling resources to the detriment of traditional bureaucracies (in theory, PASE in Campeche) were put on hold. Competing proposals had been on Zedillo's desk since late 1996. Therefore, it seems that Zedillo paused to assess the damage to his party and, after a disastrous showing at the polls, sided with Sedesol. Future events may render Zedillo a strong or weak president, but from 1995 to August 1997 he regulated the distribution of social welfare resources according to his political timetable and not that of his party, the bureaucracy, opposition political forces or civil society. His reaction to the election of July 1997 reconfirms that the traditional constraints associated with maintaining executive legitimacy remain a crucial factor in the management of established social resources.

It is unwise to divorce post-1994 public policy from the budgetary and macroeconomic reality, yet genuine policy divisions existed in the Zedillo government. Torres (1996: 71) demarcates three concurrent social welfare programmes since 1995. Carlos Rojas engineered the first (before May 1998) through the Sedesol apparatus. Rojas advocated the government's capacity to secure loyalty among the low-income population by joining state and society in partnership (or *concertación*) under centralised, executive management. Luís Téllez and Santiago Levy of the Presidential Assessors Office are at the front of a second programme where decentralisation via Branch 26 is a neoliberal alternative to the first programme. For Torres, pessimism pervades the second policymaking group, notably over the future of the dislocated rural poor and the government's potential to ameliorate the situation. The third programme is what Torres designates the 'militarisation' of social policy, or the overlapping of distributive decisions and strategies of national security. Not surprisingly, Torres' preoccupation is with Zedillo's Chiapas programme, ascribed to the state-level but run by Sedesol, producing a hybrid of decentralisation and centralisation. He identifies this third case – though his main concern is with programmes one and two – in order to demonstrate that generating electoral support (populism/neo-populism, or programme one) or decentralisation (neoliberalism/technocracy, or programme two) excludes a piece of the contemporary puzzle. He therefore proposes listing 'national security' alongside more familiar variables when studying Mexican social policy.

González de la Rocha's (1997) mid-term review of social policy relies on two coherent models rather than miscellaneous, disconnected programmes. She wrote in late 1997, a full year after Torres, and concludes: 'Mexico's recent social policy path has been one of switchbacks and changes in direction' (González de la Rocha, 1997: 3). Oscillation is the by-product of a transition from an old conceptual and organisational model to a new one. The former, dubbed the 'participatory state' model, is closely linked to Mexico's experience with import-substitution-industrialisation (ISI). Where the state has 'acted as mediator, producer, and *social agent*' (González de la Rocha, 1997: 3). Alternatively, there is the 'human capital' or World Bank model, dedicated to preparing Mexicans for the private market, where the state is a regulator and neo-social agent. González de la Rocha views current policy as a transitional phase in a linear process from one model to the next.

Finally, Rodríguez (1997) couches social policy within the norms and contingencies of her 'distributive state' framework. This framework, rather than budget fluctuations, social conditions 'on the ground', or rival political and civil society pressure, indicates that the key variable guiding social policy becomes political legitimacy, itself dependent on a complex, multi-layered structure of exchange relationships. Rodríguez characterises Zedillo and his two predecessors as reluctant disciples of decentralisation, who only diluted power and resources when faced with no other alternative.

It is important to repeat that Torres and Rodríguez formulate conclusions based on events in 1995 and 1996. Naturally, Zedillo's unprecedented moves toward decentralisation under his *federalismo nuevo* platform (in particular in health and education services) overshadowed their findings. González de la Rocha, one year later, reverses course and depicts social policy as 'bureaucratic.... Macro-level strategies dominate...The state allocates resources, and recipients have virtually no voice in suggesting or choosing what they receive' (González de la Rocha, 1997: 3). She is therefore in general agreement with Torres' first programme and basically breaks with the Rodríguez message that decentralisation is inevitable. González de la Rocha's comments are explained by the fact that they coincided with Zedillo's August 1997 announcement of Progresa and the decision to centralise resources at Sedesol.

To place the PASE/Progresa experience within a wider context, it is best to borrow from and adjust these available frameworks and incorporate this book's focus on continuity and discontinuity. Each author perceives disharmony layered in current policymaking; however, the origin of this feature is in dispute. At Fidelist, post-1994 events illuminate three 'poles of bureaucratic alignment/affiliation' within the policymaking arena. It will soon be obvious that the intention is not to discard 'models' or 'miscellaneous programmes' as building blocks for general analysis. This research simply seeks to acknowledge that the policymaking environment at Fidelist appeared too muddled or fragmented to warrant either term.

Individuals with long-term training and experience at Conasupo form a first pole. They propound both overtly and covertly an antiquated, state-centred development model and observe formal and informal institutions forged under dominant-party rule ('continuity'). For instance, such individuals exhibit hostility toward greater pluralism among political parties and do not differentiate between the 'government' and the 'PRI' – which generates a discourse punctuated with references to 'us' versus 'them'. Moreover, borrowing from González de la Rocha, the domestic market and bolstering the urban middle class takes priority. In part, this is the 'developmental state' popularised in the 1960s and 1970s on the heels of the Japanese miracle, albeit one that blends Mexico's unique corporatist institutions. Such individuals defend Conasupo programmes, expect to remain in their office beyond the short-term, and acknowledge partisan loyalties. No one disputes the existence of this first pole, although there is a consensus that it is in decline. These individuals nonetheless persist and continue to influence policy decisions and, for two reasons, it is a mistake to write them off as inevitable victims of modernisation or neoliberalism. First, one often finds that such individuals are qualified in terms of education, training and experience to succeed in their posts and advance up the occupational pyramid. Second, in general there is a reluctance to leave a professional career in the bureaucracy with this group, a sharp contrast with younger, more technically proficient employees found at Conasupo who envision a future career in the private sector. This trend appears in the questionnaire data recorded in appendix 6.0.

Solidarity (now *ramo 26*) and Sedesol demarcate a second pole that is ignored by González de la Rocha and undeveloped by Torres. The political economy circumstances peculiar to 1988 and 1989, namely, an executive legitimacy crisis, unparalleled party competition, and general economic instability, set the context and shaped the parameters of Solidarity and later Sedesol (Guevara Sanginés, 1995: 153).. Traditional channels, corporatist or otherwise, underwent a process of fragmentation, pitting traditional (for example, Conasupo) and new (Sedesol) bureaucratic agents against one another.

A third pole, again returning to González de la Rocha, represents the human capital and decentralisation proponents. She highlights the World Bank and Inter-Development Bank as catalysts behind Progresa's official discourse on the structural conditions of poverty. At the level of official discourse this may be true. But this investigation of Progresa's formative period (late 1996 to August 1997) found that the Treasury Ministry fit this role. Furthermore, interviews with technical personnel who perform statistical analysis and monitoring functions at Fidelist (but who exist outside the policymaking arena) indicate a pessimistic view of traditional Conasupo activities and the partisan politics that surround them. These groups represent a third pole.

This tripartite conception of the policy arena at Fidelist came into focus more or less sharply depending on the type of policy and where, in terms of the bureaucracy, the policy was articulated. For example, the three currents were in place in (1) the design of operations in Campeche, (2) the national PASE proposal, and (3) the post-May 1995 integration of Fidelist, Diconsa, and Liconsa into Sedesol.

In the first case, mid-level technical personnel (pole three), below Fidelist's four main supervisors (a mixture of pole one and two), handled policy decisions. Sedesol (pole two) did not interfere in Campeche. Fidelist organisers designed and executed the PASE pilot programme according to a coherent neoliberal/technocratic agenda. The second case involved four principle architects, of which two can be viewed as members of pole one, and two from the second pole. A mutual interest in securing resources united both poles and masked genuine disagreement. Consequently, amid the final Progresa accord there are countervailing bureaucratic interests: on the one hand, there is a reliance on Diconsa, and, on the other hand, there is 'community participation' from the Solidarity toolbox – the latter was something that never surfaced in Campeche and therefore emerged only after Sedesol entered the policy arena.

In the third and final case, Sedesol officially controls Fidelist, Liconsa, and Diconsa. However, after May 1995 Diconsa expansion continued unabated, and Zedillo maintained the Milk and Tortilla Programmes. Likewise, there have been no steps to reform Liconsa or Fidelist operations in Mexico City. Sedesol therefore conducts *concertación* dialogues with community and union leaders and initiates major policy shifts, but this does not amount to a radical policy change. In the end, this tripartite framework has maintained a balance between continuity and discontinuity, and encouraged incremental rather than radical policy innovations.

Summary

Three issues link Zedillo's management of traditional Conasupo resources with observations in earlier chapters: Conasupo's generation of political capital, its capacity to be 'recreated' and the differences between 'targeting' under de la Madrid and Salinas and 'bundling' under Zedillo. In section one the general discussion as well as the specific observations of Progresa reveal certain areas of continuity. It appears that traditional demands for legitimacy still impose constraints on the development of neoliberal policies. After 1994, another PRI administration promised radical reform across the social sector (i.e., *federalismo nuevo*). Yet its execution has been partial rather than comprehensive; in turn, some programmes have been decentralised (such as health and education resources) while others have not (Progresa and traditional Conasupo consumption programmes).

Conasupo's traditional infrastructure of stores and *lecherías*, plus the Tortilla Programme, continued to expand after 1994. Thousands of communities entered *concertación* dialogues with either Humberto Mosconi or Carlos Rojas between 1994 and 1997. However, the magnitude of the recent economic crisis seems to have denied the PRI the votes that traditionally flow from these programmes. For example, Conasupo's strategic client population in and around Mexico City contributed to the PRD's victory in the July 1997 D.F. mayoral election.

Earlier chapters concluded that incremental innovation under the CMP would not preclude another 'recreation' in the future. In some ways, the decision to split Conasupo in May 1995 marked another recreation, driven by a climate of crisis and pressure for innovation at the beginning of a six-year cycle. Splitting Conasupo gave the impression that, like Solidarity, it would soon disappear. Yet while production services have been reduced, there has been little innovation of the consumption programmes analysed in this book.

Finally, it is too early to assess whether a policy shift toward 'bundling' under Progresa can succeed where 'targeting' failed before and under the CMP. However, there have been some troubling developments. Lessons from Campeche and from the process that led to Progresa suggest that the pressures for continuity and discontinuity are still salient and still likely to impose constraints on radical policy innovation. Indeed, this chapter presents good reasons to be cautious about a broadly neoliberal operation in Campeche being expanded to accomplish the official goals of Progresa.

Appendix 6.0 Survey of Employees Opinions

From 5-24 April 1997 a questionnaire was circulated at the Office of Social Programmes (OSP) and Office of Planning and Information at Fidelist. Both are located along Mexico City's busy *Avenida Insurgentes*. Questions range from simple data collection (name, age, birthplace, etc.) to more detailed opinions.

OSP was a product of the Conasupo *Modernización* Plan. It first appeared in October 1990 to co-ordinate the Tortilla and Milk Programmes under one roof and to inject technical skills into the administration, planning and assessment of these programmes. Fidelist took over the Tortilla Programme in 1992. Opinion at Fidelist shows the different bureaucratic currents referred to in Chapter Six. This information provides a flavour of the viewpoints that prevail at Conasupo after the experience described in the preceding chapters.

Questionnaire: (SAMPLE)

Section#1:
1. Job title
2. Age and birthplace
3. Experience at Conasupo
4. Experience at other Conasupo branches
5. Education
6. Previous job
7. Can you see yourself working for Conasupo in 5 years time?

Section#2:
Given that the Salinas administration modernised Conasupo, please describe the level of changes in the following areas. Answer: (i) increased moderately, (ii) no change, (iii) reduced moderately or (iv) reduced.

1. The capacity to distribute basic products
2. The capacity to help domestic producers of basic products
3. The capacity to help the working class
4. The capacity to operate independently of external political actors

Section#3:
- Describe how the situation will be at Conasupo in 5 years time, for example will Conasupo have a larger or smaller budget, more or less employees, the same social responsibilities that exist today and the same programmes that exist today.
- How would you describe the social function and responsibility of Conasupo during the Zedillo and Salinas administrations?

Number#1

Section#1:

Job	Department sub-boss (Fidelist)
Age and Birthplace	34 years Mexico, D.F.
Experience at Conasupo	3 years
Experience in Conasupo System	Impecsa
Education	7th Semester (University)
Previous Job	Administrator in an insurance company
Do you see working at Conasupo in 5 years?	No

Section#2:

1. Reduced moderately	3. Reduced moderately
2. Reduced moderately	4. Reduced moderately

Section#3:
- I don't believe so. I believe that Conasupo will go under and that currently it does not act towards the aim to which it was created.
- I believe that currently Conasupo does not comply with its objectives. It could provide a lot more social assistance and this does not happen.

Number#2

Section#1:

Job	Department sub-boss (Fidelist)
Age and Birthplace	25 years, Mexico, D.F.
Experience at Conasupo	2 years
Experience in Conasupo System	No
Education	Undergraduate degree, Economics, Uni. Panamericana
Previous Job	Conasupo Analyst
Do you see working at Conasupo in 5 years?	No

Section#2:

1. No change and Reduced	3. Reduced moderately
2. (no answer)	4. Rcduced

Section#3:

- I believe that Conasupo is a business that, politically, is difficult to end (*desaparecer*), although hopefully this will happen because the existing programmes change at the whim (*al antojo*) of the people that are in power, *sexenio* to *sexenio*. Perhaps they will assign Conasupo a smaller budget.
- Mediocre, because intervention of Conasupo in the importation of grains (corn, beans, etc.) seems to only obstruct fixing prices in the free market and prejudices the true Mexican *campesinos* while only benefiting the organised *Mafia of supposed producers*.

Number#3

Section#1:

Job	Department boss (Fidelist)
Age and Birthplace	33 years, Mexico, D.F.
Experience at Conasupo	3 years
Experience in Conasupo System	No
Education	Undergraduate degree (UNAM)
Previous Job	National Provincial Group (Insurance company)
Do you see working at Conasupo in 5 years?	No

Section#2:

1. Reduced moderately	3. Reduced
2. Reduced	4. Reduced

Section#3:

- I believe that in less than a year Conasupo will disappear. They have been limiting its activities since 1991, on the instructions of our government (read: the United States of America).
- It has been gradually disappearing; it does not have any social function currently.

Number#4

Section#1:

Job	Department sub-boss (Fidelist)
Age and Birthplace	35 years, Mexico, D.F.
Experience at Conasupo	3 years
Experience in Conasupo System	Liconsa
Education	Undergraduate degree in Social Work
Previous Job	Technical secretary to the director of the Milk Programme
Do you see working at Conasupo in 5 years?	No

Section#2:

1. Increased moderately
2. Increased moderately

3. No change
4. Increased moderately

Section#3:

- In fact, social programmes that attract beneficiaries are not part of Conasupo any more because the tortilla as with the milk are now inside the budget of SEDESOL. Perhaps Conasupo will remain as it is today without any increases in its institutional power.
- During the Salinas period it was a disaster and this has been gradually discovered now. Currently with Zedillo Conasupo seems vindicated and it seems to have new strength.

Number#5

Section#1:

Job	Administrative Supervisor (OSP)
Age and Birthplace	34 years, Mexico, D.F.
Experience at Conasupo	16 years and 9 months
Experience in Conasupo System	No
Education	Secondary level
Previous Job	No
Do you see working at Conasupo in 5 years?	No

Section#2:

1. Reduced
2. Reduced

3. Reduced
4. Reduced

Section#3:
- I consider that Conasupo, if it does survive five years, will have a smaller budget and logically less workers. Perhaps less social responsibilities, or rather no social responsibilities. Conasupo will not be responsible for social programmes. It will have another function, such as marketing.
- During Carlos Salinas, Conasupo was losing its social presence in favour of the Solidarity programme and it has been thus during the administration of Zedillo, although, Solidarity as such, I believe has disappeared. But Conasupo so far has not recuperated its social functions for which it was created in 1965.

Number#6

Section#1:

Job	(No title) OSP
Age and Birthplace	40 years, Mexico, D.F.
Experience at Conasupo	20 years
Experience in Conasupo System	No
Education	(No response)
Previous Job	Only Conasupo
Do you see working at Conasupo in 5 years?	Yes

Section#2:

1. Reduced moderately	3. Reduced moderately
2. Reduced	4. Reduced

Section#3:
- I consider that Conasupo will maintain its social activities, perhaps with less employees.
- (No response)

Number#7

Section#1:

Job	Sub-manager (OSP)
Age and Birthplace	29 years, Teloapon, Guerrero
Experience at Conasupo	6 years
Experience in Conasupo System	Diconsa
Education	University degree
Previous Job	Systems analyst for CPAR
Do you see working at Conasupo in 5 years?	Yes

Section#2:

1. Reduced moderately	3. 'Not Applicable' (answered)
2. Reduced moderately	4. 'Not Applicable' (answered)

Section#3:

- Budget – depends on the programmes [that Conasupo runs]. Employees – depends on the functions [that Conasupo performs]
- Conasupo has the same social function

Number#8

Section#1:

Job	Department boss (OSP)
Age and Birthplace	28 years, Mexico, D.F.
Experience at Conasupo	4 years
Experience in Conasupo System	No
Education	University degree, Engineering (UNAM)
Previous Job	Systems Assessor at MMC (Large transport firm)
Do you see working at Conasupo in 5 years?	No

Section#2:

1. Reduced moderately	3. Reduced
2. Increased moderately	4. Reduced moderately

Section#3:
- The possibility exists for the transformation of the business and a possible merger or reduction of its activities; perhaps with more responsibilities.
- Salinas = Reduction of responsibilities   Zedillo = Definition of objectives

Number#9

Section#1:

Job	Analysis unit boss (Fidelist)
Age and Birthplace	26 years, Mexico, D.F.
Experience at Conasupo	3 years
Experience in Conasupo System	No
Education	Undergraduate degree, economics, Univ. Panamericana
Previous Job	Analyst specialist at INEGI
Do you see working at Conasupo in 5 years?	No

Section#2:

1. Reduced moderately	3. Reduced moderately
2. Reduced moderately	4. Reduced moderately

Section#3:
- Conasupo will merge with another governmental institution, with less employees and other social responsibilities. I do not believe that Conasupo will reach the same number of beneficiaries.
- Salinas: There existed an increase in support for the *campesinos* and he created new support programmes.
Zedillo: Has diminished the size and capacity of support.

Number#10

Section#1:

Job	Technical studies department boss (OSP)
Age and Birthplace	29 years Mexico, D.F.
Experience at Conasupo	4 years
Experience in Conasupo System	No
Education	Undergraduate (Univ. Americana)/Masters (ITESM)
Previous Job	Administrative Co-ordinator, ITESM
Do you see working at Conasupo in 5 years?	Perhaps, but I am not really sure

Section#2:

1. Reduced
2. No change
3. No change
4. Increased moderately

Section#3:

- I think that through the restructuring, the Conasupo budget will decrease, Conasupo employees will decrease and a better definition of Conasupo functions will occur.
- It has changed substantially. I would say that the social function has disappeared in the majority of Conasupo activities. Now, Conasupo only markets and guarantees the supply of beans, corn and powdered milk.

Number#11

Section#1:

Job	Department boss (Fidelist)
Age and Birthplace	31 years, Cuautla, Morelos.
Experience at Conasupo	5 years
Experience in Conasupo System	No
Education	Undergraduate degree I.R.
Previous Job	First job
Do you see working at Conasupo in 5 years?	No

Section#2:

1. Reduced moderately	3. Reduced moderately
2. Increased moderately	4. No change

Section#3:

- It will be a marketing business with much fewer employees and with a different role in the government and in Mexican society.
- The social function and the responsibility will continue to be the same, unfortunately the high (*alto*) functionaries have distorted these functions for their own self-benefit.

Number#12

Section#1:

Job	Executive spokesperson to the Office of Corn Marketing (OSP)
Age and Birthplace	33 years Mexico, D.F.
Experience at Conasupo	8 years
Experience in Conasupo System	No
Education	Undergraduate degree, economics (UNAM)
Previous Job	Only Conasupo
Do you see working at Conasupo in 5 years?	Yes

Section#2:

1. Reduced	3. Reduced moderately
2. Reduced	4. No change

Section#3:

- A smaller budget; fewer employees; more selective responsibilities; more normative programmes than operative programmes.
- A marked tendency to liberalise the markets, evolving gradually from an operative role to a normative role.

Number#13

Section#1:

Job	Inter-institutional co-ordinating sub-manager (OSP)
Age and Birthplace	42 years Mexico, D.F.
Experience at Conasupo	10 years
Experience in Conasupo System	No
Education	Undergraduate degree, economics (UNAM)
Previous Job	Analysts Specialist at the Treasury Ministry
Do you see working at Conasupo in 5 years?	(No response)

Section#2:

1. Increase moderately
2. Increase moderately

3. Reduced
4. Reduced moderately

Section#3:

- It will have to adapt to the changes that appear with the variables in macroeconomic policy.
- Good. They redesigned the objectives and functions of Conasupo, concentrating resources principally on the rural population, and therefore the real social impact improved in this sector.

Number#14

Section#1:

Job	Manager (OSP)
Age and Birthplace	48 years Mexico, D.F.
Experience at Conasupo	6 years
Experience in Conasupo System	4 years at Diconsa
Education	Undergraduate degree (UNAM)
Previous Job	Sub-manager (OSP)
Do you see working at Conasupo in 5 years?	No

Section#2:

1. Reduced   3. Reduced
2. Reduced   4. Reduced

Section#3:

- For certain Conasupo will have to go back to its former responsibilities. The former responsibilities which consisted of being a corporation of parastatal businesses that had a social focus and was efficient.
- With Zedillo, Conasupo totally reduced its social responsibilities and functions. In the first Salinas period it still had the required importance but with the privatisations it turned into its present state.

Number#15

Section#1:

Job	Analysts Specialist (Fidelist)
Age and Birthplace	28 years Mexico, D.F.
Experience at Conasupo	6 years
Experience in Conasupo System	No
Education	Secondary-level
Previous Job	Analyst
Do you see working at Conasupo in 5 years?	No

Section#2:

1. Reduced   3. Reduced
2. Reduced moderately   4. Reduced

Section#3:

- It tends to disappear.
- I suppose that it has less responsibility and also its image is somewhat tarnished because of its administration, it tends to have a smaller social function.

Notes

[1] All 29 department managers and office directors at Diconsa's Mexico City headquarters and 37 of 40 Diconsa subsidiary (i.e., regional, state and local) managers possess a minimum qualification of an undergraduate degree. Fidelist's headquarters in Mexico City exhibits the same pattern.

[2] One factor that justifies this assumption is the frequent communication between Fidelist, Diconsa and Liconsa. In the first place, this has to do with former employment relationships. In the second place, Fidelist co-ordinates certain programmes with the other two agencies, the most important is Progresa.

[3] Under Zedillo, rates of social spending continue to increase as total public spending declines. The 1997 social development budget of ($US) 28.6 billion or 9 percent of GDP, followed increases in 1995 and 1996. Moreover, under his policy of *federalismo nuevo*, state and municipal authorities manage customarily centralised budgets for public education and health services. Zedillo also boosted locally-managed Municipal Development Funds (MDFs) from ($US) 830 million in 1995 to ($US) 941 million in 1996 and to ($US) 1,033 million in 1997 (*Informe de Gobierno*, 1997).

[4] On election day in July 1994, La Botz (1995: 213) notes the comments of a woman, left off the election list, and questioned about her anxiety over not voting: 'Because', said the woman, 'I was told that if I did not vote for the PRI that my child could no longer go to school, and I would lose the milk program. So I have to prove that I voted'. La Botz continues: 'What is particularly important about this story, is that it is not just one story about one mother. While interviewing voters and observers, I heard this same story, with slight variations, told several times about different women in different towns all over Mexico'.

[5] 'To bring women in as allies under Progresa is one of the social policy successes of the Zedillo presidency…[however]… Although plurality has become a feature of Mexico's social and political life, its impacts are yet to be felt in the design and implementation of social policy', notes González de la Rocha (1997: 13).

[6] The reader should note that Antonio Herrera was the Diconsa Union President in Michoacán who helped orchestrate the November 1989 national protest against the threat to CTM jobs at Diconsa (see Chapter Five).

[7] This was the official version, but I was told that a national PASE was always going to be under Sedesol's Branch 20 (e.g., a centralised programme) (Interview, Mexico City, Office of Fidelist, 4 April, 1997). For a discussion of the origins of Branch 26, see Bailey (1995: 178).

7 Clientelism and Neoliberalism: Lessons from Conasupo

Introduction

Scholars of Mexican state-society relations continue to contest the scope, pace and direction of shifts and innovations that date back to the 1982 economic crisis. The factors that are seen as exerting pressure on the old model are familiar: economic constraints and subsequent restructuring, changes to the political rules of the game, and the ascendancy of a much-heralded neoliberal, technocratic administrative class. Moreover with the transition to the first post-revolutionary, non-PRI federal administration, brought about by way of the ballot box in July 2000, it is important to reflect on the state-society legacy that the incoming Fox administration will face. Scholars of state-society relations still situate themselves between two general views: the first relies on the premise that a fundamental 'breakdown' of the old institutions is both imminent and a prerequisite to a post-clientele state-society model in Mexico. The second view depicts these institutions as resilient and flexible, capable of adapting to greater political competition and a liberalised economy; here state-society relations are bound to an incremental, controlled process of innovation.

These two views, restated in the language introduced at the start of this book, represent discontinuity (e.g., 'breakdown' or 'exit') and continuity (e.g., incremental adaptive change or 'loyalty' and 'voice'). After briefly reflecting on this larger debate, I want to turn to the lessons and the 'map' of continuity and discontinuity generated by the Conasupo case study. I will conclude by reintroducing the two central questions from the Introduction of the book: why has the process from general to targeted subsidies been so protracted? And how have patrons and their clientele politics survived after 1982? I will return to the four 'areas for discussion' outlined in Chapter One to answer these two questions.

Continuity/Clientelism and Discontinuity/Neoliberalism

Two analytic assumptions anchor the 'breakdown' or discontinuity view. The first concerns the issue of prerequisites that would need to be satisfied if Mexico is to construct a model of state-society relations where the PRI and the state are distinguishable, both institutionally and normatively. Discussions of prerequisites typically carries over into the debate on Mexico's 'democratic' transition, where it is believed that Mexico's traditional institutions are too illegitimate for the political opposition and a sceptical Mexican society, who are both well-versed in the tacit norms (informality, arbitrariness, personalism, centralised decision-making, etc.) and formal institutions (corporatism, formal *concertación*, parastatals, etc.) after decades of interaction, but whose participation will ultimately legitimise a new model. However the issue of 'what comes next' is not a chief concern of this research, rather our attention has been devoted to interpreting developments after 1982 and especially between 1988-1994.

Stepping back from considerations of 'what comes next', a second assumption is that there is a threshold or a 'critical point' beyond which Mexico's clientele pattern of state-society relations cannot continue without systemic change. Theoretically, the idea is linked to both classical modernisation theory and the 'virtuous circle' of neoliberal proponents. Looking back at the 1980s, it also reflects empirical lessons learnt from the 'authoritarian transitions' witnessed elsewhere across Latin America. In one guise or another, the main view in the Mexican case has been that, beginning with the 1982 crisis, the maintenance costs or constraints associated with the authoritarian state-society model have increased due to pressure on public spending, splits in the PRI elite, NAFTA, opposition party challenges and the development of a more pluralistic Mexican civil society (that is, greater media freedom, NGO development, popular movements). The relentless pressure to innovate and recreate institutional mechanisms to legitimate the old model has focused attention to possible 'triggers' that might spark a collapse – for example, economic and foreign policy crises in Argentina in 1982, unified political opposition in Chile in 1988, and the collapse of external constraints in Eastern Europe in 1989. However, neither the economic crises in 1982-1983, 1986-1988, and 1995-1996, nor the various political crises since 1982 (fraudulent elections and the Mexico City earthquake in 1985, the PRI split in 1987, the Chiapas rebellion and political assassinations in 1994, opposition control of the lower house as of 1997, etc.), nor the end of the Cold War have triggered a free-fall in Mexico.

By contrast, the incrementalist view that tries to evaluate the factors that encourage continuity downplays the idea of a rapid linear progression toward inevitable rupture.[1] Here scholars agree that there is a continuous exertion of pressure on old patterns of state-society relations, both at the level of tacit norms and at the level of formal institutional channels. But they choose to concentrate and accentuate the contextual circumstances peculiar to Mexico and the resiliency of Mexican institutions, specifically their capacity to keep respective clients loyal to the traditional rules of the game. The causal relationship is often reformulated so that pressure is shown to lead to innovation and steps toward politically pragmatic cost reduction. In this vein, Craske's (1994a: 43) investigation of the PRI's Popular Sector organisations during the Salinas years concludes: 'The most prevalent outcome has been the modernisation of authoritarianism' ... 'The development of the Mexican political system has never been unilinear, but has been continuously renegotiated *vis-à-vis* society'.

Continuity is therefore rooted in the strong propensity of institutions and clients to adapt to new political and economic circumstances rather than electing to incur the risks that would inevitably follow a complete breakdown. Loyalty, in most cases, comes down to a combination of limited options at the local and national levels due to severe economic realities for large numbers of Mexicans coupled with the state's often insurmountable resource advantage in the contestation for political power. This combination is at the centre of most studies that try to come to terms with the resiliency of the PRI's corporatist branches after 1982 and in most studies that try to explain why the rural and marginal poor continue to vote for the PRI. In the context of this current investigation, one might ask why changes such as transparent national elections and new space for opposition parties – illustrations of 'discontinuity' – should disrupt interaction among clients and Conasupo? These relationships are formulated against a background of a society characterised by high income inequality, a serious deficit in basic services, and no national experience with multi-party democracy. Is it logical to expect that clients might elect to 'throw the bums out' or 'demand a new deal with the state'?[2] Until the barriers that preclude such a radical realignment of norms and perceptions are tackled then the logic behind continuity and *certain segments* of the Mexican population may remain in place; it is not clear that market development and cleaner elections can achieve this by themselves.

How do we situate this study of Conasupo amid these two contrasting views of state-society relations? In some respects, Conasupo challenges and supports the core assumptions of either view. This case study does not dispute the premise that a profound rupture is a prerequisite of a new state-society model in Mexico; in fact, it provides further justification. Conversations at Conasupo, laden with references to 'us' (PRI and the state) and 'them' (PAN, PRD, opposition elected officials, the United States government, etc.), lend more empirical weight to this premise. Yet, despite this normative issue, Conasupo – in particular, its management during the Salinas years – exemplifies the types of post-1982 private and public norms, institutional arrangements and 'systemic adaptability' that continued to push a final breakdown into the future.

Likewise, the Conasupo case study poses certain problems for the breakdown view's premise about 'legitimate institutions'. It is the archetypal institution steeped in the norms of clientele state-society relations, but whether it is 'illegitimate' requires further comment. Before Raúl Salinas came to symbolise everything that was wrong with his brother's administration, Conasupo was a legitimate enterprise in (1) the eyes of much of Mexican society, and, though this may seem somewhat counterintuitive, (2) the political opposition most threatened by PRI-Conasupo clientelism, the PRD. While the PRD advocates sweeping reform of traditional Conasupo programmes, it has never, even after the experience of the Salinas years, supported the liquidation of Conasupo.

'External candidates' represented 45 percent of the PRD's candidate list in the 1997 election and the highest concentration was found in the DFMA and the state of Veracruz (*Reforma*, 19 March 1997). It is interesting that Demetrio Sodi de la Tijera, Conasupo's most vocal PRI supporter in 1987-1990, won a federal deputy seat in the D.F. under the PRD banner in 1997. Alejandro Ordorica, another ex-PRI member, who also succeeded Sodi de la Tijera at the office of social provision in the D.F. (under Salinas), won another seat for the PRD in the D.F in 1997. One could speculate that, given the stance of the Cárdenas administration in the DFMA, in particular its attempt to compete with Liconsa via the 'old norms' (clientelism), a Cárdenas presidential victory in the year 2000 would not have necessarily undermined the legitimacy of the types of traditional institutions evaluated in this case study – albeit, new managers and emblems would be expected. Likewise, although the PAN officially supports liquidating Conasupo, it is worth remembering the episode between ex-PAN governor Vicente Fox and Fidelist that took place in early 1997 (see Chapter Six). Fox did not advocate the end of the Tortilla Programme, but rather he wanted such patronage to operate at the state level, where the PAN enjoys more power.

Assessing the link between the 'costs' of maintaining clientele norms and a future breakdown, Conasupo pushes us to reconsider some conventionally accepted parameters. Let us first distinguish between political and economic 'costs' because the trigger for different scholars typically focuses on one more than the other.[3] The comments above on legitimacy and Conasupo suggest that the 'political costs' associated with traditional Conasupo operations were not too dissimilar before and after 1982 (e.g., objections from the PAN, domestic business, and World Bank/IMF). What is more interesting is the issue of economic costs and a clientele breakdown in the narrow context of Conasupo. De la Madrid elected to increase the Conasupo budget as well as its modes of intervention (rural distribution, processing activities, etc.), while the policy of Salinas did the opposite on both accounts. Thus the former loosened the main constraints on Conasupo (budgetary and distributional) while the latter attempted to tighten them. What is paradoxical yet revealing is that Conasupo, as this research has shown, served more clients under Salinas than de la Madrid. This experience raises a concern for those who would contend that Mexico's clientele model relies upon an expanding resource pie (Morris, 1991).

Similarly, Rodríguez's (1997) broader study of decentralisation in Mexico concludes that constant pressure on state-society relations forces the PRI-led government, paradoxically, to decentralise or 'give up power' at the centre – a move that spreads the cost of governing more widely – as an effective strategy to maintain control at the centre. The logic of economic efficiency underpins this view; the Mexican state resembles a private firm that 'sub-contracts' less essential activities so that it can concentrate on core decision-making. Conasupo has followed a similar logic. Pressure to cut public spending implied that to maintain continuity among strategic populations (corporatist branches, lower-income DFMA consumers, etc.)

general subsidies had to be scrapped and replaced by a policy of targeting and rationalisation of non-essential activities (processing of basic goods, marketing non-basic grains, etc.) so that the parastatal could focus its limited resources on priority, legitimacy generation commitments.

Policy Success at Conasupo during the Salinas Years

In Chapter One, policy success was defined in terms of Conasupo's capacity to generate political capital for the executive, within some not very precise budget and distributional constraints, arguably Conasupo's central *raison d'être*. In turn it was also suggested that political capital flowed from two sources: 'final output' and a 'process' (informal, arbitrary, centralised) that joined lower-income Mexicans, political elites and the corporatist branches of the PRI around the logic of social justice. In theory, the switch to a neoliberal social policy should have increased Conasupo's budgetary and distributional constrains, shifting the balance from continuity to discontinuity. However, while neoliberal/technocratic rationality was not absent, it was more a loose boundary around an entity with a more familiar political rationale. Two types of indicators can help shed light on the issue of political capital and Conasupo: voting behaviour of typical Conasupo beneficiaries (final output) and the maintenance of preferential commitments with the corporatist sector (process).

Table 7.0 Votes for Parties in Congressional Elections (1988-1997)

Year	PRI	PAN	Cárdenas/PRD
1988 (%)	50.4	17.1	29.6 (Cárdenas)
1991 (%)	61.4	17.7	8.9 (PRD)
1994 (%)	50.3	26.8	16.7 (PRD)
1997 (%)	40.0	27.2	26.3 (PRD)

Source: Wallis (1998: 166)

Table 7.0 summarises party support in Congressional elections between 1988 and 1997. At this general level, I suggested in Chapter One that we should focus on support for Cárdenas/PRD. Not only did the challenge on the Left capture a large portion of the 'official' vote in 1988 (29.6 percent), more important is that the typical Cárdenas/PRD voter roughly coincided with Conasupo's beneficiaries – more often lower-income or working class, unionised, and located in the D.F. or central Mexico. From table 1.0 (Chapter One, p.27) these groups largely contributed to the PRD's decline in 1991 (8.9 percent). On the specific issue of the PRI's 1991 turnaround, evidence from the Conasupo case study reinforces the position of Varley (1996), Domínguez and McCann (1995), and others, who believe that the provision of basic services was a decisive factor because the types of voters who switched their votes were those who clamoured for basic services. It is worth pointing out that women, the members of the household who came into contact with Conasupo daily, represented one of the largest defections from the PRD – according to table 1.0, 20 percent of females voted for Cárdenas in 1988 yet the figure fell to 5 percent in 1991. Turning to 1994, the PRD electoral support improved on its 1991 total but fell far short of the Cárdenas performance in 1988 and at no time in the 1994 campaign did it pose a real threat to the PRI. One could look at a few interesting developments with core beneficiaries of Conasupo: in 1988 Cárdenas won 24 percent of the working class vote and 20 percent of the female vote, but in 1994 managed 8 percent of the working class vote and 8 percent of female voters.

Yet, the electoral landscape was shook profoundly in 1997, when the PRD registered 26.3 percent of the total vote and more relevant for our purposes Cárdenas secured a landslide victory in the DFMA. Here we find Conasupo's core clients abandoning the PRI en mass. The unprecedented economic crisis that hit Mexico in 1995 and 1996 in general, together with the Raúl Salinas/Conasupo scandal that played out on the front pages of national papers throughout 1996 and 1997 in particular, of course eroded the 'political capital' accumulated during the Salinas years. However, it is too soon to speculate on whether this spells a breakdown of traditional clientele norms in this area of state-society relations or a situation similar to 1988.[4]

Switching from elections to the matter of corporatist commitments or 'process', Conasupo again seems to have generated meaningful political capital. President de la Madrid, in moments of instability in 1983 and 1986, secured the loyalty of the CTM and CNC partly through a wide array of preferential, informal and clientelistic Conasupo *concertación* agreements. I will elaborate on the issue of corporatist commitments and Salinas below; here it suffices to note that President Salinas continued the informal, preferential treatment of official unions, especially during the height of his legitimacy crisis (1989-1991). By 1994, though Conasupo lost its processing infrastructure, wholesale services (Impesca) and large-sized urban stores, it still delivered subsidies to record numbers of grain producers and final consumers and maintained its corporatist commitments – a classic case where we observe a traditional institution recreating itself to adapt to a new environment, while reinforcing its *raison d'être*.

Expanding the discussion of 'process' beyond patrons and clients, it is also possible to identify a macro political economy achievement outside these aggregate statistics from the Salinas years. Despite Conasupo's clandestine growth – that is, its simultaneous exit and re-entry in food markets – observers ranging from academics outside and inside Mexico, the domestic media and the World Bank all greeted the Conasupo *Modernización* Plan (CMP) of October 1989 as an assault on the parastatal and its customary duty as a bridge between the executive, the PRI and segments of Mexican society. Mexican sociologist Gurza Lavalle (1994) writes that, by 1994, the CMP had redefined the post-revolutionary meaning and boundaries of both the public sphere and strategic activities for government intervention. Meanwhile, as late as 1997, members of the Mexican media depicted Conasupo as 'withering on the vine' under Salinas.

In this way, skilful management and packaging of the reform process at Conasupo produced what, on the surface, seemed unattainable. President Salinas negotiated and 'delivered the goods' to new and old intermediaries. He convinced the World Bank otherwise, to the point that it funded reforms in Mexican food markets throughout the Salinas years. Finally, he manipulated the domestic media into believing that Conasupo's days were numbered or, after 1991, that the technocratic-driven, neoliberal and popular Solidarity apparatus had taken over the parastatal. In so doing, Conasupo generated political capital (and votes) for Salinas beyond the parameters of our definition of policy success.

Conasupo: Redrawing the Continuity-Discontinuity Map

This book started with two questions: Why has a government that managed radical reform elsewhere in the public sector, found it so difficult to deliver consumption and production subsidies to poor households? And at a more theoretical level, how, under significant economic and political change, did the abstract 'patron' survive, along with the legitimacy of their informal, clientele politics, when both modernisation theory and the 'virtuous circle' of neoliberalism predicted the contrary? One could posit a variety of answers to these questions in the context of the Conasupo case study and I propose to proceed by returning to the 'four areas for discussion' outlined in Chapter One.

(1) Parameters for Policymakers and Institutional Reform

The first area for discussion concerns the idea that a small circle of technocrats may not be able to impose tightly defined neoliberal policies ('technocratic revolution from above') to long-running services when the executive prescribes *reform* but prohibits full *privatisation* or *parallel* administrative and operational structures. In part, this returns us to the normative assumption of the 'breakdown' view. However, one of the principle contentions of this research is that the last three presidential administrations have demonstrated a strong capacity for dismantling traditional public institutions, but they have not shown the ability to reform certain areas of the public sector where liquidation is not feasible.

Commencing in 1983, a series of unsuccessful efforts to replace Conasupo's general subsidies with a coherent and efficient policy of needs-based targeting illustrates that the obstacles to reform are highly obstructive. This conclusion concurs with pre-1982 research on Conasupo (see appendix 1.0). Moreover, in discussions with decision-makers who served during the de la Madrid, Salinas and Zedillo years, there is still a tendency to point to lower-level 'intermediaries' as the chief impediment blocking or distorting official objectives. Earlier I cited Austin and Fox's assertion that the Conasupo bureaucracy 'bent' official policy before 1982 (appendix 1.0), an observation that points to a marked imbalance in bureaucratic agency *vis-à-vis* reformist goals imposed from above. In theory, the switch to a market-oriented development model in general and the targeting of social resources in particular, aimed at reversing this predicament. This case study, however, has shown that bureaucratic agency at Conasupo, and the general tendency of official policy to be bent to meet the needs of old patrons and clients, continued into the 1990s and sometimes stymied reformers outright.

Admittedly, this interest in policy parameters and technocratic reform stems from the decision of Salinas in 1989 to consider imposing a neoliberal agenda at Conasupo, and a general suspicion that, in practice, reformers inside the Mexican government enjoy limited manoeuvrability when reforming highly politicised and entrenched institutions. Conasupo's history of recursive administrative reforms between 1961 and 1988 testifies to this situation, and it is not self-evident why this time around should have been different.

Regarding the CMP, its policy formation period (1988 to late 1989) boiled down to a struggle over policy parameters for the next six years. When candidate Salinas contemplated the discontinuation of the parastatal on the 1988 campaign trail, he sent up a trial balloon to test the public's appetite for radical innovation. He figured that, after black markets in Conasupo goods had cropped up around Mexico City in the inflationary climate of 1986-1988, Conasupo had perhaps stopped generating political capital among its intended beneficiaries. If this was true, it seems probable that Salinas would have decided to scrap Conasupo altogether and divert free-upped resources into Solidarity, a general policy preference that he exercised elsewhere. Bailey (1995) and Rodríguez (1997) point to 'recentralisation' of this type under Salinas. But his disputed victory at the polls and the defection of traditionally loyal PRI constituencies (and Conasupo clients) to Cárdenas, together with a public, corporatist and partisan backlash regarding Conasupo's future, forced Salinas to step back and eventually to instruct the Secretary of Commerce (Secofi) to formulate a compromise. So the strategy to 'recreate Conasupo' under the guise of Solidarity was dropped for a plan more suited to the prevailing political threats to the government. Secofi in turn elected to sell non-priority Conasupo assets and to launch a six-year agenda to reform the exiting administrative and operational apparatus – in other words the CMP.

Policy uncertainty resulted from the political environment that engulfed Conasupo in 1988 and 1989. Initially, the threat to the PRI appeared on the right, as the 1980s witnessed PAN strength grow among the urban middle class and small business class, particularly in northern states. Liquidating Conasupo, particularly its retail operations (Diconsa) and processing factories (Iconsa), both of which competed with local businesses (recall Alberto Santos' role in Monterrey), appeared as a rational response to the prevailing political challenge; likewise, Conasupo's old clients could always be placated via Solidarity. However, the Cárdenas rise in the 1988 election and his challenge on the issue of 'social justice' reconfigured the direction of Conasupo policy; it was now employed to reverse the slide among the government's core clients (the urban and rural poor and unionised workers). This experience during 1988 and 1989 reiterates how some traditional institutions can readily adapt to challenges thrown up in the constant process to legitimate the old state-society model.

Not surprisingly given the politics involved, the CMP was 'bent' almost instantly. Until 1988, Conasupo-producer arrangements had revolved around a geographically confined network of warehouses and rail/highway transportation facilities, neither of which changed under the CMP. Chapter Three showed that the transition from general (12 grains) to targeted (2 grains) subsidies unfolded so as to encourage long-serving Conasupo producers, often commercial growers who had previously cultivated wheat and sorghum, to take up subsidised corn production and remain beneficiaries of Conasupo resources. The scope of this switch, coupled with the near halt of Conasupo's corn imports after 1990, inflated the total number of affiliated Conasupo grain producers to an unprecedented level through 1994. Here again Conasupo 'gave up some control' (i.e., 10 grains) in a way that eventually reinforced its position as a patron in rural Mexico.

It is hard to misconstrue the evidence on the consumer side of Conasupo operations. Starting in 1983, innovations to the Tortilla Programme led to wild distortions in the field and sometimes local clientele arrangements hijacked entire regional allotments of subsidies. Salinas and his Conasupo team acknowledged and used this history, first on the 1988 campaign trail as a rationale for discontinuing the parastatal, and later as a justification for their six-year reform agenda – for example, *tortibono* abuse justified the exchange of coupons for computerised cards. As this sophisticated technology came on line in 1991-1992, the new tortilla scheme officially operated a beneficiary list of 6,000 households in the DFMA. Yet, when Fidelist replaced Diconsa in October 1992, it found 600,000 cards circulating around the DFMA, a level of abuse or 'bending' that rivalled earlier schemes.

As for the Milk Programme, Liconsa constructed around 1,300 *lecherías* from 1978 to 1988; however, the total surpassed 6,000 by 1994, and most of this construction had been realised before 1992. In fact, Salinas constructed 500 *lecherías* to benefit 2 million DFMA households in his administration's first 100 days alone. Following the discovery of widespread abuse by independent investigators in October 1993, Salinas conceded that the task of reorienting Liconsa awaited his successor because the 'appropriate conditions to proceed' did not exist. This candid admission was curious for any Mexican executive, not to mention one that enjoyed a 70 percent approval rating going into the final year of his term. Unprecedented resources flowing through traditional intermediaries (and subsequent 'bending') almost certainly contributed to a recovery of PRI electoral support after 1988 in the DFMA, among the urban poor, and among unionised workers. Returning to Varley's general interpretation of the PRI's electoral turnaround after 1988, Salinas gave the urban poor basic services, their central demand of the political system – something Cárdenas convinced voters in 1988 that only he would do.

The CMP prompted an urban-to-rural transfer of Diconsa resources, as it privatised 589 centrally located, warehouse-type urban stores and opened over a thousand smaller stores per year in marginal urban and rural communities. Diconsa offers another example where policy was able to adapt to prevailing circumstances: (1) the figure of 589 stores slated for privatisation and calls for cutting Diconsa's budget, first appeared in a 1986 World Bank policy report; (2) the top area of Diconsa re-investment of funds generated from the privatisation of certain assets was the union-run Infonavit Diconsa stores (table 3.8, Chapter Three), thus safeguarding and 'targeting' traditional union interests; and (3) the negotiation of new stores brought Salinas (actually his brother) in direct consultation with thousands of lower-income communities that may have been vulnerable to the PRD.

After the PRI's electoral landslide and the PRD's collapse in the 1991 election, Conasupo's 1989-1991 policy of courting the urban poor and official unions yielded to a policy of consolidation and efforts to improve efficiency so that Conasupo might, at some later date, be recreated into a legitimate component of a neoliberal state-society model (i.e., needs-based, transparent and accountable distribution). Original policy parameters were dropped and parallel structures emerged inside Conasupo: first, the unanticipated construction of Fidelist in 1992, and the subsequent centralisation of administrative functions in the newly-formed and executive-controlled Technical Committee. It should be reiterated that in no way did the CMP in October 1989 foreshadow these administrative changes.

At the start of a new *sexenial* cycle, President Zedillo collapsed these parallel administrative institutions as well as Liconsa, Diconsa and Fidelist into Sedesol, severing their link with Conasupo and essentially 'recreating Conasupo' in the guise that Salinas first envisioned back in 1989. As I argued in Chapter Six, it remains an open question whether steps taken under Zedillo have curbed bureaucratic agency and bending, or should be viewed as radical redrawing of the old parameters for policy-making. Bureaucrats from the old Conasupo apparatus are still in control of a nation-wide apparatus where the old norms of informal, centralised and arbitrary decision-making have not disappeared. Thus, future 'discontinuity' or another CMP-style 'recreation' (something that I would not preclude) must ultimately depend on how the government chooses to negotiate, operate, supply and monitor retail stores and tortilla and milk subsidies.

Finally, it should be mentioned that, in January 1999, Conasupo consumption services were 'officially' transferred under parallel arrangements at Sedesol, while President Zedillo authorised the discontinuation of Conasupo grain purchases as well as the entire parastatal. However, the 'privatisation of Conasupo' does not signal an end to traditional Conasupo services (Liconsa, Diconsa and Fidelist) that contributed to effective political management under Salinas, nor should it be mistaken for a cost induced 'breakdown' of old state-society arrangements. Traditional programmes continue under other administrative arrangements, new programmes continue to emerge, and it is unclear whether Conasupo's producer programmes have been 'discontinued' or moved under the control of the Secretary of Agriculture.

(2) *Post-1982 Executive Management of Parastatals*

A second area for discussion concerns executive management of parastatals. Many have speculated that the neoliberal/technocratic wing of the PRI has dominated state operations and public policy since 1983, and that 'neoliberalism' is connected to specific policy decisions and shifts in state-society relations. Here one would then expect that 'neoliberal' executives would manage parastatals such as Conasupo differently than 'populist' executives.

With the limits and logic of the *sexenial* cycle, if an incoming president was serious about reforming Conasupo's position in state-society relations, he had to be willing to break preferential ties to the PRI's corporatist branches and end general access enjoyed by both middle-income consumers in and around Mexico City, and commercial producers located around Conasupo's rural grain infrastructure. It was well known inside the government that this complex of arrangements could not deliver a neoliberal alternative.

President de la Madrid's National Development Plan 1983-1988 increased the level of consumption subsidies offered by Diconsa to aid vulnerable segments of the population during Mexico's economic crisis. In this context 'vulnerable' constituted households earning below two times the national minimum wage, Diconsa's criteria since 1965. However, Chapter Four's review of the de la Madrid years (in particular, table 4.2) found that these benefits accrued to official corporatist unions disproportionately.

President Salinas touted that his agenda represented far-reaching neoliberal reform based on the principle of catering to those most in need. Yet he embarked on a reckless expansion of Conasupo subsidies, largely, though not exclusively, through corporatist channels. Distribution commitments between official unions and Conasupo were renewed in March 1989 and, again, in his first 100 days Salinas and his team negotiated, most via the CNOP, 500 *lecherías* in the DFMA. At this time when there was much confusion about the traditional 'rules of the game' these actions transmitted a strong and well-known message about the road ahead to would-be bureaucratic reformers, to corporatist intermediaries and to clientele populations. In the DFMA, in particular, the new executive, following his predecessors, appeared committed to managing Conasupo as a channel to negotiate and 'deliver the goods' to loyal communities. Likewise,

Salinas took steps to assure labour unions that his intention was not to abandon them – besides resource commitments, he also pledged to hire CTM employees at all new Diconsa stores and construct Infonavit Diconsa stores.

Leaving aside lower-income grain producers and the fact that the CMP increased the CNC's participation in Conasupo operations (it was Salinas who brought the CNC into the Administrative Council of Boruconsa), why did the CMP encourage Conasupo's commercial clients to take up subsidised corn production? By 1991, a mixture of bureaucratic agency and the volition of commercial grain producers combined to 'bend' the CMP, yet there was a reluctance by the Salinas administration to alter the established guidelines. Perhaps, in part, the insistence of the Mexicans in 1991 that corn should be added to the NAFTA agreement (against the advice of the United States negotiators) can be interpreted as a response to the decisions of producers in 1990. Even if this is true, it does not diminish the fact that Conasupo's producer subsidies were maintained between 1990 and 1994, and that Conasupo-producer arrangements at the end of the Salinas term resembled those in place in 1988. Logically, as it became apparent that things had gone wrong (by the end of 1990) the Salinas administration should have altered the criteria for Conasupo grain purchases, so as to realise the official goal of the CMP in this area, that is, targeting of subsidies to lower-income producers. In a backdoor way, President Salinas did this through a parallel scheme, the Programme of Direct Subsidies for Agricultural Producers (Procampo, 1993-present).[5] Bolívar *et al.* (1993: 67) note that 2.2 million of the 3.2 million producers that got aid from Procampo in 1993 and 1994 were producers that had no previous access to government support. But regarding traditional Conasupo clients, Salinas left the matter to his successor, another indication of the difficulty and perceived political costs in reforming the types of long-standing relationships and institutions under review.

Executives stamp their imprint and reveal their policy orientations through the appointment of Conasupo personnel. In December 1988, President Salinas left Conasupo operations in the hands of two *politicos*, Ignacio Ovalle and Raúl Salinas. The first Salinas team departed for more prestigious positions in the public sector in the final months of 1991 and early 1992. This period marked the end of Conasupo's reckless expansion of consumer and producer subsidies, the beginning of a more coherent and intense reform agenda, and the restoration of single-party dominance at the polls. Chapter Five found, in 1992, that a new team, many possessing unquestionable technocratic credentials, took over and immediately demonstrated a new level of neoliberal/technocratic ambition.

If, as I am suggesting, political economy logic guided executive management in this area, then perhaps continuity in state-society relations can be seen as a pre-requisite for imposing neoliberal reform. This would help to explain the discrepancies in policy management between 1988-1991 and 1992-1994. Consider, in addition to the examples reviewed above, the timetable for privatising various Conasupo assets – this part of the CMP was under tight executive control. Iconsa, a minor component of the Conasupo apparatus, was classified as a 'non-priority activity' in 1989. Its factories were privatised, with the proceeds recycled into Conasupo's consumption infrastructure. However, in the Administrative Council's annual meeting in October 1991, 'non-priority' encompassed Impesca, Miconsa, and Liconsa (factories and not *lecherías*). In a relatively brief span, the same executive-run Administrative Council authorised two strikingly different visions of the parastatal's future infrastructure. Given that the Mexican government faced a relatively propitious budgetary climate in 1991 (compared to 1989), it is clear that this policy shift corresponded to a new executive mandate at Conasupo, handed down around October 1991.

Our discussion of Progresa offers an indication of whether comparable executive management continued under Zedillo. The Campeche pilot programme had a neoliberal profile and treasury officials exerted pressure on its financing between its launch in 1995 and the July 1997 mid-term election. However, Chapter Six showed that the PRI's loss at the polls coincided with a redirection of policy toward traditional institutions. Zedillo even stipulated restrictions to curb the future influence of treasury officials on Progresa's financial structure, the best illustration of this was the adoption of mandatory inflation adjustments.

(3) *Traditional Parastatals and Methodology*

A third area for discussion raises a methodological preoccupation and essentially expands the discussion to a more general level: in some areas of public policy there is a tendency for a political economy calculation to transcend a neoliberal or technocratic paradigm shift among policy makers.

Although Conasupo offers an example to support this contention, it is an oversimplification to reduce this case study to a simple 'either/or' dichotomy because the more accurate depiction is one of two causal factors which overlap: neoliberal policy solutions and the relentless pressure to innovate to maintain legitimacy. This overlap comes into view at different points in this case study. For instance, there was a general intellectual shift at the beginning of the 1980s away from universal subsidies in favour of needs-based targeting, yet a highly politicised execution of this new policy ensued in the 1980s and 1990s. In fact, Chapters Three (producer subsidies), Four (consumer subsidies) and Five (bureaucratic reform) discovered a conspicuous and consistent gap as well as wild distortions of policy that started as broadly neoliberal.

Repeating the findings of earlier studies of Conasupo, there are conceptual problems when the components of policy are analysed according to a strict 'efficiency' criterion. Successive fiascos in schemes to target handouts would suggest general technocratic '*in*competence', or minimally, an aversion to jeopardise broader legitimacy concerns for gains in administrative efficiency – in which case the empirical and normative significance of the terms 'technocrat' and 'neoliberalism' breaks down. How does one square the circle of Secofi's internationally acclaimed and executive-supported neoliberal technocrats, and their ill-conceived, inefficient policy decisions at Conasupo? Secofi, via the Administrative Council, acted on President Salinas' policy preferences, and it designed or approved the various schemes in the CMP that upheld old partisan and/or corporatist commitments. Secofi delineated eligibility guidelines for Conasupo services under the CMP based on strict socioeconomic considerations; however, it also elected to filter resources through the PRI's corporatist intermediaries – a past recipe for failure. In this way, the overlap of neoliberalism and political contingencies are best analysed in the context of the executive's larger agenda to secure public support.[6] Briefly discussing the competence of decision-makers underscores the danger one faces if policy prescriptions are divorced from their broader political context in this area of public policy.

Perhaps the most striking display of the neoliberal-political overlap was in Conasupo's policy inside and outside the DFMA. Conasupo abandoned any attempt at a coherent or assertive reformist agenda inside the DFMA, yet in the geographic areas where the Salinas administration provided the Tortilla and Milk Programmes for the first time, it realised meaningful steps and registered success toward needs-based distribution. So whilst we see an attempt made at encouraging neoliberal delivery of Conasupo subsidies, this attempt progressed in a way that stopped at the edge of old distribution agreements.

Finally, to examine Progresa on its initial 'neoliberal/technocratic merits' would overlook issues that might determine its future success. Another intellectual shift (the 'bundling' of social resources according to the Chilean model) provided the impetus to reorient a number of social programmes in Mexico, including the Milk and Tortilla Programmes. By 1996 there were various blueprints and funds available to turn a small pilot programme into a national bundling scheme. The process laid in limbo for approximately a year awaiting executive approval. Chapter Six's analysis of this interval revealed a great deal about the balance between the resolve to adopt neoliberal solutions and the relentless pressure to uphold traditional political commitments. The development that broke the impasse seemed to be, again, consideration of a political nature rather than neoliberal (or macroeconomic). Before the decision was made, it was the view of Fidelist employees and the managers of the pilot scheme that Zedillo sided with a 'neoliberal blueprint' sponsored by treasury officials. As Salinas backtracked on the 'neoliberal option' following the rejection of the PRI at the ballot box in 1988, that same cycle appears to have been repeated in July 1997, for Zedillo soon left Progresa in the hands of the traditional social sector.

(4) *Continuity and Clientele Norms*

A fourth and final area for discussion considers why there might be reasons that clientele norms can survive as old patterns of reciprocity come under threat. Research on Mexican state-society relations, from the neoliberal, the modernisation, or the pluralist viewpoints, often assume that a degeneration of 'old bargains' – via the market (specialisation, free trade, etc.), processes of modernisation (i.e., education, technology or information), or shifts in power among political groups – is *a priori* sufficient for more efficient, modern or multi-actor modes of exchange. While these views accurately characterise developments across a broad spectrum of relations between state and society in Mexico, they do not describe events at Conasupo. On several occasions (with grain producers, the ongoing switch from general to targeted subsidies, urban consumer services, etc.) a more accurate picture is one of concurrent and repeated episodes of liberalisation and re-intervention, attacks on clientelism and fresh opportunities for clientelism.

After January 1990, faced with an erratic international grain market or taking steps to remain with Conasupo, many commercial grain producers who marketed their wheat, sorghum and soybeans to the parastatal in the past, made the decision (and incurred the adjustment costs) to switch into corn production – one step forward, one step back. The decision to discontinue 589 large supermarkets and subsequently re-deploying thousands of Diconsa stores to impoverished rural and marginal urban areas presents a comparable scenario. Here, transfers from urban to rural zones promised more rational use of social assistance in the fight against poverty. Yet the fact that there were no guidelines to structure negotiations between executive representatives (in this case the President's brother) and community leaders before 1993 (Chapter Five), well after the boom in store construction, ensured that, again, state-society bargaining took place according to the informal, arbitrary, and executive-driven logic that has long been the norm underpinning Mexico's old state-society model. Ignacio Ovalle responded to a question about the best way to use Solidarity funds for the construction of Diconsa stores and *lecherías*:

> The PRI will demand that Solidarity provide support to our members. And if other people organise themselves, let them receive benefits too, but not at the expense of the organisation that good *PRIistas* have already achieved (Dresser, 1991: 28).

On balance, the substance of the bargain or slice of the pie fluctuated for some old Conasupo clients during the Salinas years; nevertheless, the result did not mark a radical transformation or, in areas long served by Conasupo, an environment any less clientelistic – that is, less selective, less partisan and less informal. Here we observe how it was possible for abstract patrons inside or outside the parastatal, and their clientele politics and long-serving networks, to survive neoliberal policy prescriptions such as targeting, agricultural price liberalisation, Total Quality Control Management, privatisation, meritocratic recruitment, and so forth.

So far we have focused on the state without commenting on society. How beneficiaries responded to neoliberal innovations at Conasupo is also revealing. It reflects the complexity of laden social norms and expectations incorporated in the area of state-society relations that has been served by Conasupo. To give one example, Conasupo beneficiaries were offered free rather than merely subsidised tortillas in 1990, and the immediate reaction of this population was to walk from *tortillería* to *tortillería* using cards multiple times. It seems that the inducement of free tortillas fostered no conviction to comply with the government's official eligibility guidelines (one free kilo per day), and sparked more and novel kinds of abuse.

However, other social reactions to neoliberal solutions turned up in this case study; for example, Fidelist employees openly acknowledged a shadow pricing system in operation at its affiliated though privately owned *tortillerías*. Surveys from the Campeche pilot programme found that beneficiaries often preferred traditional Conasupo services; thus, rather than embracing the opportunity to utilise consumption subsidies on a range of goods at local markets (i.e., the Campeche PASE scheme), respondents favoured access to free tortillas and heavily subsidised Liconsa milk according to the old rules and through the old intermediaries that lie outside the marketplace. Perhaps parallels can be drawn with Aitken's (1996: 31) observation on Mexican political culture: 'A corrupt cacique who fulfilled his role as a patron and responded to his people in moments of crisis may be preferable to a bureaucrat who applied the rules in a form that did not respond to the people's needs, even if the bureaucrat were honest'.

Conclusion

The answers to our two questions as well as broader implications concerning state-society relations flow from the above areas for discussion. First, the relentless pressure to innovate and legitimise the old state-society model surrounded Conasupo and caused the protracted and unfinished switch from general subsidies to needs-based targeting. The last three Mexican presidents have refused to take the steps that might precipitate a 'breakdown' of old clientele arrangements. Meaningful policy innovation was not absent from successive episodes of 'recreating' Conasupo, but at the level of state-society relations such changes produced incremental, protracted changes rather than a fundamental breakdown of the old norms, institutions and tacit bargains.

Second, resilient patrons and the legitimacy of their clientele politics are tied to the specific policy decisions that underpinned this incremental process of innovation. Close empirical inspection of policy-making revealed an unwillingness to sever links to the PRI's corporatist branches and to end the informal and arbitrary nature of Conasupo agreements in general. This provided plenty of opportunities for new and old clientele arrangements or 'bending' of policy that started as neoliberal. Neither de la Madrid nor Salinas challenged the old norms and expectations categorically. Across Conasupo, this reinforced the expectations that the 'old rules of the game' were still in place and that the message from above was one that still prioritised *loyalty* (clientele arrangements) rather than *exit* (coherent needs-based or neoliberal distribution) – of course the centralised control of Conasupo policy precluded *voice*.

As far as 'society' is concerned, for the lower-income population that relies on Conasupo benefits, challenging the legitimacy of clientele norms (*exit*) implies enormous risks. In Mexico half the population could not afford the daily basket of basic goods in 1997. The state's particular blend of neoliberal innovations and respect of old intermediaries and clientele norms raised the costs to *exit*. In this way policy-making both created the space for patrons and nurtured the necessary conditions that reinforced the legitimacy of clientele arrangements.

Finally, the Conasupo case study offers insight into broader patterns of state-society relations. First, evaluating Conasupo as opposed to a parallel programme like Solidarity reveals the ways in which neoliberal solutions respond to traditional bureaucratic agency. Long-term vested interests nurtured under the old 'rules of the game' operated inside the Conasupo policy arena. Although these old rules delayed parallel institutions, a process of 'recreation' was the endpoint after trial and error, representing a protracted (and still not achieved) stage before a 'final breakdown'. Innovations in the 1980s, the CMP, international consultants, 'smart cards' and computer systems, and Total Quality Control Management training only delayed the split and later 'recreation' of Conasupo under Zedillo. In the end neoliberal solutions succumbed to the old institutional norms and logic, failing either to deliver efficient, needs-based distribution or de-legitimatise clientele reciprocity. This contributed to continuity or an incremental process of innovation. Arguably, this map of post-1982 state-society relations strikes a more accurate balance between continuity and discontinuity than the conventional depiction developed in Chapter One. Indeed, Conasupo illustrates the types of uncertainties and accommodations that can be expected to have confronted post-1982 (and perhaps future) efforts to impose neoliberal policy in other areas of the public sector, such as the judiciary (notably Mexico's autonomous courts with special jurisdiction in labour, electoral, administrative, tax and agrarian disputes), the police force, the customs services, revenue generation services, the consumer protection agency (Profeco) and other parastatals (Infonavit, Pemex, IMSS, DIF, etc.). In these areas, it is plausible that the political costs or practical constraints furnish similar conditions to those at Conasupo.

Second, the Conasupo case study also suggests that at different stages of the six-year presidential term, the balance of continuity and discontinuity is apt to be tipped in one direction or the other. Hence there may be a general timetable with respect to continuity and discontinuity in state-society relations. At the beginning of the term, constraints such as *concertación* with the corporatist sector lock in a measure of continuity while the need to pursue the unrealised goal of 'social justice' necessitates the appearance of constant innovation. If there is too much drift in the direction of continuity or discontinuity, then such constraints reassert themselves – too much corruption precipitates policy innovation and too much neoliberalism leads to 'bending'. In the end, this produces a sense of policy continuity, that is, incremental adaptive change that avoids a clear breakdown or policy stagnation.

Third, Cornelius (1995: 149) writes:

The experience of Mexico under Salinas shows that distributive and redistributive programs, however carefully designed and well funded, can work only where powerful political and economic interests do not prevent them from reaching their target populations.

Though couched in a general discussion of Mexican social policy, Cornelius's chief interest is Solidarity. He mentions Conasupo, yet it hardly fits the 'carefully designed' characterisation or his underlying argument. This view misleadingly directs our attention regarding the abstract 'constraints' on social policy (and state-society relations) away from the executive who, rather than remaining passive or falling victim to 'powerful political and economic interests', had everything to do with Conasupo resources not finding their intended beneficiaries. It is also hard to sustain that Mexican executives (in particular, President Salinas) are not able to check abuses if they choose to do so. That resources do not always find targeted beneficiaries is actually part of the political capital generated by Conasupo (in addition to generating votes, promoting the ideals of the Revolution, etc.). If low-income populations secured resources by a neoliberal rationale, then the need to negotiate ('enter the process') with the executive and the various channels of the PRI disappears. More importantly, the 'shared interests' joining political elites and Mexicans loyal to the old model regarding the logic of securing social justice (e.g., 'we all agree that this is our central goal and that it has not been achieved yet') would breakdown – and along with it the old model of state-society relations.

Fourth and finally, at a general level, Mexico stands apart from other cases in Latin America and the rest of the developing world because of its remarkable continuity in state-society relations. This is what makes Mexico so fascinating. Conasupo is revealing in this respect, because one could point to comparable programmes across the developing world during the last four decades (notable examples include Egypt, India, Brazil, Peru and Venezuela). However, the difference is Conasupo's permanence; Mexico could enter GATT under de la Madrid, enter NAFTA under Salinas, and form an independent central bank under Zedillo, and negotiate its foreign debt in the 1980s and 1990s, while still having room for Conasupo, or some 'recreation' of it. Thus it continues where similar programmes have been abandoned as a country switches national development strategy, manages external constraints (for example, in agreements with the IMF and World Bank) or experiences sharp swings in domestic politics. In this way, the Conasupo experience offers some clues concerning the unique Mexican case.

Writing of Conasupo, Ochoa (1994: 322) ends his historical investigation by speculating on the Salinas years:

> Although the State Food Agency has been dismantled by President Salinas and replaced by subsidies targeted for certain poor producers and poor consumers, which is likely to be more cost-effective, its political viability remains to be seen.

Though his reference to 'dismantled' and optimism regarding who benefited from targeting misread the Salinas years, this current investigation heeds the call to examine the correlation between innovation and the parastatal's capacity to provide legitimacy for the old state-society model. The interpretation that has emerged shows the relentless pressure to legitimate the system, coupled with the expectations of patrons and clients, matter as much as neoliberal solutions. This investigation therefore offers insight on a meaningful source of continuity in state-society relations among strategic populations and the Mexican government.

Notes

[1] Although Philip's (1986: 130) observation understates the degree of recent change, his caution remains relevant: 'A series of delicate relationships have grown up within the system which it is difficult or dangerous for the political elite to disturb. Thus, despite the rapid rate of superficial change, the system is in many ways profoundly rigid and conservative. It is very difficult to carry through major reforms'.

[2] A national opinion poll (*Reforma* 2 March 1997) asking 'what is the most grave problem of the country' found: 'economic issues' 74 percent, 'public security' 7 percent, 'corruption' 4 percent and 'lack of good government' 3 percent. The same poll asked which political party could resolve the country's most grave problem: PRI 16 percent, PAN 15 percent, PRD 7 percent, other 2 percent, 'none of them' 45 percent, and no opinion 15 percent.

[3] Smith (1998) in a recent paper emphasises that the 'economically excluded' masses in Mexico must soon trigger off a breakdown; while the numerous studies of party development and democratisation in Mexico point to the evolution of voting practices, the emergence of NGOs, and the maturing and spreading of opposition political parties.

[4] Though DFMA voters defected from the PRI and supported the PRD in July 1997, it is still interesting that the PRI's official campaign strategy in the DFMA demanded that their candidates start their day with a visit to the local *lecherías*. Similarly, in the last days before the November 1996 local election in the State of México, the PRI campaign hired

1,000 vans to make sure that *lecherías* around the populated area of Nezahualcóyotl provided housewives with their daily milk quota (*Reforma* 7 November 1996).

[5] Interestingly, interviews with present and past Conasupo employees did not confirm this connection between Conasupo and Procampo. However, a document prepared by the Administrative Council claims that Procampo 'replaced' traditional Conasupo subsidies. See Conasupo (8 August 1995).

[6] Gibson (1996: 360) makes the following observation of social provision during the Salinas years: 'Tensions between technocratic elites in the executive branch and the PRI's traditional *políticos* running the peripheral coalition [his surrogate for 'political machine'] were very real in Mexico....However, a marriage of convenience was sustained by the interest of both groups in holding on to their quota of state power. It provided an unlikely alliance between internationalized technocrats and parochial politicians that saw the reform process through'.

Bibliography

Acedo Angulo, B. (ed.) (1995), *Solidaridad en Conflicto: el funcionamiento del Pronasol en municipios gobernados por la oposición*, Nuevo Horizonte Editores, Mexico City.

Aitken, R. (ed.) (1996), *Dismantling the Mexican State?* Macmillan Press Ltd., London.

Almond, G., and Verba, S. (1963), *The Civic Culture: Political Attitudes and Democracy in Five Nations*, Princeton University Press, Princeton.

Ames, B. (1987), *Political Survival: Politicians and Public Policy in Lain America*, University of California Press, Berkeley.

Appendini, K. (1992), *De la milpa a los tortibonos: la reestructuración de la política alimentaria en México*, Instituto de Investigaciones de la Naciones Unidas para el Desarrollo Social, Mexico City.

Austin, J. and Esteva, G. (1987), *Food Policy in Mexico: The Search for Self-Sufficiency*, Cornell University Press, Ithaca, NY.

Bailey, J. (1988), *Governing Mexico*, St. Martin's Press, New York.

Barry, T. (1995), *Zapata's Revenge: Free Trade and the Farm Crisis in Mexico*, South End Press, Boston.

Camp, R. (1993), *Politics in Mexico*, Oxford University Press, Oxford.

Centeno, M. A. (1994), *Democracy Within Reason*, The Pennsylvania State University Press, University Park.

Colclough, C. and Manor, J. (eds) (1991), *States or Markets? Neoliberalism and the Development Policy Debate*, Clarendon Press, Oxford.

Cornelius, W. (1996), *Mexican Politics in Transition: The Breakdown of a One-Party-Dominant Regime*, Center for U.S.-Mexican Studies, San Diego.

Cornelius, W., Craig, A., and Fox, J. (eds) (1994), *Transforming State-Society Relations in Mexico: The National Solidarity Program*, Center for U.S.-Mexican Studies, San Diego.

Cornelius, W., Gentleman, J., and Smith, P. (eds) (1989), *Mexico's Alternative Futures*, Center for US-Mexican Studies, San Diego.

Cornelius, W. (1975), *Politics and the Migrant Poor in Mexico City*, Stanford University Press, Stanford, California.

Cothran, D. (1994), *Political Stability and Democracy in Mexico: The 'Perfect Dictatorship'?*, Praeger, London.

Cox, A., Furlong, P. and Page, E. (1985), *Power in Capitalist Society: Theory, Explanations and Cases*, Wheatsheaf Books Ltd., Brighton.

Craske, N. (1994a), *Corporatism Revisited: Salinas and the Reform of the Popular Sector*, Institute of Latin American Studies, London.

Dahl, R. (1982), *Dilemmas of Pluralist Democracy: Autonomy vs. Control,* Yale University Press, New Haven.

Dahl, R. (1961), *Who Governs?* Yale University Press, New Haven.

Economic Commission for Latin America (ECLA) (1995), *Economic Survey of Latin America and the Caribbean 1994-1995,* United Nations Publishing, Santiago, Chile.

Fagen, R., and Tuohy, J. (1972), *Politics and Privilege in a Mexican City,* Stanford University Press, Stanford, California.

Foweraker, J. and Craig, A. (1990), *Popular Movements and Political Change in Mexico,* Lynne Rienner Publishers, Boulder.

Fox, J. (1992), *The Politics of Food in Mexico: State Power and Social Mobilization,* Cornell University Press, Ithaca, NY.

Fox, J. and Aranda, J. (1996), *Decentralization & Rural Development in Mexico,* Center for U.S.-Mexican Studies, San Diego.

Gamble, S.H. (1970), *The Despensa System of Food Distribution: A Case Study of Monterrey, Mexico,* Praeger Publishers, New York.

Garduño Ríos, S. and González Vega, G. (1998), *Los indicadores de bienestar en México 1940-1995,* Instituto de Investigación Económica y Social Lucas Alamán, Mexico City.

González de la Rocha, M. (1991), *Social Responses to Mexico's Economic Crisis of the 1980s,* Center for US-Mexican Studies, San Diego.

Grindle, M. (1980), *Politics and Policy Implementation in the Third World,* Princeton University Press, Princeton.

Grindle, M. (1977a), *Bureaucrats, Politicians, and Peasants in Mexico,* University of California Press, Berkeley.

Gurza Lavalle, A. (1994), *La reestructuración de lo público El caso Conasupo,* Universidad Nacional Autónoma de México, Escuela Nacional de Estudios Profesionales Acatlán, Mexico City.

Hansen, R. (1971), *The Politics of Mexican Development,* Johns Hopkins Press, Baltimore.

Harvey, N., and Serrano, M. (1995), *Party Politics in 'An Uncommon Democracy': Political Parties and Elections in Mexico,* The Institute of Latin American Studies, University of London, London.

Hellman, J.A. (1983), *Mexico in Crisis,* 2nd Edition, Holmes and Meier, London.

Hirschman, A. (1970), *Exit, Voice, and Loyalty: Responses to Decline in Firms, Organizations, and States,* Harvard University Press, Cambridge, Mass.

Ingram, H. and Mann, D. (1980), *Why Policies Succeed or Fail,* Sage Publications Ltd., London.

International Development Bank (IDB) (1994), *Economic and Social Progress in Latin America 1994 Report,* The Johns Hopkins University Press, Washington D.C.

Kaufman Purcell, S. (1975), *The Mexican Profit Sharing Decision: Politics in an Authoritarian Regime*, University of the California, Berkeley.

Kiewiet, R. and McCubbins, M. (1991), *The Logic of Delegation*, Chicago University Press, Chicago.

La Botz, D. (1995), *Democracy in Mexico: Peasant Rebellion and Political Reform*, South End Press, Boston.

Lomelí, V. (ed.) (1996) *¿Devaluación de la política social?* Red Observatorio Social, Mexico City.

Lustig, N. (1992), *Mexico: The Remaking of an Economy*, Brookings Institute, Washington, D.C.

Maier, C. (ed.) (1989), *Changing Boundaries of the Political*, Cambridge University Press, Cambridge.

March, J., and Olsen, J. (1989), *Rediscovering Institutions: The Organizational Basis of Politics*, The Free Press, New York.

Maxfield, S. (1990), *Governing Capital: International Finance and Mexican Politics,* Cornell University Press, Ithaca, NY.

Mesa Lago, C. (1989), *Ascent to Bankruptcy: Financing Social Security in Latin America*, University of Pittsburgh, Pittsburgh.

Mény, Y. (1993), *Government and Politics in Western Europe*, Oxford University Press, Oxford.

Morris, S. (1991), *Corruption and Politics in Contemporary Mexico*, University of Alabama, Tuscaloosa.

Nord, B. (1994), *Mexican Social Policy: Affordability, Conflict and Progress*, University Press of America, Inc., New York.

Philip, G. (1992), *The Presidency in Mexican Politics,* St. Martin's Press, New York.

Robertson, D. (1985), *A Dictionary of Modern Politics*, Europa Publications Ltd., New York.

Rodríguez, V. (1997), *Decentralization in Mexico: From Reform Municipal to Solidaridad to Nuevo Federalismo*, University of Texas, Austin.

Roett, R. (ed.) (1995), *The Challenge of Institutional Reform in Mexico*, Lynne Rienner Publisher, Boulder.

Roniger, L. (1990), *Hierarchy and Trust in Modern Mexico and Brazil*, Praeger, New York.

Rubio, L. and Newell, R. (1984), *Mexico's Dilemma: The Political Origins of Economic Crisis*, Westview Press, Boulder.

Russell, P. (1994), *Mexico Under Salinas.* Mexico Resource Center, Austin, Texas.

Salinas, R. (1988), *Diconsa la modernización comercial y la regulación del abasto popular*, Instituto Naciónal de Administración Pública, A.C., Mexico City.

Serrano, M., and Bulmer-Thomas, V. (1996), *Rebuilding the State: Mexico After Salinas*, The Institute of Latin American Studies, London.

Smith, C., Acuna, C., and Gamarra, E. (eds) (1994) *Latin American Political Economy in the Age of Neoliberal Reform*, Lynne Rienner, Boulder.

Smith, P. (1979), *Labyrinths of Power: Political Recruitment in Twentieth-Century Mexico*, Princeton University Press, Princeton.

Story, D. (1986), *The Mexican Ruling Party: Stability and Authority*, Praeger Publisher, New York.

Ugalde, A. (1970), *Power and Conflict in a Mexican Community*, University of New Mexico Press, Albuquerque.

Ward, P. (1990), *Welfare Politics in Mexico and Mexico City*, Allen and Unwin, London.

Ward, P. (1989), *Corruption, Development and Inequality: Soft Touch or Hard Graft?* Routeldge, London.

Weir, M., Orloff, A.S., and Skocpol, T. (1988), *The Politics of Social Policy in the United States*, Princeton University Press, Princeton.

Williams, H. (1996), *Planting Trouble: The Barzón Debtors' Movement in Mexico*, Current Issue Brief 6, Center for U.S.-Mexican Studies, San Diego.

World Bank, (1992, 1991, 1990c, 1989, 1988a, 1987), *The World Bank Annual Report*, The World Bank, Washington D.C.

Yates, P.I. (1978), *El Campo Mexicano*, Ediciones el caballito S.A., Mexico City.

Articles, Journals and Unpublished Documents

Alisky, M. (Winter 1973), 'Conasupo: A Mexican Agency which makes low-income workers feel their government cares', *Inter-American Economic Affairs*, Vol.27, No.3, pp.47-59.

Ames, B. (1999), 'Approaches to the Study of Institutions in Latin American Politics', *Latin American Research Review*, Vol.34, No.1, pp.221-36.

Anagnoson, T. (1980), 'Targeting Federal Categorical Grants: An Impossible Dream?' in Ingram and Mann, *Why Policies Succeed or Fail*, Sage, London.

Appendini, K. and Liverman, D. (1994), 'Agricultural policy, climate change and food security in Mexico', *Food Policy*, Vol. 19, No. 2, pp.149-64.

Appendini, K. (Oct 1991), 'Los campesinos maiceros frente a la política de abasto: una contradicción permanente', *Comercio Exterior*, Vol.41, No.10, pp.976-984.

Arce, D. (1999), 'The Political Economy of the Neoliberal Transition', *Latin American Research Review*, Vol.34, No.1, pp.212-20.

Austin, J. and Fox, J. (1987), 'State-Owned Enterprises: Food policy Implementers', in Austin and Esteva (eds), *Food Policy in Mexico*, Cornell University Press, Ithaca.

Bachrach, P. and Baratz, M.S. (1962), 'Two Faces of Power', *American Political Science Review*, Vol.56, pp.947-952.

Baer, D., 'Misreading Mexico' (Fall 1997), *Foreign Policy*, pp.139-50.

Baer, D. and Weintraub, S. (1994), 'The Pressure for Political Reform in Mexico', in Baer and Weintraub (eds), *The NAFTA Debate: Grappling with Unconventional Trade Issues*, Lynne Rienner, Boulder.

Baer, D. (1993), 'Mexico's Second Revolution: Pathways to Liberalization', in Roett (ed.), *Political and Economic Liberalization in Mexico: At a Critical Juncture?*, Center for US-Mexican Studies, San Diego.

Bailey, J. (1995), 'Fiscal Centralism and Pragmatic Accommodation in Nuevo León', in Rodríguez and Ward (eds), *Opposition Government in Mexico*, University of New Mexico Press, Albuquerque.

Bailey, J. (1994), 'Centralism and Political Change in Mexico: The Case of National Solidarity', in Cornelius, Craig and Fox (eds), *Transforming State-Society Relations in Mexico: The National Solidarity Strategy*, Center for US-Mexican Studies, San Diego.

Bailey, J. (1987), 'Can the PRI be Reformed? Decentralizing Candidate Selection', in Gentleman (ed.), *Mexican Politics in Transition*, Westview Press, Boulder.

Bailey, J. (1986), 'What Explains the Decline of the PRI and Will It Continue?' in Camp (ed.), *Mexico's Political Stability: The Next Five Years*, Westview Press, London.

Bartra, A. (Jan-Feb, 1991), 'Pros, contras y asegunes de la apropiación del proceso productivo', *El Cotidiano*, Vol.39, pp.46-52.

Bohórquez, G. (Sept-Oct 1989), 'Tendencias actuales del movimiento urbano popular en México', *El Cotidiano*, No.31, pp.50-56.

Bolívar, A. (Dec 1993), 'El lento camino de la modernización', in *El Cotidiano*, No.59, pp.64-73.

Booth, J. and Seligson, M. (1984), 'The Political Culture of Authoritarianism in Mexico: A Reexamination', *Latin American Research Review*, 19, pp.106-124.

Brachet-Márquez, V. (1995), 'Mexico: The Search for New Parameters', *Latin American Research Review*, Vo.30, No.3, pp.163-176.

Brachet-Márquez, V. and Sherraden, M.S. (1994), 'Political Change and the Welfare State: the case of Health and Food Polices in Mexico (1970-93)', *World Development*, Vol.22, No.9, pp.1295-1312.

Bruhn, K. (Jan 1996), 'Social Spending and Political Support: The 'Lessons' of the National Solidarity Program in Mexico', *Comparative Politics*, Vol.28, No.1, pp.151-178.

Camp, R. (1985), 'The Political Technocrat in Mexico and the Survival of the Political System', *Latin American Research Review*, Vol.20, No.1, pp.97-118.

Casanueva, E. (1996), 'El maíz, la dieta y la salud en México', in Torres (ed.), *La Industria de la masa y la tortilla*, UNAM, Mexico City.

Castillo, J.S. (Jan-Feb 1992), 'La elecciones locales en 1992', *El Cotidiano*, Vol.52, pp.19-24.

Centeno, M.A., and Maxfield, S. (Spring 1992), 'The Marriage of Finance and Order: Changes in the Mexican Political Elite', *Journal of Latin American Studies*, Vol.24, No.1.

Collier, D., and Collier, R. (Dec 1979), "Inducements versus Constraints: Disaggregating 'Corporatism'," *American Political Science Review*, Vol.73, No.4, pp.967-987.

Collier, D., and Collier, R. (1977), 'Who Does What, to Whom, and How: Toward a Comparative Analysis of Latin American Corporatism', in Malloy (ed.), *Authoritarianism and Corporatism in Latin America*, University of Pittsburgh Press, Pittsburgh.

Cornelius, W. (1995), 'Designing Social Policy for Mexico's Liberalized Economy: From Social Services and Infrastructure to Job Creation', in Roett (ed.), *The Challenge of Institutional Reform in Mexico*, Lynne Publishers, Boulder, CO.

Cornelius, W. (1987), 'Political Liberalization in an Authoritarian Regime: Mexico, 1976-1985', in Gentleman (ed.), *Mexican Politics in Transition*, London: Westview Press.

Cox, N. (1985), 'Changes in the Mexican Political System', in Philip (ed.), *Politics in Mexico*, Croom Helm, London.

Craig, A., and Cornelius, W. (1980), 'Political Culture in Mexico: Continuities and Revisionist Interpretations', in Almond and Verba, *The Civic Culture Revisited*, Little, Brown, Boston.

Craske, N. (1994b), 'Women and Regime Politics in Guadalajara's Low-income Neighbourhoods', *Bulletin of Latin American Research*, Vol. 13, No.1, p.61-78.

Davis, D. (1994), 'Failed Democratic Reform in Contemporary Mexico: from Social Movements to the State and Back Again', *Journal of Latin American Studies*, Vol. 26, pp.365-408.

DeWalt, B. and DeWalt, K. (1991), 'The Results of Mexican Agriculture and Food Policy: Debt, Drugs, and Illegal Aliens', in Whiteford and Ferguson (eds), *Harvest of Want*, Westview Press, Boulder.

Díaz, C. (1997), 'Electoral 'Management' of Opposition Parties by Mexico's PRI, 1970-1994: A Preliminary Model of Dynamic Preemptive and Reactive Strategies', Conference Paper, LASA, Guadalajara, April 17-19.

Domínguez, J. and McCann, J. (March 1995), 'Shaping Mexico's Electoral Arena: The Construction of Partisan Cleavages in the 1988 and 1991 National Elections', in *American Political Science Review*, Vol.89, No.1, pp.34-48.

Dresser, D. (1994), 'Bringing the Poor Back in: National Solidarity as a Strategy of Regime Legitimization', in Cornelius, Craig and Fox (eds), *Transforming State-Society Relations in Mexico: The National Solidarity Strategy*, Center for US-Mexican Studies, San Diego.

Dresser, D. (1991), 'Neopopulist Solutions to Neoliberal Problems: Mexico's National Solidarity Program', Current Issue Brief No.3, Center for U.S.-Mexican Studies, San Diego.

Elizondo, C. (1996), 'Tax Reform under the Salinas Administration', in Randall (ed.), *Changing Structure of Mexico*, M.E. Sharpe, London.

Elizondo, C. (1993), 'Property Rights in Business-State Relations: The case of the Bank nationalization', D.Phil Thesis, Oxford University.

Escalante, R. and Rendón, T. (1988), 'Neoliberalismo a la Mexicana su impacto sobre el sector agropecuario', in *Problemas del Desarrollo*, Vol. XIX, No. 75, pp.115-152.

Escobar Latapi, A., and Roberts, B. (1991), 'Urban Stratification, the Middle Classes, and Economic Change in Mexico', in Escobar Latapi and González de la Rocha, M. (eds), *Social Responses to Mexico's Economic Crisis of the 1980s*, Center for US-Mexican Studies, San Diego.

Ferrer Pujol, J. (1996), 'Racionalización de subsidios y liberación de precios del sector', in Torres *et al., La industria de la masa y la tortilla: desarollo y tecnología,* UNAM, Mexico City.

Fox, J. (1994), 'The Difficult Transition from Clientelism to Citizenship: Lessons from Mexico', in *World Politics,* Vol.46, No.2, pp.151-184.

Fox, J. (1991), 'Popular Participation and Access to Food: Mexico's Community Food Councils', in Whiteford and Ferguson (eds), *Harvest of Want: Hunger and Food Security in Central America and Mexico,* Westview Press, Boulder.

Fox, J., and Gordillo, G. (1989), 'Between State and Market: The Campesinos' Quest for Autonomy', in Cornelius, Gentlemen and Smith (eds), *Mexico's Alternative Futures*, Center for US-Mexican Studies, San Diego.

Fox, J. and Moguel, J. (1995), 'Pluralism and Anti-Poverty Policy: Mexico's National Solidarity Program and Left Opposition Municipal Governments', in Rodríguez and Ward (eds), *Opposition Government in Mexico*, University of New Mexico Press, Albuquerque.

Friedmann, S. (1995), 'Mexico: Social Spending and Food Subsidies during Adjustment in the 1980s', in Lustig, *Coping With Austerity*, Brookings Institutions, Washington D.C.

García Falconi, S. (1996), 'Un análisis del Programa Mujeres en Solidaridad', in *La Pobreza en Querétaro, VI Foro de Sociología Querétaro*: Facultad de Sociología, Universidad Autónoma de Querétaro.

Gavaldón Enciso, E. and Pérez Haro, E. (mayo-junio, 1987a), 'A propósito de la 'Debilidad y fortaleza de Conasupo', in *El Cotidiano*, No. 17, pp.182-187.

Gavaldón Enciso, E. and Pérez Haro, E. (nov.-dic, 1987b), 'Conasupo: un esfuerzo sistemático', in *El Cotidiano*, No. 20, pp.409-413.

Gentleman, J. (1987), 'Mexico After the Oil Boom: PRI Management of the Political Impact of National Disillusionment', in Gentleman (ed.), *Mexican Politics in Transition*, Westview Press, London.

Gershberg, A. I. (1994), 'Distributing Resources in the Education Sector: Solidarity's Escuela Digna Program', in Cornelius, Craig and Fox (eds), *Transforming state-society relations in Mexico: the national solidarity strategy*, Center for US-Mexican Studies, San Diego.

Gibson, E. (Apr 1997), 'The Populist Road to Market Reform: Policy and Electoral Coalitions in Mexico and Argentina', in *World Politics* 49, pp.339-370.

González de la Rocha, M. (Fall 1997), 'Where we are: current programs and emerging trends in Mexican social policy', in *Enfoque: Economic and Social Policy, The Zedillo Administration at Midterm*, publication of the Center for U.S.-Mexican Studies, San Diego, pp.3-13.

Grindle, M. (1995), 'Reforming Land Tenure in Mexico: Peasants, the Market, and the State', in Roett (ed.), *The Challenge of Institutional Reform in Mexico*, Lynne Rienner Publishers, London.

Grindle, M. (1977b), 'Patrons and Clients in the Bureaucracy: Career Networks in Mexico', in *Latin American Research Review*, Vol. 12, No. 1, pp.37-66.

Grindle, M. (1977c), 'Policy Change in an Authoritarian Regime: Mexico under Echeverría', in *Journal of Interamerican Studies and World Affairs*, Vol.19, No.4, pp.523-552.

Guevara Sanginés, A. (1995), 'Poverty Alleviation in Mexico: The Socio-Economic Aspects of Pronasol', in Serrano and Bulmer-Thomas (eds), *Rebuilding the State: Mexico After Salinas*, The Institute of Latin American Studies, London.

Guttmen, M. (1998), presentation at the conference 'Popular Social Culture', April 22, 1998. Centre for U.S.-Mexican Studies, San Diego.

Haber, P. (1994), 'Political Change in Durango: The Role of National Solidarity', in Cornelius, Craig and Fox (eds), *Transforming State-Society Relations in Mexico*, Center For US-Mexican Studies, San Diego (1994).

Hall, L. and Price, T. (Nov, 1982), 'Price policies and the SAM', in *Food Policy*, Vol.7, No.4, pp.302-314.

Heath, J. (1985), 'Contradictions in Current Mexican Food Policy', in Philip (ed.), *Politics in Mexico*, Croom Helm, London.

Hellman, J. A. (1988), 'Continuity and Change in Mexico', in *Latin American Research Review*, No.2, pp.133-45.

Heredia, B. (1992), 'Mexican Business and the State: The Political Economy of a "Muddled" Transition', Working Paper #182, The Helen Kellogg Institute for International Studies, University of Notre Dame.

Hernández, L. (Mar-Apr, 1990), 'Las convulsiones rurales', in *El Cotidiano, 34*, pp. 13-21.

Hernández, L. (Jan-Feb, 1991), 'Respuestas campesinas en la época del neoliberalismo', in *El Cotidiano*, Vol. 39, pp.53-58.

Herrasti Aguirre, E. (1993), 'La promoción inmobiliaria popular autogestiva ¿tendrá futuro?' *El Cotidiano*, No. 57, pp. 17-22.

Hewitt de Alcantara, C. (1987), 'Feeding Mexico City', in Austin and Esteve (eds), *Food Policy in Mexico*, University of Berkeley Press, Berkeley.

Inglehard, R. (Dec 1988), 'The Renaissance of Political Culture', in *American Political Science Review*, Vol.82, No.4, pp.1203-1230.

Jusidman de Bialotovsky, C. (1987), 'SAM's Successor: PRONAL', in Austin and Esteve, *Food Policy in Mexico*, Cornell University Press, Ithaca.

Kaufman, R. and Trejo, G. (Oct 1997), 'Regionalism, Regime Transformation, and PRONASOL: The Politics of the National Solidarity Programme in Four Mexican States', *Journal of Latin American Studies*, Vol. 29, pp. 717-746.

Kaufman Purcell, S. (1981), 'Mexico: Clientelism, Corporatism and Political Stability', in Eisenstadt and Lemarchand (eds), *Political Clientelism, Patronage and Development*. Sage Publications, London.

Kaufman Purcell, S. and Purcell, J. (Jan 1980), 'State and Society in Mexico: Must a Stable Polity Be Institutionalized?', in *World Politics*, Vol. 32, No.2, pp.194-227.

Kennedy, R. (1994), 'Sovereign Debt Restructuring Since 1982: A Practical Theoretical Interpretation', D.Phil. thesis, Oxford University, Oxford.

Kimber, R. (1994), 'Interest Groups and the Fallacy of the Liberal Fallacy', in Richardson (ed.), *Pressure Groups,* Oxford University Press, Oxford.

Knockenbauer, G. (Sept 1990), 'La modernización del agro en México', in *Comerico Exterior*, Vol. 40, No. 9, pp.830-837.

León Chaín, E. (1996), 'Organizaciones sociales en Querétaro', in *La Pobreza en Querétaro, VI Foro de Sociología Querétaro*: Facultad de Sociología, Universidad Autónoma de Querétaro, Querétaro.

Levy, D. (1986), 'The Political Consequences of Changing Social Patterns', in Camp, *Mexico's Political Stability: The Next Five Years*, Westview Press, London.

Lindau, J. (1996), 'Technocrats and Mexico's Political Elite', in *Political Science Quarterly*, Vol. 11, No. 2, pp.295-332.

Lozano, L. (ed.) (Aug 1991), 'La canasta básica de los trabajadores en México', in *El Cotidiano*, Vol.42, pp.30-46.

Lustig, N. (1991), 'Fiscal Cost and Welfare Effects of the Maize Subsidy in Mexico', in Pinstrup-Anderen (ed.), *Food Subsidies in Developing Countries: Costs, Benefits, and Policy Options*, The Johns Hopkins University Press, Baltimore.

Lustig, N. and Martín del Campo, A. (julio-septiembre 1985), 'Descripción del funcionamiento del sistema Conasupo', in *Investigación Económica*, No. 173, pp.215-243.

Martin, C. (1993), 'The 'Shadow Economy' of Local School Management in Contemporary West Mexico', in *Bulletin of Latin American Research*, Vol.12, No.2, pp.171-188.

Martín del Campo, A. and Calderón Tinoco, R. (Oct-Dec 1990), 'Restructación de los subsidios a productos básicos y la modernización de Conasupo', in *Investigación Económica*, No. 194, pp. 55-108.

McFarland, A. (1987), 'Interest Groups and Theories of Power in America', in *The British Journal of Political Science*, Vol.17, pp.129-147.

Meissner, F. (Feb 1982), 'SAM – A baby with many faces', in *Food Policy*, Vol.7, No.1, pp.83-84.

Meissner, F. (Nov 1981), 'The Mexican Food System (SAM): A Strategy for Sowing Petroleum', in Food Policy, Vol.6, No.4, pp.219-230.

Mitastein, M. (1996), 'Las dos caras de la tortilla: de lo urbano a lo rural', in Torres *et al.*, *La industria de la masa y la tortilla: desarollo y tecnología*, UNAM, Mexico City.

Moctezuma, P. (May 1993a), 'El espejo desenterrado', in *El Cotidiano*, Vol.54, pp.49-54.

Moctezuma, P. (Aug-Sept 1993b), 'Del movimiento urbano popular a los movimientos comunitarios', in *El Cotidiano*, Vol.57, pp.3-10.

Moguel, J. (Dec 1993), 'Procampo y la agricultura: ¿Por un México sin campesinos?' in *El Cotidiano*, Vol. 59, pp. 53-58.

Moguel, J. and Bartra, A. (July-Sept 1995), 'El sector agropecuario mexicano. Un balance sobre el desastre (1988-1994)', in *Problemas de Desarrollo*, Vol. 26, No. 102, pp.173-197.

Moreno, M. (1987), 'Strategic Thrusts of the New Policy (PRONAL)', in Austin and Esteve (eds), *Food Policy in Mexico*, Cornell University Press, Ithaca.

Moreno, F. (Aug-Sept 1993), 'Representación vecinal y gestión urbana en el D.F.', in *El Cotidiano*, No.57, pp.38-44.

Muñoz Rodríguez, M. (1990), 'Límites y potencialidades del sistema de la leche en México.' In *Comercio Exterior*, Vol.40, No.9, pp.886-893.

Nicholson, C. (1995), 'Mexico's Dairy Sector in the 1990s: A Descriptive Analysis', A publication of the Cornell Program on Dairy Markets and Policy, Ithaca, NY.

Ochoa, E. (1994), 'The Politics of Feeding Mexico', doctoral dissertation, University of California, Los Angeles.

Ovalle Fernández, I. (Sept 1990), 'El ejido y sus perspectivas: un enfoque jurídico', in *Comercio Exterior*, Vol. 40, No. 9, pp. 845-848.

Osorio Goicoechea, J. (1996), 'La pobreza y su combate: prioridad de la política pública en un contexto de crisis crónica', in Valencia Lomelí (ed.), *¿Devaluación de la política social?* Red Observatorio Social, Mexico City.

Outlaw, J. and Nicholson, C. (Apr 1994), 'An Overview of the Mexican Dairy Sector', in *Dairy Markets and Policy: Issues and Options*, M-14, Cornell University's Program on Dairy Markets and Policy.

Perea, A.E. and Moscoso Rodríguez, I. (1995), 'León', in Acedo Angulo (ed.), *Solidaridad en conflicto*, Nuevo Horizonte Editores, Mexico City.

Pérez Haro, E. (Mar-Apr 1990), 'La modernización en el sistema Conasupo', in *El Cotidiano*, 34, pp.22-26.

Philip, G. (1998), 'The New Populism in Spanish South America', in *Government and Opposition*, Vol. 33, No. 1, pp. 81-97.

Philip, G. (1992b), 'Venezuelan Democracy and the Coup Attempt of February 1992', in *Government and Opposition*, Vol. 27, No. 4, pp.455-469.

Philip, G. (1988), 'The Dominant Party System in Mexico', in Randall (ed.), *Political Parties in the Third World*, Sage Publications, Beverly Hills.

Philip, G. (1986), 'Mexican Politics and the Journals', in *Bulletin of Latin American Research*, Vol.5, No.1, pp.121-132.

Polanco, E.R. (Sept 1990), 'La crisis y la alimentación nacional: opciones de desarrollo', in *Comercio Exterior*, Vol. 40, No.9, pp. 859-867.

Quezada, S. A. (1993), 'The Inevitability of Democracy', in Mexico in Roett (ed.), *Political and Economic Liberalization in Mexico: At a Critical Juncture?* Center for US-Mexican Studies, San Diego.

Ramírez de la O, R. (1998), conference paper, 11 May 1998, the Centre for U.S.-Mexican Studies, San Diego.

Redclift, M. (Nov 1981), 'The Mexican Food System (SAM): Sowing Subsidies, Reaping Apathy', in *Food Policy*, Vol.6, No.4, pp.231-235.

Robles, R. and Moguel, J. (Mar-Apr 1990), 'Agricultura y proyecto neoliberal', in *El Cotidiano* 34, pp. 3-12.

Romero. J. J. (Mar 1997), 'Campeche y el viejo PRI', in *Nexos*, (electronic copy).

Rubin, J. (1996), 'Decentering the Regime: Culture and Regional Politics in Mexico', *Latin American Research Review*, Vol.31, No.3, p.85-126.

Ruiz Dueñas, J. (Apr-June 1990), 'El redimensionamiento del sector paraestatal, 1982-1988: hacia un balance del sexenio', in *Foro Internacional*, pp.789-813.

Sachs, J. (Summer 1989), 'Making the Brady Plan Work', in *Foreign Affairs*, Vol.68, No.3, pp.87-104.

Salcedo, S. (Apr 1993), 'Política agrícola y maíz en México: hacia el libre comercio norteamericano', in *Comercio Exterior*, Vol.43, No.4, pp.302-310.

Salas-Porras, A. (1996), 'The Mexican Business Class and the Processes of Globalization Trends and Counter Trends', Ph.D dissertation, London School of Economics, London.

Salinas, C. (1991), 'A New Hope for the Hemisphere', in *New Perspective Quarterly*, Vol.8.

Salinas, C. (1984), 'Production and Participation in Rural Areas: Some Political Considerations', in Aspe and Sigmund (eds), *The Political Economy of Income Distribution in Mexico*, Holmes and Meier Publishers, Inc., New York.

Salinas, R. (Sept 1990), 'El Campo mexicano ante el reto de la modernización', in *Comercio Exterior*, Vol. 40, No. 9, pp. 816-829.

Sánchez Daza, A., and Vargas Velázquez, S. (Sept-Oct, 1986), 'Debilidad y Fortaleza de Conasupo', in *El Cotidiano*, No. 13, pp.40-46.

Serra Puche, J. and Garcia-Alba, P. (1983), 'Financial Aspects of Macroeconomic Management in Mexico', Joint Research Program Series 36, Institute of Development Economics, Tokyo.

Sloan, J. (1985), 'The Mexican Variant of Corporatism', in *Inter-American Economic Affairs*, Vol.38 No.4, pp.3-18.

Smith, P. (11 May 1998), 'Democratization and U.S.-Mexican Relations: Long-Term Perspectives on Short-term Uncertainty', Conference on *Mexico and the United States in the Next Decade*, University of California, San Diego.

Smith, P. (1989), 'The 1988 Presidential Succession in Historical Perspective', in Cornelius, Gentlemen and Smith, *Mexico's Alternative Futures*, Center for US-Mexican Studies, San Diego.

Smith, P. (1986), 'Leadership and Change: Intellectuals and Technocrats in Mexico', in Camp (ed.), *Mexico's Political Stability: The Next Ten Years*, Westview Press, Boulder.

Sodi de la Tijera, D. (1988), 'El sector social en la comercialización: Factor de justicia y eficiencia', in Labra (ed.), *El Sector Social de la Economía*. UNAM, Mexico City.

Solís, L. (1984), 'Food Marketing and Income Distribution', in Aspe and Sigmond, *The Political Economy of Income Distribution in Mexico*, Holmes and Meier Publishers, Inc., New York.

Sosa, J.L. (Mar-Apr 1990), 'Dependencia alimentaria en México', in *El Cotidiano*, No. 34, pp. 39-43.

Spalding, R. (July 1981), 'State Power and Its Limits: Corporatism in Mexico', *Comparative Political Studies*, Vol. 14, pp.139-161.

Stevens, E. (1977), 'Mexico's PRI: The Institutionalization of Corporatism?' in Malloy (ed.), *Authoritarianism and Corporatism in Latin America*, University of Pittsburgh Press, Pittsburgh.

Tharp Hilger, M. (Nov 1980), 'Decision-Making in a Public Marketing Enterprise CONASUPO in Mexico', in *Journal of Inter-American Affairs and World Affairs*, Vol.22, No.4, pp.471-494.

Thelen, K. and Steinmo, S. (1992), 'Historical institutionalism in comparative politics', in Steinmo, Thelan and Longstreth (ed.), *Structuring Politics: Historical Institutionalism in Comparative Analysis*, Cambridge University Press, Cambridge.

Torres Torres, F. and Delgadillo Macías, J. (Apr-June 1991), 'Competencia y desigualdad. El nuevo modelo de abasto alimentario en México', in *Problemas de Desarrollo*, Vol. XXII, No. 85, pp. 135-153.

Torres, G. (1996), 'La redefinición de la política social: entre la política de estado y la política desde la sociedad', in Lomelí, *¿Devaluación de la política social?* Mexico City: Red Observatorio Social.

Varley, A. (1996), 'Delivering the Goods: Solidarity, Land Regularisation and Urban Services', in Aitken (ed.), *Dismantling the Mexican State?* MacMillan Press Ltd., London.

Varley, A. (1993), 'Clientalism or Technocracy? The Politics of Urban Land Regularization', in Harvey, *Mexico: Dilemmas of Transition*, Institute of Latin American Studies, London.

Wallis, D. (1998), 'The end of the PRI in Mexico?' in *Politics*, Vol.18, No.3, pp.165-171.

Ward, P. (Oct 1993), 'Social Welfare Policy and Political Opening in Mexico', in *Journal of Latin American Studies*, Vol.25, No.3, pp.613-628.

White, S. (1996), 'Depoliticising development: the uses and abuses of participation', in *Development in Practice*, Vol.6, No.1, pp.6-15.

Womack, J. (2 March 1997), 'PRI: la guerra interna', in *Reforma*, special supplement - *Enfoque*, No. 164.

World Bank (1996), *Trends in Developing Economies 1996*, The World Bank, Washington, D.C.

World Bank (1995), *Agricultural Research in an Era of Adjustment: Policies, Institutions, and Progress*, The World Bank, Washington D.C.

World Bank (1990a), 'MEXAGMKTS: A Model of Crop and Livestock Markets in Mexico', Policy, Research, and External Affairs: Agricultural Policies. Working Paper WPS 446, The World Bank, Washington D.C.

World Bank (1990b), 'Analyzing the Effects of U.S. Agricultural Policy on Mexican Agricultural Market Using the MEXAGMKTS Model', Policy, Research, and External Affairs: Agricultural Policies. Working Paper WPS 447, The World Bank, Washington D.C.

World Bank (1988b), *Rural Development: World Bank Experience, 1965-1986*, The World Bank, Washington D.C.

World Bank (1986), 'Mexican Agricultural Sector Report', No. 7609-ME.

World Bank (1983), 'Targeting Food Subsidies for the Needy.' World Bank Staff Working Papers#617.

Work Bank (1987), 'Measuring Project Impact: Monitoring and Evaluation in the PIDER Rural Development Project-Mexico', Staff Working Paper 332.

Government Documents

Consejo Consultivo del Programa Nacional de Solidaridad, *El Programa Nacional de Solidaridad* (1994), Fondo de Cultura Económica México, Mexico City.

Crónica del Gobierno de Carlos Salinas de Gortari 1988-1994 (1994), Fondo de Cultura Económica, Mexico City.

El Gobierno Mexicano. Presidencia de la República (1994), Dirección General de Comunicación Social, Mexico City.

(1994a) 'Toma de Posesión de la Directiva del Congreso del Trabajo', (25 Oct 1989/b) pp.122-124.

(1994b) "Audiencia a Miembros de la Unión General de Obreros y Campesinos de México 'Jacinto López'," (25 Oct 1989/a) pp. 125-127.

(1994c) 'Estado de México' (19/20 Oct 1989) pp. 208-215.

(1994d) 'Confederación Interamericana de Ganaderos y Agricultores' (13 Oct 1989) pp.198-207.

(1994e) 'Ceremonia de Entrega de la Relatoría de los Servicios CONASUPO', (22 Aug 1989) pp.35-39.

(1994f) 'Toma de Posesión de la Directiva del Congreso del Trabajo' (27 July 1989) pp.122-124.

(1994g) 'Consejo Nacional Ordinario del Sindicato de la Industria Azucarera', (27 July 1989) pp.71-72.

(1994h) 'Asamblea General Ordinaria del Consejo Nacional Agropecuario', (23 June 1989) pp.98-102.

(1994i) 'Asamblea General de Asociados de la Fundación Mexicana para la Salud', (14 June 1989) pp. 86-88.

(1994j) 'Clausura de la Asamblea Nacional Constitutiva del CAP', (26 May 1989) pp.103-113.

(1994k) 'Audiencia a Representantes de la CNC', (23 May 1989) pp.100-102.

(1994l) 'Clausura de la Asamblea General del Infonavit', (28 Apr 1989) pp. 98-103.

El Sector Alimentario en Mexico edition 1996 (1996), INEGI/CONAL, Mexico City.

El Sector Alimentario en Mexico edition 1992 (1992), INEGI/CONAL, Mexico City.

El Sector Alimentario en México, (1990) INEGI, Comision Nacional de Alimentacion (CONAL), Mexico City.

Estudio de Campeche: evaluación de beneficiarios (1996), Sedesol, Mexico City.

Informe de Gobierno. Statistical Annex. (1983 through 1999), Presidencia de la República, Mexico City.

Manual de organiszación del gobierno federal 1974: organismos descentralizados y empresas de participación estatal (1974), Secretaría de la Presidencia, Mexico City.

Plan Nacional de Desarrollo 1989-1994 (1989), Presidencia de la República, Mexico City.

Programa Nacional de Modernización del Campo, 1990-1994 (1990), Mexico City: SARH, Mexico City.

Programa Nacional de Modernización del Abasto y del Comercio Interior, 1990-1994 (1990), Secofi, Mexico City.

Conasupo Documents

Fidelist, Dirección de Planeación e informática, gerencia de planeación: importe/kilogramos de la liquidación durante 1995/1996 (1997).

Canasta Basica Campeche (Dec 1996).

Conasupo en cifras (Oct 1996).

Croquis de Comercios y Clínicas que participarán en la Prueba Piloto Campeche (1996).

Fidelist, PASE, Document Number 000381, Produced by Lic. Francisco Laren Najeza (25 Oct 1995).

Conasupo: su función social (8 Aug 1995).

Canasta Básica Alimentaria Para el Bienestar de la Familia: Prueba Piloto Para el Estado de Campeche (June 1995).

Programa de apoyo a la alimentación y nutrición familiar: prueba piloto en el estado de Campeche (May 1995).

Estatuto orgánico de la compañía nacional de subsistencias populares (1994a)

Informe de autoevaluación correspondiente a 1994 (1994b).

Memoria de gestión del período comprendido de diciembre de 1988 a agosto de 1994 (Sept 1994).

Manual de normas y procedimientos del programa de subsidio a consumo de tortilla (Nov 1994a).

Dirección de programas sociales: memoria de actividades 1990-1994 (Nov 1994b).

Informe de autoevaluación correspondiente a 1993 (1993).

Informe de autoevaluación correspondiente a 1992 (1992).

Informe de autoevaluación correspondiente a 1991 (1991).

Conasupo en cifras: consolidado 1990 (1990).

Conasupo: CNC - Conasupo, 50 años de lucha por la alimentación, Mexico City: distribuidora e impulsora comercial Conasupo (1988a).

Modernización y Bienestar Social: La Experiencia de Diconsa (1987a).

Política Social y Empresa Publica: El Caso Conasupo (1987b).

Diconsa: programa de la sucursal la viga (1985a).

Diconsa: programa de sucursal culiacan (1985b).

Diconsa: manual de funcionamiento del almacén (1985c).

Diconsa: 1983: las tiendas serán centros intergrales de distributión y servicios conasupo (1985d).

Diconsa: Informe al consejo de administración diciembre de 1984 (1984a).

Diconsa: primer seminario para la desecentralización del abasto (1984b).

Conasupo ahora (1984c).

Diconsa en cifras (1984d).

Diconsa: informe del presidente del consejo de administración (1983).

Index

References from Notes indicated by 'n' after page preference

Fideicomiso para la Liquidación al Subsidio de la Tortilla (Fidelist) 38, 130-141, 160, 166 (8n, 9n, 10n, 11n), 170, 179-182, 191, 207 (12n)
Foreign Debt Negotiations 50-52
Fox, V. 128, 137, 218, 256, 260, 264

Galletera Mexicana S.A. (Gamesa) 73-74, 82 (16n)
García Suárez, E. 54, 55
Garnica Márquez, I. 56
General Assembly of the National Agricultural Council (CAP) 50, 62-63
German Carcoba, L. 55
Giordano, S. 79, 115, 180, 189, 206 (4n)
Gómez, V. 115
González Barrera, R. 12, 82 (13n, 14n, 16n, 17n), 115-116, 121 (32n)
González Curi, A. 229
Granados Chapa, M.A. 76, 81 (9n)
Grajeda Alvarado, E. 55
Guerra Díaz, R. 232
Gurría, J.A. 51, 68

Hank González, C. 12, 43, 69, 74, 81 (10n), 206 (2n)
Herrejón, I. 79
Herrera, A. 196, 232, 255 (6n)
Hirschman, A. 5

IMF 50-51
Impulsora del Pequeño Comercio (Impecsa) 38, 70, 87, 90-92, 112, 114, 121 (27n), 170, 192
Industrias Conasupo, S.A. (Iconsa) 38, 73-74, 79, 81 (13n), 84, 89-90, 110-117, 120 (22n, 23n, 24n, 27n), 160, 174-175, 266, 271

Institute for Social Security and Services for Public Employees (ISSSTE) 4, 86
Institutional Revolution Party (PRI) 1-2, 7-9, 23-24, 29, 35, 43, 54-59, 79-80, 83 (17n), 110, 115, 123, 127-128, 148, 220-221, 228-229
Instituto Tecnológico y Estudios Superiores de Monterrey *(ITESM)* 148-149, 156-157, 200-204

Labour Congress (CT) 50, 61, 64, 66-68, 81 (11n), 119 (10n), 127, 130, 147, 152-153, 165 (3n) 166 (10n)
Land Titling Policy 118 (8n)
Leche Industrializada, S.A. (Liconsa) 38, 65, 72, 87, 92, 111-115, 121 (26n, 27n, 28n, 29n), 127, 142-151, 160, 167 (15n, 16n, 17n, 18n), 170, 179-182, 186, 196, 207 (7n), 210, 213-217, 225, 227, 230, 241, 255 (2n), 259, 267-268, 271, 275
Levy, S. 238
López Portillo, J. (Conasupo policy) 31, 39, 44, 52-53, 73-74, 101, 118 (1n), 142-143, 154

Maíz Industrializado, S.A. (Miconsa) 38, 69-70, 79, 87, 90, 113-116, 121 (6n), 271
Mastreta, J. L. 55
Medina Plascencia, C. 218
Mexican Food System (SAM) 31, 39, 44, 89, 106, 108
Mexican Social Security Institute (IMSS) 4, 42, 51, 86, 167 (16n), 216, 277

Milk Programme 26, 38, 58-59, 72, 89, 92, 96, 114, 119 (12n), 121 (26n), 122, 142-151, 154, 158-159, 162-164, 166 (15n, 16n), 167 (17n, 18n, 21n), 184, 196, 224, 226, 231, 243, 246, 255 (4n), 267, 273

Ministry of Agrarian Reform (SRA) 9, 90, 152

Molinos Aztecas (Maseca) 34, 69-73, 82 (13n, 14n), 115-116, 121 (31n, 32n), 135-136, 181, 216

Mosconi, H. 82 (18n), 212, 214, 242

National Action Party (PAN) 7, 11, 26, 29, 47 (14n), 50, 55, 58, 94, 120 (22n, 25n), 163, 197, 218-219, 229, 259-261, 265

National Basic Foods Company (Conasupo) 2, 14-15, 37-45, 89

National Confederation of Popular Organisations (CNOP) 16, 127, 130, 147, 152, 166 (10n), 167 (21n), 269

National Development Plan 1989-1994 (NDP) 85-89, 101

National Food Programme (Pronal) 15, 31, 40, 47 (20n)

National Housing Fund (Infonavit) 9, 14, 61-62, 67, 91-92, 113, 164, 168 (22n), 216, 267, 270, 277

National Peasant Confederation (CNC) 24, 32, 61-67, 75, 78, 86, 98, 109-110, 117, 152, 155, 214, 220, 263, 270

National Popular Housing Fund (Fonhapo) 16

National Programme for the *Modernización* of Supply and the Domestic Market 1990-1994 (NPMSDM) 85-90, 101

National Solidarity Programme (Solidarity/Pronasol) 2, 7, 15-16, 46 (2n, 9n), 54, 60, 65, 79, 111, 118 (8n), 133, 153, 160, 162, 164, 168 (22n), 177, 180, 206 (1n, 3n), 210, 214-218, 226-227, 233, 235, 237, 240-242, 248, 263, 265, 266, 274, 276, 278

Neoliberalism 2-4, 94, 117, 120 (22n), 122, 127, 147-148, 169, 238, 240, 257, 264, 269, 272, 277

North American Free Trade Agreement (NAFTA) 46 (5n), 69, 145, 257, 270, 278

Ovalle, I. 49, 56, 60, 64, 66, 71, 74, 76-79, 85, 90-91, 95, 115, 118 (3n), 119 (10n), 120 (24n), 128-129, 145, 164, 167 (22n), 171, 176, 189, 195, 204, 206, 206 (2n), 270, 274

Ordinary Assembly of the National Agricultural Council 63

Ortega, M.T. 189

Pasalagua Branch, J.M. 79, 180, 189, 206 (4n)

Peón Escalante, F. 79

Political Culture 5, 19

Popular Defence Committee (CDP) 15, 216

Popular Kitchen Programme 91, 118 (10n), 167 (16n)

Popular Urban Movement (MUP) 24

Privatisation 17, 47 (13n), 51, 66-67, 78, 82 (14n), 84, 90-93, 110-117, 120 (24n), 121 (26n, 28n, 29n), 145, 155, 160, 162, 164, 174-177, 181, 188, 192, 196-198, 264, 267-268, 274

Programme for the *Modernización* of Public Enterprises 1990-1994 (PMPE) 85-88, 174-177